WHAT THE SURVIVORS KNEW . . . AND THE PEOPLE DIDN'T.

The survivors remember all too well the hunger and the fear, the disorganized and sometimes murderous squalor of the retreat to the coast, and the scurry into the boats that only the kindness of the weather made possible. But the British people in mid-1940 needed more than bare reality. The Navy and the Air Force would protect the island against attack from across the sea, but they had no power to return the heavy blows that the enemy was bound to inflict upon them. Words were the necessary and the only weapons, to foster the faith that Britain would eventually triumph, and to rally the support of Britain's friends around the world.

The story of Dunkirk was instantly, and without dictation from any effective national propaganda organisation, forged into the main armament of Britain's moral warfare. It was embellished, simplified, made glorious. . . .

The truth cannot hurt them now.

―――――――――――

DUNKIRK

The Necessary Myth

NICHOLAS HARMAN

JOVE BOOKS, NEW YORK

This Jove book contains the complete, revised
text of the original hardcover edition.
It has been completely reset in a typeface
designed for easy reading, and was printed
from new film.

DUNKIRK

A Jove Book / published by arrangement with
the author

PRINTING HISTORY
Hodder and Stoughton edition published 1980
Coronet edition published 1981
Also published by Simon and Schuster
Jove edition / May 1990

ISBN: 0-515-10306-3

Jove Books are published by The Berkley Publishing Group,
200 Madison Avenue, New York, New York 10016.
The name ''JOVE'' and the ''J'' logo
are trademarks belonging to Jove Publications, Inc.

PRINTED IN THE UNITED STATES OF AMERICA

10 9 8 7 6 5 4 3 2 1

For Connie

CONTENTS

Part Four
THE DUNKIRK SPIRIT

Introduction

DUNKIRK
THE NECESSARY MYTH

"So long as the English tongue survives, the word Dunkerque will be spoken with reverence. For in that harbor, in such a hell as never blazed on earth before, at the end of a lost battle, the rags and blemishes that have hidden the soul of democracy fell away. . . . This shining thing in the souls of free men Hitler cannot command, or stain, or conquer. . . . It is the great tradition of democracy. It is the future. It is victory."
— The New York Times, June 1st, 1940

"Personally I feel happier now that we have no more allies to be polite to & to pamper."
— KING GEORGE VI, letter to the Queen Mother, June 27th, 1940

Every spring they come back to Dunkirk to remember their dead comrades, and to commemorate one of the greatest defeats and one of the most extraordinary triumphs in British history, a nine-days' wonder that changed the world. Fifty years on, they swing a bit stiffly past the Town Hall saluting-base and wheel into position to hear the speeches that cele-

1

brate the glories of their youth. The veterans of 1940 are all too conscious now that their ranks grow thinner year by year. But they are bound together by history. They were there when it was made.

How would we behave, how could we endure, amid the hardship and the suffering that they recall with humour as well as with pride? Since they were young, Europe has lived through its longest period of international peace since nations were invented. Dunkirk itself will do as a symbol of the transformation of a continent.

In seventy years the city was bombarded three times by German guns, in 1871, in 1917, and again at its fall in 1940. Now the dangers it faces, such as they are, come from prosperity, on a frontier that nobody bothers to defend, beside a Channel under which they are digging a tunnel. The steelworks and refineries give it some of the dirtiest air in western Europe. To westward looms the nuclear power-plant at Gravelines. Along the beaches to the east towards Belgium, where once the soldiers waited for the boats that never came, topless sunbathers shun the oil-clots. This may not be the Europe the men of 1940 thought they were fighting for; but if they had given in to Hitler, it would certainly be worse.

It was a close-run thing. On May 10th Hitler's armies swept westwards out of Germany into the neutral Low Countries, lured the Anglo-French forces out of their prepared defences and fell upon their disorganised rear. Ten days later the German spearhead had reached the sea, cutting off the Allies' northern front from the main army in France. Two weeks later again, the British had been driven off the Continent, the Belgians forced to surrender, and the French sent reeling towards defeat.

Against all the odds, against every prediction from every side, 220,000 British soldiers, 110,000 French, and a few hundred Belgians were brought across the sea to Britain. The French returned at once to France, and reformed into combat units just in time to surrender to the Germans when their national government collapsed. The British on their island kept on fighting. Their army had left most of its weapons and all of its transport behind in France. But the men became the nucleus of the new alliance that, five years later, won the Second World War.

Winston Churchill, Britain's new prime minister, came to power amid the confusion of those terrible days. He warned the House of Commons against calling the evacuation from Dunkirk a victory. It was, he said, a deliverance. It meant more than most victories. As the last men landed in the ports of southern England, the tales of providential rescue took root and grew into legend. The uneasy yoke of the alliance with France fell away, the domestic recriminations of the phoney war were forgotten. The whole nation arose and cheered the gathering in of its soldiers.

The survivors remember all too well the hunger and the fear, the disorganised and sometimes murderous squalor of the retreat to the coast, and the scurry into the ships that only the kindness of the weather made possible. But the British people in mid-1940 needed something more than bare reality. Their army had left its arms behind in France. The navy and the air force would protect the island against attack from across the sea; but they were powerless to return the heavy blows that the enemy was bound to inflict. Words were the necessary and the only weapons, to foster the faith that Britain would eventually triumph, and to rally the support of Britain's friends around the world.

The story of Dunkirk was instantly, and without dictation from any effective national propaganda organisation, forged into the main armament of Britain's moral warfare. It was embellished, simplified, made glorious. It told of how a gallant band of soldiers, betrayed by their allies, fought their way to home and safety, being conveyed across the last few crucial miles of water by an armada of small boats manned by volunteer civilians.

This was part of my childhood faith. I was seven years old in 1940, at the age when life's beliefs are being formed. With a whole generation throughout the English-speaking world, I was nurtured on the story of Dunkirk that sustained Britain's cities through the blitz, and fortified its people, military and civilian alike, for the ordeal by combat that ended in 1945. Still today, after all, the British are often urged to invoke the "Dunkirk spirit," that combination of improvisation and dogged refusal to acknowledge the reality of failure. That the weather itself was on Britain's side in 1940 only strengthens the faith. The German soldiers of the time had *Gott mit uns*—

God is with us—on their belt-buckles. The British had it in their hearts.

But it was not quite like that. When I began to write this book, for the fortieth anniversary of the evacuation in 1980, I had expected, perhaps naïvely, to retell in modern form the uplifting story on which I was reared. But as I talked to the veterans and read the dusty papers in the archives, the moral tale began to slide away. It became clear that, as with all good working myths, parts of the traditional Dunkirk story are reliable. The truth of other parts is poetic rather than literal.

In particular I struggled for a while to substantiate the belief that an armada of civilian "little ships" had played a significant part in the rescue of the army. It was almost with distaste that I came to understand that this was false. The little ships operated only on the last two days of the British evacuation, and then to very little effect. It was impossible that civilians could have volunteered earlier for service at Dunkirk, since the whole affair was kept secret from the public until three-quarters of the army was safe at home.

It was much the same with the belief that Britain was let down in 1940 by her French and Belgian allies. Certainly the armies of those two countries were badly beaten. But the British army was badly beaten too; and, far from being betrayed by their allies, the British political and military authorities practised upon the French and Belgians a methodical deception which enabled the British to get away with their rear defended.

The men who served at Dunkirk are, on the whole, by no means shocked by this conclusion. They are simply glad that they got away. I spent many hours with survivors, in groups and on their own. Their courtesy and patience were extreme, as they faced memories that were often painful, often shielded in protective jokes. ("Look round this bar and you'll see a dozen men who were the last out of Dunkirk, and there are as many more in the bar next door.")

Soldiers remember battles as women remember childbirth, through a merciful screen of selective oblivion. No fighting man can know the significance of his own part in a general conflict. At Dunkirk, even the strategists and staff officers were improvising in the dark. The radios did not work, the telephones did not connect with each other, the messages never arrived in the frantic improvisation of defeat. The planners left a mass of documents—Cabinet papers, war diaries, orders, technical instructions, radio scripts, and the later, self-justifying publications of generals and political leaders. Those sources, many of them famous, many more (because of Britain's bizarre rules of "official secrecy") unavailable to anybody writing before the present author, tell of chaos along the Flanders coast.

Others, too, have reason to remember those days; Germans in their moment of what seemed like historic victory, Belgians and Frenchmen in the agony of defeat. For them Dunkirk was a sideshow. Britain's army in France formed only a small part of the forces in conflict, and the British decision to disengage, while a surprise (to put it mildly) to her allies, seemed of no great significance to her enemies.

Myths, given time, become certainties, and the truth makes people nervous. For the BBC I wrote and presented an hour-long documentary film based on this book. Our production team felt tugs from high in the corporate ranks: were we really, they asked, going to state that the "little ships" and their volunteer crews were of no significance in the evacuation? So we found some more eyewitnesses to confirm it.

The *Sunday Telegraph* of London published long extracts from the book, in successive weeks. They asked for no changes at all. But reaction to the first instalment must have worried the then editor, who asked if I would mind him prefacing the second with an explanation that I had myself been a fighting soldier. I was not sure how a bad wound in Korea increased my credibility as a chronicler of the Second World War, but several *Telegraph* readers wrote to say they felt happier as a result.

Anyway, I don't think anybody who has actually read the book could regard it as disrespectful of the men who did the fighting. I have had more than 200 letters from people who were there. Their main concern has been to write down, for good or ill, their own part in the story, to insist that the names of men and units, and the details of their weapons, be remembered right, before it is too late. To my gratification (and, I must admit, my surprise) nobody has complained that I made any significant error. Lately, I fear, I heard a reputable commentator dismisss the book as a "classic account" of Dunkirk. I hope it is not that dull.

All the armies in the field, including Britain's, were sometimes heroic. Sometimes, too, they stole, shot civilians out of hand, drank, slaughtered their prisoners. There were sailors who refused to go to France, as well as sailors who returned again and again to face the bombs and the machine-guns and the corpses drifting in the oily water. The men of Dunkirk behaved as people do behave under the most appalling stress. Europeans, fighting in Europe, they behaved in war just as, in more recent conflicts, soldiers from other continents have behaved when fighting on stranger shores.

In Europe in 1940 the stakes were terribly high. The penalty of permanent failure by the Allies does not bear thinking about. Whatever the motives and whatever the conduct of the British, they were at least on the right side against the right enemy. Of the giant powers whose part in the defeat of Hitler was in the end to be decisive, the Russians were at the time passively entwined in alliance with the Nazis. The Americans were worrying not about the future of freedom in the wide world, but about their own domestic future, and in particular about whether to elect Franklin D. Roosevelt to a third term in the White House.

If the British in 1940 told, and enjoyed, and embroidered, some versions of the story, they did so because that helped them to stay in the war. Like the veterans of Dunkirk itself, they did the best they could with the weapons they had, and they survived to fight again. That was enough. The truth cannot hurt them now.

This, then, is the story of Dunkirk. About half of this book consists of a day-by-day account of the evacuation, and is centred on the town of Dunkirk and the fifteen kilometres of shelving beach that stretch across the Belgian border to the little seaside resort town of La Panne. In order to make sense of the story of the evacuation, the book tells first the separate but interlocking stories of how the French, Belgian and British armies came to be where they were, with their backs to the Channel. The first cause of that was the triumphant progress of the German Army, and with that we begin.

Part One
ALLIES AND ENEMIES

1
BLITZKRIEG

Hitler's Germany was a war machine. Aggressive imperialism, disguised as the redressal of old wrongs and the reacquisition of usurped Germanic territory, was the *raison d'être* of the Nazi regime. War production, and an approach to full employment in the armed forces and the industries producing armaments, was the motor of the country's economic recovery in the 1930s, and thus of its leader's growing popularity. The Army, with political stiffening from the parallel military structure of the National Socialist "security force," the SS, was the regime's chosen instrument. Against the democracies that hankered after peace, and would accept almost any humiliation to secure the hope of it, stood a nation dedicated to war.

By his brilliant campaigns of the spring of 1940 Hitler extended German dominance through north-western Europe, leaving in opposition to him only the one European nation whose traditions, and whose imperial institutions, he truly admired. But his real ambitions lay eastwards. His book *Mein Kampf* ("My Struggle"), written in jail in 1924, had laid out his programme for Germany. First, the Germans were to claim the lands to the east where sizeable German-speaking communities lived. Then they were to conquer the grain-producing territories inhabited by the peoples speaking Slav languages. Thus would be established on the Eurasian landmass a great self-sufficient empire dominated by the inherently superior Germanic "race."

The democracies of western Europe and North America might try to obstruct this world-historical process, because they were so foolish and decadent as to allow cosmopolitan Jewish conspirators to dominate their economies and to manipulate their policies. But because of this Jewish dominance the democracies lacked the strength effectively to oppose the Germans and their leader. They could inconvenience, but not in the end deny, the progress of Germany to its destiny.

Reasonable men outside Germany regarded this as poisonous nonsense, which of course it was. They therefore failed to realise that every word of it was meant in earnest, not as a vision but as a plan of action. Faced with Hitler's unreasonable demands, the democracies met them with reasoned concessions. Unopposed, Hitler was permitted to take over first the Saar-land, then Austria, then Czechoslovakia, acquiring each time more manpower and more factories capable of producing arms. By the autumn of 1939 it was Poland's turn. The governments of Britain and of France declared, reluctantly, that this time they would stand by the commitment they had made in law and in honour to defend the government in Warsaw.

Hitler believed he could call their bluff again. On September 1st German forces marched across the Polish border, having trumped up the usual pretext that they were acting to "liberate" a Germany minority under alien rule. On September 3rd, with the German advance prospering, the Allied powers bit on the bullet. At 11 a.m. that day Neville Chamberlain, prime minister of Great Britain, announced on the radio that his country was now at war with Germany. With even greater reluctance the French government of M. Daladier announced at 5 p.m. its own belligerence.

As Hitler had foretold, the Allies did nothing effective to protect the nation on whose behalf they had gone to war. In eighteen days the German Army put an end to organised resistance in Poland. For the first time the world witnessed the spectacle of blitzkrieg, the lightning war—literally witnessed it, since the victorious Germans methodically recorded on film the savagery of their advance, and distributed the film not only to cheering audiences at home but also to horrified, and sometimes intimidated, audiences abroad.

For five centuries the marching infantryman and the horse-drawn piece of artillery had been the tools of war in Europe. The coming of the railways had helped to concentrate more men and more munitions in one place than ever before. In the First World War that had increased the amount of slaughter, but not altered the nature of the battle. Now, by Hitler's Germany, the technology of the twentieth century was unleashed. The internal-combustion engine changed the way in which weapons could be transported, on land and in the air. Wireless communications transformed the possibility of controlling armies on the move.

The Polish defence consisted of infantrymen armed with rifles and machine guns, with artillery to their rear. Reinforcements were available to be moved into position by rail. This was the technique on which the French were to rely the following year. It was irrelevant to the new German method of attack. Tanks, deployed in masses, drove straight through the infantry lines and fell on the guns behind. The victory of the tanks was consolidated by infantry in cross-country transports. The defenders' reinforcements were immobilised by air attacks. The theory of this new form of warfare had been pondered and published for fifteen years and more, first in Britain and then around the world. The Germans tried it out in practice, and showed that it worked.

Instead of trains they used trucks, or even transport aircraft, to supply the forward units of their advance. Instead of slow-moving heavy guns they used dive-bombing planes, of infinitely greater range. They deliberately planned to sow panic and confusion in the enemy rear; the dive-bombers were fitted with howlers, to make their attack more frightening both to the defending soldiers and to the civilians who ran onto the roads and hampered the movement of their fighting men. They let it be known—sometimes truthfully—that Germany could call upon a network of spies and traitors, thus spreading suspicion between their opponents' troops and civilians. Most of the German army in Poland was perfectly conventional and followed conventional tactics. But the Germans played down this aspect of the campaign. They were out to frighten and demoralise their enemies, both actual and potential. It was total war.

So Poland fell. On October 6th, less than five weeks after the Allies had declared war, Hitler addressed the Reichstag, his servile parliament. He offered the Allies a negotiated peace. The terms, he broadly hinted, could be easy. From Britain he expected only a guarantee of friendship and, perhaps, the return of a few bits of the former German Empire that had been incorporated in the British Empire after the First World War. A second war, he suggested, was not worth pursuing for an extinguished cause.

Two neutral monarchs, the King of the Belgians and the Queen of the Netherlands, offered their joint good offices for mediation between the powers whose *casus belli*, Poland's independence, had been eliminated. They hoped, it seems, to avert by conciliation the threat that war would spill over their peaceful and barely defended borders with Germany. Others had done likewise before.

Hitler's peace offer would have legitimised the conquest of Poland. It went unanswered. Three days later he ordered the preparation of an invasion of France through the territories of his neutral benefactors, Holland and Belgium. On January 11th, 1940, a German transport plane was forced down by bad weather in Belgium. From the wreck the Belgian police secured both the German staff officer on board and the plan he was carrying. It clearly showed that Germany intended to disregard the neutrality of the Low Countries. Some on the Allied side took the revelation of this scheme as a carefully planned German deception, meant to cause confusion. Neither the two governments whose existence was threatened by it, nor the French and British to whom it was communicated, did anything to guard against the invasion of which they had now been warned.

The German plan of attack was modified, finalised and set in motion as the earth dried up after the winter, making all firm for their unrivalled assembly of tanks and vehicles. The French intelligence services anticipated its precise date, but their warnings were ignored. Indeed, even the Germans were uncertain until the last day whether they would be able to move. At midday on May 9th, their meteorologists made a firm forecast of clear skies on the following morning. Hitler

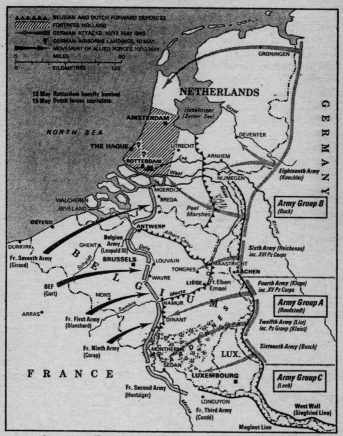

gave the met officer a medal on the spot. But nobody had discovered or guessed the massive audacity of the scheme that Hitler had himself selected from the options presented by his eager staff.

By traditional military doctrine the attackers should have feinted on one front and attacked in full strength on another. Instead they threw everything they had into a massive double offensive. Brilliantly it exploited the triple strength of the German Army—the new-model armoured panzer divisions, the airborne shock troops, and the solid mass of conventional divisions with horse-drawn guns and foot-slogging infantry.

Germany's western frontier runs roughly north from Switzerland, confronting four nations: France, Luxembourg, Belgium and the Netherlands. The French had walled up their border with Germany itself by the Maginot Line of fortifications that ran from Switzerland to the corner of Luxembourg; on this front the Germans did nothing. To northward of the end of the Maginot Line, where France meets Luxembourg and Belgium amid the hill country of the Ardennes, the attack was mounted by German Army Group A. Under its commander, General von Rundstedt, were concentrated seven of Germany's ten modern armoured divisions. North of that again, across the long border with Belgium and the Netherlands, German Army Group B under General von Bock advanced at dawn on May 10th.

Bock was an officer of the old school. Back in the early 1930s he had, in a famous argument, pulled rank on one of Hitler's favourite military intellectuals, the tank theoretician General Guderian. "Tank armour prevents them from saluting properly on parade," said Bock. "Anyway you move too fast. How can you ever command all that without telephones?" "By radio," replied Guderian. "Wrong!" retorted Bock. "Wireless will never work in a tank."

Now Bock had the sort of army he liked and understood. He had a nominal three armoured divisions under his command. But they were the three weakest in the German Army, with old tanks, and under strength. Bock's tanks, like those of the defending Allied armies, were split up into small parcels, to work with infantry formations and under infantry command. The infantry were fairly well supplied with trucks and buses, but most of the soldiers had to go by train or walk. Almost all Bock's heavy artillery was horse-drawn—more reliable, said his old-style gunnery officers, and in the Low Countries there would be plenty of fodder but little tank fuel.

As Bock's men started forward the door to the Low Countries was locked for them by Hitler's most revolutionary military formations, the bomber planes and the airborne and glider troops of what the British later came to call commando units. These forces overwhelmed the strongpoints and captured undamaged most of the bridges along the Dutch and

Belgian borders. The areas behind them were subjected to terror bombing which blocked the railway junctions and drove the civilians of what had the previous day been neutral towns out in panic onto the highways. The defending armies were paralysed. Into the resulting chaos plodded Bock's troops, impeccably organised, steady against the half-trained Dutch and Belgian conscripts.

This was the attack that the Allies had expected—although they had not foreseen the terrible success of the bombing and commando assaults that opened the way for the conventional German forces. To meet the attack the French and British armies moved forward according to plan into Belgium and Holland. But there they met three surprises. First, the trenches and strongpoints they thought had been prepared for them did not exist. Second, the German advance guard was already moving up to the unprepared line of defences. Third, and most important, the Germans had attacked and broken through behind them. So the Allies turned right around and started back again, seeking a line on which to stand firm against the enemy's double thrust. They kept moving back all the way to Dunkirk.

The Dutch Army of ten divisions did not stand a chance. It fought for only three days, and was then ordered to surrender to spare further suffering by the people of the cities, under the ruthless hail of German bombs. The Belgians, seeing the Allies abandon most of their territory without a shot fired, kept on fighting all the same. Hitler was delighted with it all. When he heard of the Allied move forward into the Low Countries, he told his sycophants afterwards, "I could have cried for joy—they had fallen into the trap."

The trap was the manoeuvre of the German troops in the centre of the line, General von Rundstedt's Army Group A. His command was slightly larger than Bock's, and included the cleverest and bravest commanders, the best-trained troops and the finest machines of the German Army. His seven panzer divisions were unlike anything the Allies possessed. *Panzer* means armour-plated. The main force of these divisions consisted of tanks. But they also included infantry in cross-country transports, and their own supply organisation, motorised guns and anti-aircraft units. All the tanks and most of the transport units had radios that worked fairly reliably, at least in the daylight hours. The commanders, including the divisional generals, could thus move with the leading units of the attack, where they could see the actual fighting and modify their plans to exploit an opportunity as it arose. They wirelessed their orders back to the staff administrators behind, and to the aircraft that did for them the work that heavy guns performed for conventional army formations.

The Germans had in total slightly fewer, and lighter, tanks than the French, and smaller reserves of ammunition for their guns. But the German tanks were faster and much better deployed. The French tanks could not move without their accompaniment of slow-moving vehicles and infantry. The seven German divisions of Army Group A were organized as fully-equipped panzer striking forces. They struck, violently and fast, at a point so unexpected that the French had not even organised it into a proper line of defence.

It was received opinion among orthodox soldiers that armies could not attack through the narrow valleys of the Ardennes, in the corner of land where France, Belgium and the pocket state of Luxembourg meet. The French thought so. They did not trouble to build their Maginot Line up to cover this section of their border, and they stationed their weakest troops behind it. Most of the German high command agreed with this French judgement, which would of course have been true for an advancing army dependent on supply and reinforcements carried by rail, or on good roads.

But Hitler's generals were not all conventional soldiers. Many were dedicated to the ideology of the Third Reich. Some knew very well how the new technology of battle worked. The commander of XIX Corps, General Guderian, the chief theoretician and creator of the panzer divisions, had served as a radio officer as long ago as 1912. Other generals had no tank experience at all, like the Seventh Division's commander, Erwin Rommel. An infantryman by training, he had until three months before been in charge of motor transport at Hitler's personal headquarters, sorting out absurd squabbles about precedence between various Nazi Party thugs. He soon learned his job. It was another keen Nazi, General von Manstein, who had persuaded Hitler to adopt the plan of attack through the Ardennes.

Peter Hadley, a British infantry officer, was with a unit that captured some panzer troops in May 1940. "They were a miserable selection of men from a physical point of view, and in their tank overalls looked for all the world like a lot of stunted and undernourished coal-heavers." Behind them, though, were Hitler's dedicated generals and Hitler's wonderful plan.

The advance guard of Army Group A simply drove along the narrow valleys of the Ardennes, taking to the fields where the roads and bridges were inadequate, and swept down upon the ill-prepared French defences before the garrisons could believe they were under attack. On May 13th they were in France, and had a bridgehead across the river Meuse. Where the defenders blew up the bridges, the Germans simply built their own, of pontoons or of rubber rafts supporting planks. But most of the bridges were left intact by their defenders, unwilling to bar the way to the counter-attack they hoped to make quite soon.

The key point of the defence was the great French fortress of Sedan. As the Germans pushed across the nearby bridges, the Allies sent their planes to bomb the bridgeheads. On the fourteenth, 170 planes, 100 of them British, attacked the bridges by Sedan. Eighty-five of them, including forty-six British bombers, were shot down. The Germans moved their anti-aircraft guns with the spearhead of their attack. The Allies sent in their bombers in long lines, squadron after squadron, presenting each a perfect target. It was a massacre. Air Marshal Barratt, commanding the British air forces in France, wept at the news and ordered his surviving aircraft to move back to bases in Britain.

By May 15th Sedan had fallen. The weight of German bombing and of German tank attacks had overwhelmed the incredulous defenders. Once across the Meuse and clear of the strongpoints there was nothing in the way of the panzers. The Allies had no reserves available. The vast bulk of the Allied armies had marched soberly up into Belgium to meet Army Group B's more conventional assault. Unopposed, the panzers could now motor ahead. The French thought they would advance on Paris, and moved all their available mobile forces to block that avenue. Instead the Germans headed due west toward the English Channel coast.

The route west lay along the north bank of the river Somme. This was where the most murderous battles of the First World

War had been fought, and the place-names in the corps commanders' reports were full of dreadful memories for both sides. But this time the advance ran not from the north, against the grain of the French landscape, but along the roads in the valley bottom that offered the line of least resistance.

Hitler and his high command feared, as well they might, a flank attack by the French from the south that could have cut off the precious tank spearhead from its base. The panzer divisions carried fuel for two hundred kilometres on the road. There were three days' rations with the tanks, three in the regimental supply vehicles, three more in divisional supplies on the move behind the fighting front. But even this generous self-sufficiency could have been badly dented by a flank attack.

There were cautious men, as well as daring gamblers, among the German staff. Hitler listened to the advice of both factions, nervous, ready to react to any emergency. He infuriated his professional staff officers, who thought it was a supreme commander's job to lay down a broad strategy and then imperturbably refrain from interfering. General Halder, the chief of staff at Army headquarters, noted in his diary on May 17th: "Führer is terribly nervous. Frightened by his own success, he is afraid to take any chance and so would rather pull the reins on us." But the Führer's nerve held for long enough. It was the gamblers in the Army, not the cautious soldiers from staff college, who had his ear.

After their victorious ride through Poland the previous autumn, the Germans had feared that France would be a tougher nut to crack. They found the going easier. The roads were better, the bridges were stronger, local resistance was non-existent. The Royal Air Force, which might conceivably have stopped them, was between May 15th and 22nd busy organising its withdrawal from bases in France to airfields in England: it played no serious part in trying to attack the panzers. The Germans were desperately short of military maps; instead they took from garages ample supplies of Messrs. Michelin's excellent touring maps, with roads and short cuts, well-stocked filling stations and garage workshops, all clearly indicated at an advantageous *prix publicitaire*. Poland was never like this.

The fighting commanders at the front contemptuously watched the French give up. Swarms of elderly reservists pathetically asked the Germans what to do with the weapons they were eager to surrender. General Rommel was amazed when, in the end, he met a French colonel who refused to co-operate in the disarming of his men. Regretfully, Rommel sent him off to be shot.

But the German high command could not see all this, and were reluctant to believe it. On May 17th General von Brauchitsch, the supreme commander, with Hitler's agreement, ordered the panzers to stop and consolidate their flank against a counter-attack. (Brauchitsch, in 1939, had told a colleague he did not believe France could be defeated.) General Guderian, in charge of the spearhead and in constant conversation by radio with the leading commanders, was furious at this delay. He resigned his command in protest. His immediate superior, fearing the Führer's wrath if his favourite were thus to be suddenly withdrawn from the battle, persuaded Guderian to reconsider his resignation. By a face-saving compromise Guderian was allowed to carry on with his advance "for reconnaissance only"—*nur für Kampfaufklärung*.

It turned out more than a reconnaissance. In triumph, during the night of May 19th–20th, Guderian's foremost units reached Noyelles, where the Somme goes out through its canalised mouth to the salt sea. By the evening of the following day, May 20th, the German Army was in control of Abbeville, where the last road and rail bridges cross the Somme, carrying the track south to Paris and the main body of the French Army.

Still the panzer divisions refused the counsels of prudence. With only one day's rest they turned north to the next vital links in the Allies' chain of communications, the Channel ports of Boulogne and Calais. Frantically the British rushed token forces over to stiffen the French garrisons of the ports, foot guards to Boulogne, light infantrymen to Calais. The guards were promptly shipped back to England and safety; the light infantry were left to surrender on May 26th. The way was clear to the last of the Channel ports remaining in Allied hands, Dunkirk.

But now at last the prudent faction of the German high command prevailed. All across France the tanks had been moving through ideal country, where the fields as well as the roads can bear the weight of tracked vehicles. But from Calais eastwards the land runs flat and soggy into the reclaimed

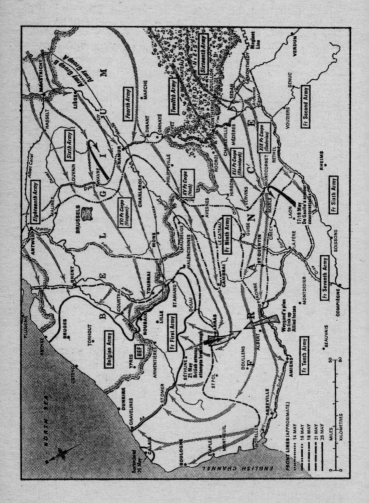

salt marshes of the Low Countries. Dunkirk itself is built entirely on land reclaimed from the sea. It is surrounded by a ring of broad, navigable canals, and a fantasy of smaller dykes and ditches which the locals call *les watergangs*. Half-way between Calais and Dunkirk the wide, canalised river Aa meets the sea at Gravelines, the fortress-town whose walls, designed by Louis XIV's great military architect Vauban, still dominate even the vast nuclear power plant nearby.

Even the panzers could not cross this obstacle. Thirty kilometres inland, at St.-Omer, a German unit did succeed in crossing the Aa. It was the regiment of the *Schützstaffel*—the Nazi party's private army, the SS—called the *Leibstandarte Adolf Hitler*, the Adolf Hitler Lifeguards. They were opposed by a few French and British gunners. The armoured vehicles could not move off the roads on the marshy ground. If a single tank or truck was hit by the enemy the entire column was immobilised. This happened several times. In particular the SS commander, a revolting bully called Sepp Dietrich, spent several hours sheltering in a drain to get away with his life. The regular army officers who rescued him were delighted to see him spattered with duckweed. The impression soon got across that the Aa should not be tackled lightly.

The panzer troops were a precious resource, ideal for fighting in open country but intensely vulnerable if tied to the roads by boggy terrain, and dependent for their progress over waterways on bridges strong enough to bear a tank. By now half their tanks were out of service, more through wear and tear than through enemy action. They needed to stop and refurbish. The objective of the German campaign was to defeat France. Only with a strong panzer force could they start their new rush down towards Paris, to sweep up the main body of the enemy.

On May 24th, with the battle for Boulogne still in progress and that for Calais scarcely under way, General von Rundstedt finally issued the long-expected order for the panzers to stop their advance. They were not to move east of the river Aa towards Dunkirk and the roads leading to that town. Hitler confirmed Rundstedt's order. The Air Force, he said, should be left to deal with the Allied troops bottled up in Flanders. Field Marshal Goering, the Luftwaffe commander, said his men could prevent any trouble from that quarter. The general in command of air operations in France, Kesselring, was not so sure: "From May 13th continuous operations had literally consumed all the personnel and material of our Air Force. After three weeks, units fell to fifty percent and even thirty percent of establishment." Anyway, even if the Luftwaffe failed, the slow-moving Army Group B was moving down through Belgium towards Dunkirk with its foot soldiers and its horse-drawn guns; if there was to be a siege on boggy ground it should be left to them, not to the unsuitable panzer divisions.

None of the panzer commanders seems to have seriously disagreed with Rundstedt's order to stop on the Aa, as confirmed by Hitler. Later, with the usual hindsight of frustrated conquerors, some claimed that they could have finished the job if left alone by the top brass. After the war General Guderian was interrogated by a man he much admired, the British theorist of tank warfare Captain Liddell Hart. Guderian tried to put the blame for the halt at the Aa—as for so much else—on Adolf Hitler: "We were not informed of the reason for this . . . We were utterly speechless."

Hitler, after the staff meeting at which he confirmed the order to stop, had made one of his familiar orations about his admiration for Britain, and for the British Empire as the supreme example of racial domination. From this evidence Liddell Hart elaborated a theory that Hitler let the British army escape from Dunkirk on purpose, meaning to make a separate peace with the British after the defeat of France. Hitler did not want a separate peace with Britain. His army did hold back from the final assault on Dunkirk, allowing the British to escape behind a screen of French defenders. But it is fantastic to suppose, as Guderian ingratiatingly suggested, that he let them get away on purpose.

The stop order on the Aa line was countermanded after two days, when Calais fell to the Germans on May 26th. But the renewed advance followed a new strategic pattern. Hitherto the panzers of Army Group A had slashed ahead, while Army Group B dealt in its slower way with the Belgian front. General Halder, the chief of staff, put the change clearly in his diary:

I wanted [Army Group] A to be the hammer, B to be the anvil. Now they are making B the hammer, A the anvil. Since B has a strongly held front against it, that will cost a lot of blood and last a long time. What is more, the Luftwaffe, on which we rely, is held up by the weather. All these disagreements result in a pulling to and fro which is taking more nervous energy than the whole job of leadership. Anyway, we shall win the fight in the end.

The German Fourth Army staff noted the same day, May 25th, that the battle near Dunkirk had another new element.

For two days now the enemy has had air superiority over von Kleist's [panzer] group and sometimes over Hoth's group. This is something new for us in this campaign, and is caused by the fact that the English have their air bases ''on the island itself,'' and close by, while our units are still for practical purposes really based in Germany.

There is in retrospect little doubt that, if the panzer divisions had carried on with their gamble and pushed across the waterways towards Dunkirk on May 24th, they could have cut off the British and French armies from retreat across the sea. But they would surely have lost many tanks. Prudence won. Once the Allied armies of the north were bottled up in Dunkirk, the Germans had good reason to assume that they would stay bottled up there. The port was out of action, the Luftwaffe was bombing, Bock's troops were on their way through Belgium to besiege the town.

But Bock's advance was badly delayed by the Belgian and French resistance, and by the tedious task of organising the surrender of the entire Belgian Army on May 28th. When the two army groups, A and B, finally met, they failed to coordinate their operations against the men they had surrounded. In the gap between the two groups the British, and part of the French army, slipped back to the sea and—by the courage and organisation of the Royal Navy—across it.

From the German point of view, capturing or annihilating the British land army at Dunkirk would have been an added triumph, wholly unexpected and thus all the more glorious. But it was not part of their plan. The target for the blitzkrieg was now Paris and the heartland of France. For the French and the Germans alike the evacuation from Dunkirk was a sideshow. For the British it remained, during the few days until the last soldiers of the British Expeditionary Force got away, the key to survival as a fighting nation.

2

THE RELUCTANT ALLIES

The Second World War began in an attempt by Britain and France to preserve the independence of the small nations of Europe, and thus to prevent German hegemony on the Continent. In the first nine months of the war six nations—Poland, Denmark, Norway, Luxembourg, the Netherlands, Belgium—went down before the German onslaught. Finland, meanwhile, fell to the Russians, with German acquiescence. France on June 16th, 1940 joined her smaller Continental fellows under German control. The original anti-fascist alliance was involuntary: the Allies did not join it until they were attacked. And it was wholly unsuccessful.

War had become inevitable in the early hours of August 24th, 1939. In Moscow that day the emissaries of Hitler signed a pact of non-aggression with Stalin's Soviet Union. It was accompanied by a secret protocol dividing eastern Europe into a German and a Soviet sphere of influence, and Poland was the first casualty. On September 1st, on faked pretexts, and in accordance with a directive fixed by Hitler five months before, the German troops began their remorseless advance. The intervention in the war three days later of Britain and France did nothing to help the government in Warsaw.

Poland was overrun within a month. From the east the Russians crept in to glean the harvest of the Nazi victory. Next, with Germany's blessing, the Russians moved in on

Finland. To the amazement of the world the Finns held out all through the bitter winter, surrendering only in March 1940; but nobody helped them either. The peace of defeat settled over Germany's eastern fringes. Now it was the turn of the west.

At sea the navies of Britain and Germany were engaged in a far-flung battle of blockade and counter-blockade. The Royal Navy was stronger and more skilful. It was a struggle that the Germans were bound, in the long term, to lose. They had to strike on land, soon. Neither side dared move on the front where they faced each other directly: along the Franco–German frontier each army was in defences strong enough to deter attack. A land fight had to come on neutral ground. The neutrals, in Scandinavia and in the Low Countries, feared and expected a German attack. But they knew that any overtures to the Allies would be taken by the Germans as a preparation for war, and would call down a pre-emptive strike. So they did nothing.

The phoney war ended in Scandinavia. The German armaments industry depended heavily on iron ore which, mined in northern Sweden, was transported by rail to the north Norwegian port of Narvik, and thence by ship through Norway's neutral coastal waters to German ports. The Allies agreed to stop this trade. On April 8th, 1940 the Royal Navy violated Norway's neutrality by laying a minefield in her coastal waters. This act of war was to have been followed up, the next day, by a swift Allied occupation of the Norwegian mainland, poising an Anglo–French military and naval force strategically to Germany's north.

The Allied plan failed. It was by chance that the Germans chose the same moment to pursue the same objectives; but they did so with greater suddenness and skill, and they had Britain's prior aggression to justify them. (From neutral ground *The New York Times*, resolutely pro-British, spoke of Britain's "more humane illegality.") Hitler's troops, air-lifted, marched behind a band down the streets of Oslo on April 9th. Simultaneously they rubbed out Denmark, where they met almost no organised resistance. On May 3rd the Norwegian Army capitulated and the Germans set up a puppet government under their despised sympathiser Vidkun Quisling. All the Allied troops—superior in numbers, inferior in aircraft and in fighting ability—were lifted out of central and southern Norway by May 3rd, in a long-range rehearsal for Dunkirk.

In the far north the Allies persisted for a while in their attack on Narvik. But a tiny German force, largely of sailors fighting as infantry, held stubbornly onto their bridgehead until May 27th. Just as this small German force reached the end of its tether the Allies gave up in Norway, faced with the greater drama of the collapse of France. By June 7th the Royal Navy had lifted the entire force of 14,000 French, 8,500 British and 2,000 Polish soldiers out of Narvik to Britain, where the King and government of Norway had chosen exile rather than disgrace.

The Norway adventure was a disaster. But it did have fortunate consequences. The Royal Navy suffered heavy losses, particularly with the sinking of the aircraft carrier *Glorious*, freighted with Royal Air Force fighters and their crews. The German Navy, though, was badly beaten. On April 13th alone eight large German destroyers and one submarine were sunk by the British. The German Navy—according to Captain Roskill, the official historian of the Royal Navy—ended the Norwegian campaign with no major warship fit for sea. Britain's command of the North Sea and the Channel was assured. There could be no invasion of Britain in 1940.

Just as important, the Norway fiasco caused a wave of disgust in both the British and the French parliaments with the Prime Ministers responsible. As their majorities faded away, Neville Chamberlain resigned on May 8th and the following day Paul Reynaud offered his resignation. In Britain the King invited Winston Churchill to form a new coalition of all parties, which he completed in the afternoon of May 10th, as the news of the German attack in the Low Countries broke. (Somehow it did not matter that Churchill, as First Lord of the Admiralty, had been the Minister chiefly responsible for operations in Norway.) In France, by contrast, President Lebrun got the news of the German attack as he was considering the formation of a new coalition to replace Reynaud's team. Faced with the immediate crisis, the President asked Reynaud to stay on at the head of a caretaker government. Defiance at the top in Britain, defeatism in France—these were the consequences of parliamentary manoeuvres carried out before the scale of the German threat became apparent.

Piling on the daring, Hitler started his adventure in the Low Countries even before the success of his Scandinavian gamble was finally accomplished. He knew the Dutch and Belgian armies to be weak and ill-organised. And he did not believe that their people would resist him whole-heartedly. There was indeed much pro-German feeling in the Netherlands, not only among its German-speaking minority. In Belgium too, where the dominant French-speaking Walloon population habitually discriminated against their Flemish fellow-citizens, many Flemings had more sympathy for Germany than for France.

The chance of a concerted Franco-Belgian defence policy had been lost in 1936. In that year King Leopold had cancelled his country's defence treaty with France as a gesture of appeasement to the Germans. His decision was made easier since the left-wing Popular Front government which took office in France that year, including Communist members, had actively encouraged French-speaking Belgian Socialist politicians to take an anti-monarchist line in their home policies.

Senior French and Belgian officers had formal talks about possible cooperation in November 1939 and again in January 1940, following the capture of the German plan of attack through Belgium. Nothing followed. In April 1940 the Belgians formally refused the French permission to inspect the defensive line on the river Dyle, just east of Brussels. In fact a few French and British staff officers in plain clothes did take a look at the line. They were unofficially helped by Belgian officers, who politely but surreptitiously showed them the prepared Belgian defences. What the genteel spies did not see were the places where there were no prepared Belgian defences, and that was most of the Dyle line they were expected to man.

On May 10th the lightning struck. The German pretext for attack was, as expected, the military necessity of "forestalling a planned Franco-British action" in Belgium. From Waalhaven in the Netherlands right down to Châteauroux in Touraine, the airfields of neutrals and belligerents alike were bombed. So were the rail junctions. Paratroopers and glider troops dropped onto the bridges and strongpoints of the Neth-

erlands and of Belgium. The German success was instanta-
neous and complete. Nazi sympathisers among the Dutch and
Belgian forces played their part. Far more important were the
incompetence and unpreparedness of the loyal defenders.

By striking with bombing planes and airborne troops behind the neutrals' front the Germans wrecked their communications at once. The defenders did not know what had hit
them, and did not believe it when they found out. Some of
the German exploits were truly incredible, like the capture
of the Belgian fortress of Eben Emaël by parachutists and
glider-borne engineers who landed on its roof, and used the
new and secret technique of "shaped-charge" explosives to
blast in its walls. By midday on May 11th even this formidable redoubt, guarding the route to Liège and the key of the
Belgian waterways, was in German hands. Too late, the Belgians invited an attack by Allied bombing planes on the
bridges of the Maas and the Albert Canal. The German anti-
aircraft gunners were there in force. The French and British
bombers were badly knocked about, and their bombs failed
to hit the targets.

Thus the road was opened by the German airborne and
specialist forces for the steady advance of their conventionally
equipped Army Group B, on the German right flank. Meanwhile Army Group A, in which were concentrated the highly
mobile panzer divisions, the pride of Hitler's Army, was
pushing through Luxembourg. The resistance was not from
defending troops, but from narrow valleys, hilly terrain, bad
roads and weak bridges. All these obstacles the Germans surmounted. By May 12th the panzers were into France, ready
to cross the Meuse. The same day, too, it became clear that
the Dutch Army could not stand. Isolated units fought bravely,
but without any chance.

In so far as the Dutch had a defensive plan, it was to abandon the north east of their country to the invaders, form a
"bastion" in the centre of the country covering The Hague,
Amsterdam and Rotterdam, and wait for help. On the morning of May 10th, before Winston Churchill went to Buckingham Palace for the formal acceptance of his task as prime
minister, he had met a group of Dutch ministers who had
rushed across to look for support from Britain. But it was the

French who offered practical help to the Dutch. Two French divisions were promptly landed by ship on the islands of Walcheren and Beveland at the mouth of the Scheldt. Another French division was sent to make contact with the main body of the Dutch Army, but its route was blocked by the German advance guard, and the roads and railways were impassable. It turned back without fighting. The Dutch were on their own. Undefended Rotterdam was cruelly bombed, with no military objective.

On May 13th King George VI of England had a rude awakening. His diary recorded the circumstances:

> I was woken by the police sergeant at 5:00 a.m. who told me Queen Wilhelmina of the Netherlands wished to speak to me. I did not believe him, but went to the telephone & it was her. She begged me to send aircraft for the defence of Holland. I passed this message on to everyone concerned, & went back to bed. It is not often one is rung up at that hour, and especially by a Queen. But in these days anything may happen, & far worse things too.

No British aircraft were sent to the Netherlands as a result of the royal request. Instead King George received a further call from Queen Wilhelmina later in the day. It was from Harwich, on the coast facing Holland. The British destroyer HMS *Harvester*, sent to her rescue, had brought her across the North Sea to safety. The King went down to greet his fellow monarch on her arrival that evening at Liverpool Street Station, in the City of London, where she got off the train. The Queen had no baggage beyond the clothes she stood up in. She carried with her, and subsequently treasured, the steel helmet given to her by the captain of the destroyer that carried her into exile.

The Royal Navy, meanwhile, was looking after matters of equal strategic importance. The gold stock of the Netherlands central bank was loaded into warships and shipped over into the custody of the Bank of England. So was most of Amsterdam's treasure of industrial and gem diamonds. Fortunately there were brave Jews among the Dutch bankers, and the diamond trade was (as it still is) almost exclusively Jewish.

two divisions of Belgian troops and ten Dutch divisions. The Allied forces had many more soldiers than the Germans. They held nothing in reserve.

The Allied—that is to say the French—high command assumed that the Germans would take a couple of weeks to break down Dutch and Belgian resistance in the eastern parts of those countries, nearest to Germany. During that time, it was supposed, the Allies would be able to get their superior forces into position east of Brussels to meet the German advance. But the Germans moved too fast through the Low Countries, and their second onslaught through the Ardennes took the Allies in the rear. Since they had no reserves to face the second German attack, the French and the British turned back before they had completed their move forward. Now their lack of mobility and of radio equipment, their reliance on railways and telephone lines which the German air raids had made useless, spoiled their ability to organise themselves. Nobody could tell where the retreat would stop.

For the French collapse on the Meuse before the panzer attack there can be no excuse. The main force in the way of the Germans was the French Ninth Army. They were almost all elderly reservists. They had practically no regimental officers, no artillery, no discipline. (The British General Brooke had reviewed them in early spring and been appalled at their sullen, dispirited air.) When attacked they ran, fifty thousand men in disgrace.

Fortifications that existed on paper did not exist on the ground. The parliamentarian and champagne millionaire Pierre Taittinger had visited the sector in March 1940 and written a worried report about the state of its defences. General Huntziger had formally replied on April 8th, 1940: "No urgent measures need to be taken to reinforce the Sedan sector." This was exactly where the panzer divisions broke through. Whole companies of soldiers had been allowed to go home on *permission agricole*, the leave traditionally allowed at hay-making time in an army formed mostly of peasants. The army commander, General Corap, was an elderly incompetent. It was a rout. The penalty for desertion in face of the enemy was summary execution, and it had often been inflicted in the First World War. Any soldier found wandering without due authorisation had reason to fear death from his own side. Once separated from their units, men knew their safest course was to surrender to the enemy. If they could not find an enemy to surrender to, they shed their uniforms and army papers, and made for home in civilian dress.

In five days from their first move forward the Germans were past the French defences on the Meuse and driving down the undefended roads towards the mouth of the Somme. The only Allied troops that might have been available to stem this rush were those already in retreat from Belgium. But they had no transport and no clear orders. There were no plans to bring fuel and repair teams to the retreating army as it moved. Trucks, and the tractors for the guns, constantly broke down. The horse-drawn artillery could at least move, feeding on local forage and conscripting draught animals from the fields. But its pace in retreat was even slower than that of the marching infantry, and there were peasant carts of refugees to block the roads as well. Attacking aircraft have rarely been offered a better target. Messages could not get through. The army fell apart.

The demoralisation of defeat went right to the top with terrible speed. On May 15th the supposedly impregnable fortress of Sedan fell, and the panzer forces began their drive to the coast. The French did not know that the Germans were heading west to the Channel. They feared the enemy would drive south-west, where Paris lay undefended and closer than the Channel. Very early in the morning Prime Minister Reynaud telephoned his opposite number Winston Churchill in London. Churchill, a notorious late riser, was deeply disturbed to hear Reynaud say, "Yesterday we lost the battle. The road to Paris is open. Send all the troops and aircraft you can." But the British Prime Minister did his best to put heart into Reynaud: "All experience shows that the offensive will come to an end after a while. I remember the twenty-first of March, 1918. After five or six days they will have to halt for supplies and the opportunity for counter-attack is presented. I learned all this at the time from the lips of Marshal Foch himself." This appeal to glorious precedent seems to have calmed Reynaud. But of course it was nonsense. It took no account of the new technology of air and road supply and reinforcement that the Germans had mastered. It took no account of the state of the French Army, or the state of mind of the French high command.

Later in the morning the French Cabinet met to consider the reports, and to decline (for a few days yet) the advice of the military governor of Paris that the government and parliament should at once abandon the capital and retreat southwards to Tours. After the Cabinet meeting M. Reynaud renewed, by telegraph, his appeal to Churchill for more troops and aircraft.

The British had no troops to send. And the case for sending British air reinforcements was already lost. The previous day Churchill had argued in his own War Cabinet that the RAF should move fresh squadrons of modern fighters to France. The redoubtable Air Chief Marshal Sir Hugh Dowding, of Fighter Command, was resolutely opposed to this weakening of his power of defence, and had carefully lobbied a majority of the War Cabinet onto his side. The new Prime Minister had lost the argument. He was not likely to reopen the case now.

Churchill decided to go to Paris and see for himself. He rushed over by plane in the afternoon. He took with him the newly appointed Deputy Chief of the Imperial General Staff, General Sir John Dill, recently recalled to this high-level job from command of a corps of the British Expeditionary Force in France. In the gardens of the French Foreign Office the secret files were burning in bonfires, sending billows of smoke and scraps of charred paper flying over the Quai d'Orsay. The Englishmen met Reynaud, Daladier, the minister of defence, and General Gamelin, the sixty-eight-year-old commander-in-chief of the Army. It was a terrible scene. Churchill persisted in wondering what was really happening to the army, in which his own expeditionary force was included. "Where is the strategic reserve?" asked Churchill. No reply. In his tortured French Churchill persisted: *"Où est la masse de manoeuvre?"* The British thought the old generalissimo was weeping. They caught only one word of his reply: *"Aucune—* None."

That afternoon Gamelin was sacked. Rather, he was told that he would shortly be sacked, and was asked to carry on until his designated successor could arrive to take over. The new supreme commander was to be General Weygand, aged seventy-three, a First War hero who had been working on grand but vague plans for inter-Allied military coordination in the Middle East; he was living in Beirut, amid glories lingering from the days in the early 1920s when he had ruled as colonial administrator the protectorate of Syria. It took Weygand two days to fly by stages from the Levant to Paris. On arrival he asked for another day to reflect upon his new duties. So for three days there was in effect no Allied supreme commander. Meanwhile the German tanks were pressing on across France towards the sea, and a million men of the armies of the north were being cut off from the main body of the Allied forces.

The new supreme commander knew nothing of the German army he faced, and precious little about the French and Allied armies he commanded. He was not the only soldier to be recalled in France's hour of need. From Madrid there had arrived on the previous day the greatest living French soldier, now aged eighty-four, Marshal Pétain. Pétain had been sent as France's first ambassador to the new fascist government in Spain. He admired Franco's vision of a new Catholic order in Europe. As Reynaud said, "*Le Maréchal est devenu Hidalgo à Madrid*—The Marshal has become a grandee in Madrid." Reynaud had called him back to serve as vice-premier in the French Cabinet, to put heart in the army and inspire the people with memories of victory. The newspaper of Reynaud's Radical Party wrote: "The glorious victor of Verdun is here. At once the gloomy mists disperse, energy stands erect, and all repeat the slogan: 'They shall not pass!' " The Marshal met Weygand as the younger, white-haired man pondered his new responsibilities. "I pity you with all my heart," said the glorious victor of Verdun.

With these changes at the top in France, the newly forged tripartite alliance was doomed. For ten days, from Weygand's assumption of the supreme command (and Pétain's taking office as deputy premier) to the capitulation of the Belgian Army before dawn on May 28th, three armies were fighting on the northern front side by side, but with different objectives. The Belgians were fighting to defend Belgium, and thought they should surrender if that proved impossible. The French wanted to counter-attack away from Belgium into France, and regarded surrender as a regrettable necessity that might come

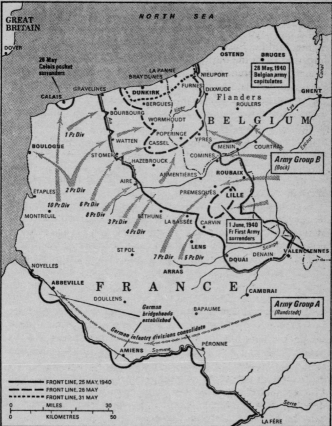

if that counter-attack failed. The British refused to think about surrender, but planned to get away to England.

To unite these disparate commands Weygand formulated a plan. It was for a counter-attack southwards across the German salient by the combined Allied armies of the northern front, and a simultaneous counter-attack northward to meet it and pinch off the German spearhead. But it was more a dream than a plan. Even if the Allies had wanted to implement it, they lacked the communications for its co-ordination.

The centrepiece of this grand confusion was Dunkirk, on the English Channel, next to Belgium, just inside France. The town—port and fortress—had a different role to play in each of the national dilemmas. For the Belgians it was the jumping-off point from which an operation could be mounted to drive the Germans out of Belgium. For the French it offered a fortified base, easily supplied by sea, for an attack southwards across the German supply lines in defence of Paris. And it was more than that too. It was, and still is, a steel town, a shipbuilding town, a great commercial and naval port, the most northerly of France's cities. It had been shelled by the Germans in the war of 1871, and again in 1914–18. To ask a French soldier to abandon it was like asking an Englishman to surrender Newcastle.

But for the British army Dunkirk was simply a convenient harbour, a transit point on the route to home and safety. That was how they hoped to use it, not as a base for a land battle. Of three allied nations, the British alone were to carry through their hope into a plan and then an achievement. But this they were at pains to conceal from their partners.

The crucial day in this divergence was May 21st, the day after the Germans had established the forward positions of this armoured southern thrust on the mouth of the Somme, at Abbeville. General Weygand had resolved to travel north to get a firm grip on the situation. Finding the land route blocked, he bravely crammed his seventy-three-year-old form into a bomber plane and flew across the German lines. He landed in the most frightful confusion at 8 a.m. on the tiny airfield of Norrent-Fontès, between Béthune and St.-Omer. The Royal Air Force squadrons that had been using it for refuelling had gone home without telling their French Air Force colleagues. A French private soldier from a logistic unit was in sole command. "They've all pissed off!" said the private to the supreme commander. "And I'm wondering what anyone wants me to do with all this fuel. Do I set it alight?"

After a while somebody flagged down a passing army truck, in which the general got a ride to a café with a telephone. While his staff officer tried to get a line to some headquarters, the general ordered an omelette. As she put it before him the *patronne* glanced up at a coloured poster on the wall showing the Allied commanders at the signing of the armistice in 1918. She recognised her man: "*Mais c'est bien vous qui êtes là, monsieur le général?*—Is that really you in the picture, General?" It was. Weygand recorded in his biography that he was much cheered by this.

Not until 3:30 p.m. did Weygand arrive at Ypres, the Belgian Army headquarters where King Leopold awaited him with Admiral of the Fleet Sir Roger Keyes, his British liaison officer. Soon afterwards General Billotte, commanding the French First Group of Armies, arrived. With him was the naval officer in command of Dunkirk, Admiral Abrial. For a long time they awaited the other essential participant in this inter-Allied conference, Lord Gort of the British Expeditionary Force. He did not show up until 9 p.m., by which time Weygand had been compelled to leave via Dunkirk in a French torpedo boat for Cherbourg, and thus by train to Paris; the supreme commander was out of touch with his headquarters for twenty-eight hours at the height of the battle.

Then and later the French believed that Gort had deliberately missed this vital conference. A signal had been sent to his headquarters telling him of it, the previous night. There is no evidence that the signal was received. Anyway, Gort had business elsewhere that day. For the first time the BEF had gone into offensive action against the Germans, even though with an absurdly small force of two tank and two infantry battalions: at Arras they had inflicted a shock on the Germans and nearly killed a divisional commander called Rommel, before being driven off in disorder (see pages 78–87). The failure of this little British attack certainly helped make up Gort's mind that there was no point in staying in France; but it seems unlikely that, before its failure became apparent, he should have been so deliberately insubordinate as to disobey a summons from the supreme commander himself.

But the Ypres conference was a total waste of time. Weygand wanted the armies of the northern front to attack southwards across the German salient, to meet a corresponding pincer movement by the main body of the French Army from south of the Somme. The King of the Belgians could not agree to the final abandonment of his national territory that this would have made inevitable. Weygand's brave flight had no consequences.

When Lord Gort did arrive, full of excuses, he had a brief meeting with King Leopold and General Billotte. It dealt with routine information and generalised but vague declarations of solidarity. The meeting broke up. Gort and Billotte drove off to their respective headquarters. Speeding down the road in the dusk, Billotte's driver crashed into a truck. The general, the one man with authority to coordinate the troops of the alliance on the northern front, was knocked unconscious. He died the next day. There was nothing in his briefcase save some personal financial documents, no plan, no record of the meeting.

The next senior available French officer was General Blanchard, commanding the French First Army. He took over Billotte's functions, but without his authority. Moreover, in the absence of orders from supreme headquarters, he felt he could not hand over command of his First Army to another. Not until May 25th did Weygand confirm Blanchard as Billotte's successor, and name General Prioux as commander of the First Army. For four crucial days neither the alliance in the north nor the largest French army within it had a full-time commander.

During that time the German advance continued, both from Belgium towards the French frontier and from the mouth of the Somme northwards towards the Channel ports. The net was tightening on the indecisive armies of the north. The Allies were caught in a bag. Its open mouth was on the coast straddling the Franco–Belgian border from Gravelines almost to Ostend, gradually being pulled shut by the twin German advances along the coast from either side. The narrow closed tip of the bag lay one hundred kilometres inland, south-east of Lille, where strong French forces and some British stragglers kept up a stout resistance.

The British decided on May 22nd that they would not stay in this bag. They began to pull their troops out of the firing line as fast as possible, to hurry them down the line to Dunkirk—not formally, yet, for evacuation, but for consolidation with a view to the evacuation that they wanted. The French, meanwhile, in the vacuum of command caused by Billotte's death and the unconfirmed status of his replacement, Blanchard, did their best to hold on to the terrain they had, and to fight the Germans off where they could. But by now the men of the British Expeditionary Force formed almost a third of the surviving fighters of the Allied armies of the northern front. Where they withdrew—and withdraw they did, in defiance of French orders which they did not feel obliged to accept because Blanchard was not officially in charge of them—they left exposed the flanks of their French neighbours, and made their withdrawal in turn inevitable.

On May 24th the British finally got what they wanted, which was a wholesale retreat towards Dunkirk. Weygand, in Paris, telegraphed in the evening to Blanchard: ''You inform me of withdrawal decided executed English in night 23/24 on Haute-Deule Canal. If this withdrawal makes impossible manoeuvre as ordered, try to establish widest possible bridgehead covering Dunkirk, indispensable for supply of battle.'' The ''manoeuvre as ordered'' mentioned here was Weygand's plan for a counter-attack southwards across the German supply lines on the Somme, which Mr. Churchill had ordered Lord Gort to join in as strongly as possible, and which offered the only possibility of aggressive action against the Germans.

The British army's move away from the enemy and towards Dunkirk had made this aggressive action impossible. Lord Gort and his staff had decided the French were hopeless. The BEF was on the move towards Dunkirk, and planning to use it as an escape route. The French were thus constrained to follow the British towards Dunkirk. But it had not occurred to the French to escape from there. For them it was to be a strongpoint in the German rear, hampering any attempt by the panzer divisions to start their march south on Paris.

The same day, May 24th, Hitler flew to the airfield at Charleville on the river Meuse, and in the control tower confirmed the order to the panzer troops to stop their advance towards Dunkirk. He had more important work for his panzers than bottling up the Allies in a coastal town from which they could not—as he thought, as the French thought, and as the British feared—escape.

The next day General Weygand frankly placed the facts before the French War Cabinet: ''France has committed the immense mistake of starting a war without having either the necessary equipment or the necessary strategic objective. She will probably have to pay a high price for this foolishness.'' It was the old hero, Marshal Pétain, who at this meeting of the *Comité de Guerre* spoke of (but did not name) the likelihood that France would do best to seek a separate armistice with Germany. The British meanwhile were refusing all talk of peace, while pulling out of the fight on the Continent. On May 26th the order went out to start Operation Dynamo, the wholesale evacuation of the BEF from Dunkirk. Neither the French nor the Belgians were informed. Indeed, Lord Gort was instructed to keep it secret. His deception kept the Belgians fighting for two more days.

At dawn on May 28th the Belgian Army capitulated. The Germans as well as the Belgians ceased fire on the eastern flank of the strip of land under Allied control. The British seized the opportunity as soon as it presented itself, moving over to fill the gap south-east of Dunkirk left by the Belgian withdrawal. This was a brilliantly organised manoeuvre, carried out by the British Second Corps under General Alan Brooke. But the French were not consulted about it. The British moved into the gap left by the Belgians. The Germans moved into the gap left by the British. Seven French divisions, half of the French First Army, were left cut off near Lille.

General Blanchard visited the headquarters of the BEF on May 28th, while this move was being carried out. He begged Lord Gort to delay his retreat for twenty-four hours, to give the First Army time to organise itself for escape. Gort flatly refused. He had received express orders from his government to subordinate everything to the safety of the BEF. Blanchard put the final question bluntly: "Will the British troops withdraw northwards [towards Dunkirk] this evening, whatever the situation of the French First Army?" Gort left the answer to his chief of staff, General Pownall, who had some fluency in French. Yes, said Pownall. The fact that the British were going home was still not mentioned.

The French First Army held out bravely in its isolated perimeter round Lille until all its ammunition was gone. The last stand tied down a large German force that would otherwise have been available to attack the perimeter of Dunkirk itself. On June 1st, in tribute to the courage of the defenders, the German victors allowed the survivors to keep their weapons for a final, ceremonial parade of surrender in the central square of Lille. Down the coast at Dunkirk the French rearguard was defending the perimeter while the British army escaped.

Part Two
THE BRITISH IN FLANDERS

4

THE SLEEPING PARTNER WAKES

In September 1939 the British sleepwalked into war in Europe. For over seven months of the phoney war the country dozed fitfully on, fighting with energy at sea, but devoting as little trouble as could be to the Continent where the reason for the conflict lay. Poland went under to the German blitzkrieg. The British could do nothing. In conspiracy with the German dictatorship, the Soviet dictatorship beat down Finland. Britain did not fight. But under the surface anger was growing in the British people, and impatience—anger with the enemy, impatience with the British government that was unwilling to act.

In the spring of 1940 Britain awoke and began to fight, first in Norway, then in France and Belgium. Neither campaign lasted long. The Norwegian campaign, begun in April, was a disaster. But it left the German fleet crippled, and provided a parliamentary pretext for getting rid of the government responsible for the plan. On May 10th Winston Churchill took office as leader of a national coalition, and the Germans attacked in France and the Low Countries. Exactly three weeks later the commander-in-chief of the British forces on the Continent waded out to a small boat on his way from Dunkirk beaches to England and a hero's welcome in defeat.

Hitler would have liked the British for his friends. He saw

their Empire as the solid achievement of his ideas of racial domination. As late as 1941 he was still saying to his entourage, ''To maintain their Empire they need a strong Continental power at their side. Only Germany can be that power.'' But the British did not know of his admiration, and would not have been interested if they had known. For several centuries Britain's European policy had been simple. It was to engage, with reluctance and often with distaste, in whatever Continental alliance would leave Britain free to pursue her imperial mission across the seas. They disliked all their allies, but they disliked the Germans even more.

From 1914 to 1918 the alliance against Germany had involved them in a war that they had won but that they had hated the winning of. The British dead in the First World War numbered just over half those of France, which in turn were far less than those of Germany. But the British remembered their dead with more pain than glory, and they were profoundly resolved never again to become stuck in the mud of Flanders.

From 1935 onwards the British government had joined, however reluctantly, in the international arms race in which aggressive Germany was setting the pace. They had reaffirmed their alliance with France. But they rebuilt their forces not for a war on land in Europe alongside the French, but for a world-wide, strategic conflict that suited the British history and temperament. It was the navy and the air force that got the new funds, the new scientific inventions, the new (but always moderate) enthusiasm of the people. By 1939 Britain was almost ready for war, but not for the war that actually had to be fought on the Continent.

The Royal Navy, guardian of the Empire and of Britain's supply routes for food and raw materials, naturally took the largest share of the new defence funds. When war came the navy was given a double role. It was to counter the expanding but still inferior German fleet of raiders and submarines. It was also to cut Germany's supply routes from the outside world, and bring the Third Reich down by attrition. While the phoney war on land continued, up to April 1940, the Royal Navy proved strikingly successful at these tasks. Its scientific achievement in finding a counter to the German secret weapon of magnetic mines was superb. Its campaign in Norwegian waters left the German Navy crippled. Its control of the narrow seas made the British army's escape from France possible. Only after Dunkirk, with Germans in every port from Norway to Brittany, did the British Navy find its resources stretched.

It was in the air that Germany's superiority first proved itself decisive, first in Poland, then in Norway, then in the Low Countries and France. The Luftwaffe at the time was primarily designed to support the army on the ground. Things were very different in Europe's second most powerful air force, the RAF.

For longer than any other air force in the world the Royal Air Force had been an independent service, with its own high command, its own traditions, and its own strategic concepts. Its leaders were naturally dedicated to formulating a distinctive role for themselves and their wonderful machines. The exciting theory of air power in the inter-war years was that strategic bombing, by striking at an enemy's factories, communications and civilian population, could do away with the messy necessity of battles on the ground. (This theory, unfortunately, lived on into the 1970s: the Americans in south-east Asia were still trying it out then.)

This notion both attracted and alarmed the British: attracted them because it implied that a naval blockade and aerial bombardment could defeat Germany without too much fighting on the Continent, and alarmed them because Britain's own big cities were terribly vulnerable to an enemy air strike. Stanley Baldwin, later to be prime minister, had encapsulated (and notably oversimplified) this view of air power in his saying of 1932: "The bomber will always get through." The RAF, following this belief, saw itself as a strategic force. In the middle and late 1930s it began to develop a fleet of long-range bombing planes far superior to Germany's. The Wellington bomber, capable of hitting towns and factories all over Germany, was to have been its main offensive arm. But far too few of them were built by 1940.

Anyway, the strategic air war failed to break out as expected at the start of hostilities. The Germans had very few long-range bombers, and could not strike effectively even at eastern England until they acquired bases in France and the Low Countries. The British did not use their bombing fleet, partly because they did not want to give the Germans the propaganda advantage of claiming the loss of innocent civilians, and much more because the French, nearer to the German air bases and with no proper system of air defence, begged the British not to start something that would call down German retaliation upon France. In the phoney war Britain's long-range bombers were used almost exclusively for dropping propaganda leaflets on German cities. There was an RAF story of the pilot who explained his late return from a mission with the excuse that the leaflets had been hard to extract from their bundles. Why, he was asked, did he not drop the whole box at once? "Oh, that might have hurt someone down below."

The RAF's real strength was in defence of the island against the expected strategic strike by the Germans. In 1936 all the RAF's fighter aircraft had been biplanes, not essentially different from those used in the First World War. With their low speed and high manoeuvrability they had been ideally suited for the imperial operations—policing the Indian frontier, terrorising villages in the deserts of Iraq—that had been the mainstay of RAF operations between the wars. The original "air component" of the British Expeditionary Force in France in 1939 included two squadrons of Gladiator biplane fighters; they were soon upgraded to match the other two squadrons with their excellent new all-metal monoplane Hurricanes.

By 1939 the RAF was already well supplied with the world's best short-range fighter aircraft. The Hurricane could match on equal terms the Germans' best fighter, the Messerschmitt 109, and its longer-range, twin-engined companion, the ME 110. Better than any was the newer Spitfire, just coming into volume production as the war began. These British planes incorporated the latest refinements in aerodynamics, engines and guns. The chief lack was of pilots to fly them, men needing not only considerable gifts of coordination, fitness and courage, but also the intelligence and training to use the sophisticated equipment that the planes carried.

Just as important as the aircraft and their pilots was the unique and highly secret system for the radiolocation of attacking planes, later called radar, axled around a network of direction finders in southern and eastern England, and linked across the vulnerable areas of the country to the fighter bases and anti-aircraft gun sites by telephone and teleprinter links. This ingenious and expensive system was solely designed to defend the cities and factories of Britain against air attack. It formed what would now be called an integrated weapons system, its outer frontier extending a maximum of forty miles from the radar ground stations. This brought the Channel ports of Boulogne and Calais within its range, took in Dunkirk on its outermost fringe, but excluded the rest of France. To employ the Hurricanes and Spitfires—scarce aircraft, their trained pilots irreplaceably scarce—outside radar range would have been to risk the RAF's main asset.

More delicate yet, it was absolutely imperative to keep the working of the radar system secret. An enemy who understood it would quickly learn to circumvent it. There could be no question of pushing the radar frontier forward over France, even of telling the French much about it. France was held to be full of spies. This, very simply, is why the RAF was carefully held back from the battle over the Continent. In May 1940, the RAF had about 1,400 ultramodern fighters. Just under 100 of them were stationed in France up to the date of the German invasion on May 10th. About 200 more were rapidly sent to France to meet the Luftwaffe. But the RAF's tragic losses over Sedan on May 14th showed the danger of committing aircraft to support of the armies in France, where there were anyway no proper maintenance facilities. By May 22nd the entire British fighter force was withdrawn from its bases in France; subsequently the Hurricanes and Spitfires fought only over the Channel coast facing Britain, flying from home bases in support of the British evacuation.

In the summer and autumn of 1940 the RAF, having been kept largely intact throughout the battle in France and Belgium, defeated the German Air Force in the Battle of Britain. But in order to keep it intact the Luftwaffe had been left largely unopposed in its operations to support the German Army on the Continent. The French believed, or claimed, that given the full force of British air support they could have held back the German Army. Even if this was untrue—and it probably was—the French had assumed that the RAF would be fully available to the alliance as a necessary supplement to the small British Expeditionary Force of ground troops. It is in any case certain that the refusal of the British to commit the RAF fully to the battle over France poisoned the relationship between the political and military leaders of Britain and of France, and contributed to the distrust whose nadir was the British deception of the French over their intention to evacuate Dunkirk, and whose culmination was the separate armistice sought by France despite her treaty with Britain.

By comparison with the navy and the air force, the British Army of 1940 was a poor relation. From the end of the First World War until the mid-1930s it had been employed largely on the routines of imperial defence, with the regular battalions rotating gently between tours at home and stints of barrack service in India. Promotion was slow, recruitment was limited by general government policies of financial stringency, and new equipment was lacking. Civilian life in the years of the Depression had few attractions for regimental officers, who hung on as ageing captains or lieutenants. Naturally this career did not attract many bright young men, who could see the promotion block of First War veterans standing in the way of their advance.

Not until 1936, with the realisation that another war could be on its way in Europe, did the possibility of modernisation start to be held out to the army. As a first stroke of modernity all horse-drawn transport was eliminated from the army in Europe by the end of 1936. (The Germans bought up a lot of the redundant animals for their own horse artillery; as well as developing a new, mechanised army they were also strengthening their traditional forces.)

Only in 1939 did the British government decide that the army should be enlarged as well as modernised. In March that year, with war now practically inevitable, the size of the part-time Territorial Army was doubled to (on paper) 210,000 men. Territorial units were made up of civilians who trained full time fourteen days a year, and occasionally on weekends and in the evenings. On the outbreak of war they were called up for full-time service. There was no serious pretence of equipping most Territorial units fully for fighting service. Many of their officers and non-commissioned officers were old hands from the First World War, unfit to fight; most units had no artillery, no signals equipment, no modern machine guns for training. Some did not even have enough rifles to go round. Over half of the men of the BEF in France belonged to Territorial units. Conscription was introduced in April 1939, with the Liberal and Labour parties voting against it in Parliament. The first conscripts—a mere 34,000 of them— were called up in July. There were very few conscripts in the BEF.

The British Expeditionary Force whose first units set off for France in September 1939 was more a symbol of Allied solidarity than an effective fighting force. Its commander-in-chief, General Lord Gort of Limerick, VC, was a man of immense personal courage and patriotism, and a protégé of the Secretary of State for War, Mr. Leslie Hore-Belisha. Gort rarely complained, even when the build-up of his force was unexpectedly delayed, and its reinforcements weakened by the detachment of trained men first for a projected expedition to fight the Russians in Finland, and then for the Norway adventure. But his report to the War Cabinet on April 11th, 1940, states that his five regular-army divisions were efficient, but not up to the standards of the BEF of 1914. The remaining eight Territorial divisions, he reported, were "fit only for static warfare." This is exactly what his own officers were saying with an air of superiority about the French Army.

But even if the five regular divisions had been up to the standard Lord Gort remembered so well from 1914, and equipped in reality as they were on paper, they would still have been unready for the campaign they had to fight. By German standards, even the full British scale of anti-tank and anti-aircraft armament was pathetic. Ammunition for practice with all kinds of weapons was desperately short, and there was nowhere to fire it off in the populous fields of northern France.

By May 1940 the BEF had only twenty-four tanks armed with two-pounder (37-mm) guns that could make a dent in an enemy tank; its seventy-six "infantry" tanks carried only a single machine gun. Lord Gort, after his return to Britain, permitted himself a plaintive note on the tank situation in his report to the War Cabinet: "Our I [infantry] tanks had succeeded in covering great distances. They had gone up to 40 miles a day, whereas they were not meant to go more than 10 miles a day . . . Perhaps our main defect was the absence of a tank with a gun. It was better to have a gun in an armoured car than a tank without a gun in it."

Incredibly, these tanks had no proper wireless. They had been designed without room inside for adequate sets, and their generators did not provide enough power for the batteries of the radios they had. Indeed, the entire signals system of the BEF was a disaster. When the army began to move, its internal chain of command virtually collapsed.

The BEF's place in the general Allied hierarchy was confused, too. As commander-in-chief of a national contingent, Lord Gort had a status higher than the strength of the forces under his command would warrant in purely military terms. Although the activities of the BEF were coordinated by the French commander, northern front, its orders came from the Allied supreme commander in Paris, General Gamelin. From these orders Gort had the right of appeal on questions of high strategy to the British War Office in London. While the Franco-British forces were standing pat along the border with Belgium this raised no particular difficulty, since all decisions had time to pass smoothly up and down along the chain of command between Paris and the operational command. But when the war became mobile, with the advance into Belgium to meet the advancing Germans, the arrangement ceased to be workable. At a conference at Ypres on May 12th King Leopold of the Belgians, as commander-in-chief of the twenty-two divisions of his national Army, agreed to integrate them with the Allies' chain of command. Gort, with his eight divisions marching into Belgium, agreed to do the same (with, of course, the full support of the government in London).

Gort thus became subject to the orders of the commander of the French First Group of Armies, General Billotte, taking an equal place in the hierarchy with King Leopold and with the generals commanding the French First, Second, Seventh and Ninth Armies. Billotte, in turn, was subject to orders from the French commander, northern front, General Georges. Georges in turn took his orders from the supreme commander, Gamelin. Gort and his staff neither liked nor for long conformed to this framework of authority. In it lay the seeds of the failure of coordination between British and French which had tragic consequences later at Dunkirk.

Billotte's army group, including the BEF, had spent the entire war so far sitting on the French side of the border with Belgium, from the Channel coast by Dunkirk to the start of the Maginot

Line and the Luxembourg border. The seaward end was held by the French Seventh Army. To their right, on the muddy plain just north of Lille, the Manchester of France, was the BEF. (This was, according to A. J. P. Taylor, the position originally held by the first BEF of 1914, who had been assigned to it under a staff plan of 1911.) To the right of the British stood, consecutively, the French First, Ninth and Second Armies.

The BEF was thin on the ground. It had three corps on the Belgian frontier. I and II Corps had the full complement of three divisions each. III Corps had only two divisions; its third, the Fifty-first (Highland) Division, had been detached to serve under French command on the Maginot Line. British units did turns in rotation there; it was a chance to see an occasional German helmet, and fire an occasional gun at long range against the enemy.

The Allies, including the BEF, had spent the worst winter on recent record preparing defensive positions on a line they were never meant to defend. If the Germans attacked, they would come through Belgium. The plan was to move forward to meet them there, well clear of French soil and the French industries of Flanders. The British Army heartily dug trenches and built strongpoints and laid wire entanglements along a line it was to abandon as soon as the first shots were fired.

This had no effect on the enemy, but caused a prominent casualty in London. The Secretary of State for War, Leslie Hore-Belisha, visited the "front" in November 1939. He was keen to push on with the construction of concrete machine-gun nests, known at the time as pill-boxes. He expressed concern that there were not enough of them. (The main reasons for the deficiency were that the frost broke up the concrete as soon as it was laid, and local contractors cheated on the supply of gravel.) Hore-Belisha's words were deliberately misinterpreted as a criticism of Lord Gort and his army for slackness. The soldiers retorted that they were building huge numbers of pill-boxes very fast, and the absurd wrangle ended with the forced resignation of the Minister. Hore-Belisha was impulsive, keen on publicity both for himself and for the army, and of Jewish origin. None of these attributes endeared him either to the soldiers or to the Conservative Party of government. The French, meanwhile, in their sector, did as little as they decently could to fortify the line, and concen-

trated on trying to keep warm and comfortable. British officers complained bitterly of being made to eat vast meals at
lunchtime when visiting their allies.

But the British too did their best to keep comfortable in
their way. Wine was cheap, and made you drunker quicker
than British beer. Apart from that, life in France was much
the same as in any other uncomfortable overseas posting. The
troops found their own forms of native entertainment. Major-
General Bernard Montgomery, commanding the Third Division, observed in his later memoirs: "It must be said to our
shame that we sent our Army into that most modern of wars
with weapons and equipment that were quite inadequate." At
the time he was critical of his soldiers as well as of their
hardware. He noted on November 15th, 1939, that in less
than a month forty-four cases of venereal disease had been
reported to his divisional medical services. He urged his junior commanders to set up more early-treatment rooms, on
the lines familiar from his last posting in Palestine. "It is no
use having one room in the battalion area; there should be
one room in each coy. [company] area; the man who has a
woman in a beetroot field near his coy. billet will not walk
a mile to the battalion E.T. room." The general pointed
out that the military police knew well where the licensed—
therefore relatively disease-free—brothels were. "These are
known to the military police, and any soldier who is in need
of horizontal refreshment would be well advised to ask a policeman for a suitable address."

This breezy document, distributed within Montgomery's division, aroused an interdenominational flutter of chaplains, who
referred the matter to the commander-in-chief himself. Lord
Gort came near to having to sack Montgomery for having issued
it. This was, perhaps, the greatest danger run by the British
Army in France during its long wait for the action to begin.

The army of the phoney war had its authorised entertainment too. The chairman of Lyons, the catering firm, advised
on improving the quality of their food. Concert parties arrived from Britain to spread the latest patriotic tunes. Gracie
Fields, the country's greatest star, sang for the lads. Even the
King came and walked benignly round selected areas. The
senior newspaper reporters gave up after that. The army had

not allowed them to report on the King's visit, and they were scooped by a handout from Buckingham Palace.

Over all these activities, military and otherwise, hung the long shadow of the First World War. All around were the awe-inspiring cemeteries—their headstones perfectly dressed, in line and in echelon, for the everlasting parade. Lord Gort himself was the embodiment of the First War tradition. As a young officer of the Grenadier Guards he had won his Victoria Cross in Flanders—they said he should have won it twice—and three Distinguished Service Orders, and the Military Cross. It is hard to know which is more astonishing, his courage or his survival.

Winston Churchill, in his racy little book *My Early Life*, written in 1930, had spoken of officers like Gort: ''I am doubtful whether the fact that a man has gained the Victoria Cross for bravery as a young officer fits him to command an army twenty or thirty years later. I have noticed more than one serious misfortune which arose from such assumptions. Age, easy living, heaviness of body, many years of promotion and success in time of peace, dissipate the vital forces indispensable to intense action. . . .'' Churchill was actually describing Sir Redvers Buller, VC, commander-in-chief in the South African War at the turn of the century. Gort was in every way a better general than Buller; but relations between the Prime Minister and the commander-in-chief of the BEF cannot have been smoothed by the words.

Major-General Spears, Churchill's waspish special emissary to the French Cabinet, described Gort in these terms: ''It has never occurred to me nor, I fancy, to any of his contemporaries to describe Gort as intelligent above the average. . . . Gort dazzled no one, but inspired confidence because he was completely trustworthy.'' The Army's public-relations officers encouraged the press to give Gort the nickname Tiger. His brother officers called him Fat Boy.

The First War traditions were affirmed right down the chain of command, in an army almost all of whose officers above the rank of captain, and many of whose warrant officers and senior sergeants, had done service last time in Flanders. The memoirs of the time resound with their nostalgia. Gordon Beckles, whose officially approved book *Dunkirk and After* was published in 1940, tells of a sergeant finding a familiar drink-shop with the same staff as it had in 1918. The pseudonymous Gun Buster, whose *Return Via Dunkirk* was published in the same year, describes "one of those incidents that, when they occur (and they occurred fairly frequently to the BEF) give one the sensation of having raised a ghost." Seeking billets for his men, he enters a ruinous farmhouse and finds it to be an old British infantry mess, never entered since its last occupants wrote on the wall: "Wipe your feet please, 1918." On a shelf lies a rusty bayonet, a Mills hand grenade, a bottle of tomato ketchup, a tin of Nestlé's condensed milk. Whether these stories be entirely true or not, the veterans who were encouraged to write for the public at the time, and to help create the myth of Dunkirk, thought them worth perpetuating. That in itself may help us to understand the backward-looking nature of the Army.

General Montgomery, in the hindsight of his memoirs, had harsh words for the BEF:

> In September 1939 the British army was totally unfit to fight a first-class war on the continent of Europe . . . In the years preceding the war, no large-scale exercises of troops had been held in England for some time. Indeed the regular army was unfit to take part in a realistic exercise.

But the British Expeditionary Force, as it awaited the start of the fighting, believed it would win glory. The soldiers were told they were better than the Germans; the Germans, indeed, were somewhat inconsistently presented in the propaganda of the time as both savage and cowardly. Hitler—who was just then preparing, under his personal direction, the most daring and successful campaign since Napoleon struck into Italy—was portrayed as a mad buffoon. Even the Germans' superior equipment was held up to ridicule. For close-quarter fighting the Germans were armed with the new Schmeisser submachine guns, the first of a generation of personal weapons that were to be adopted by every army in the world. They were, said the British newspapers, "gangster-guns," sneaking, Chicago-style devices typical of their cowardly and criminal possessors. The three weeks after May 10th were to show that bad men in an evil cause are not to be despised by their more virtuous, but less well-prepared, opponents.

5

INTO BATTLE

It was a glorious dawn on Friday, May 10th, 1940. Driver Charles Brown of the Royal Army Service Corps was in bed, asleep, at the big British fuel dump near the rail sidings at Béthune, in northern France. Twenty kilometres to the north lay the peaceful Belgian frontier, and the front line of the British Expeditionary Force. Two hundred kilometres to the east, somewhere near Aachen, there were German soldiers. Three million gallons of motor fuel in the dump were stacked in cans, in the open, to make work easier for Mr. Brown and his fellow-drivers, whose job was to distribute fuel to operational units. Naturally there was a night guard on duty. Its main job was to watch out for thieves, of whom there were plenty around. There were no anti-aircraft guns. The men on the ground, like all the BEF's supply train, had strict orders not to fire if any enemy plane came in sight. Their location was a secret, and gunfire might betray it to an enemy.

Just after 4 a.m. the sun was getting warm. A lone German monoplane appeared, buzzing in the dawn sky. From under its wing dropped a single bomb, and the plane turned away. In a blaze to match the sun the whole three million gallons went up. The secret dump was a secret no more. The phoney war was over.

Driver Brown, a commercial traveller by occupation, had volunteered for service in 1939. In the army he drove a truck, not a car, but the work was not too different. He had learned to handle a rifle and spent two half-days on the firing range. But he was trained to deliver fuel, not to fight. Now, roused from his bed by the guard to see the blaze, he had no more fuel to deliver. He was ordered forward into Belgium, to join an artillery unit as a spare driver. His convoy never found the gunners they were meant to join.

For two weeks, Mr. Brown and his colleagues drove about the crowded roads, sometimes in France, sometimes in Belgium. If they had a destination, the drivers were never told. They just followed instructions picked up at road junctions from policemen, and tried above all to keep moving. They were shelled, sometimes by Germans, sometimes by their own guns. They were bombed by high-flying aircraft and by low-swooping dive-bombers. Charlie Brown lost the rest of his convoy, and picked up the driver of a fuel truck that had blown up. Later they passed a medical convoy with ambulances, big red crosses on the roof, and they were bombed again. That time Charlie Brown was blown out of the ditch he was sheltering in, but he was not injured. Finally, with a couple of infantrymen and the driver of the bombed truck as passengers, he arrived at a canal where the military police ordered him to ditch his vehicle. He walked the final ten kilometres to Dunkirk, waited for twenty-eight hours on the beach, and finally, in an air raid, was lifted by small boat out to the destroyer HMS *Sabre*. She zigzagged across the Channel, and at four in the afternoon of Saturday, June 1st, Mr. Brown came home to Dover.

The British Expeditionary Force had planned carefully for its move forward into Belgium. At first light the German bombing began, striking at fuel dumps, rail junctions, road intersections and airfields with an accuracy that proved the meticulous work of German intelligence. But at 10 a.m., unmodified, the Allied plan of advance went ahead. The men had been told it would be a glorious battle. ''We're going to hang out the washing on the Siegfried Line,'' sang the British soldiers as their trucks rolled northwards. In five days' time they would be turning back again, trying and failing to re-establish their defence against an enemy coming from the rear as well as from the front.

So quickly did the British units move to the support of their allies that the Belgians were taken by surprise at their arrival.

General Montgomery's forward units, arriving at their assigned positions just after dark on May 10th, were fired upon
by Belgian soldiers who took them for German infiltrators.
The same day Colonel Perkins, a quartermaster officer, was
killed by a German bomb during a railway reconnaissance.
These were the first casualties for the British Army in the real
war in Flanders.

The British Expeditionary Force had been allotted a place
of honour in the Allied line of defence. Eight British divisions
were to man the eastern approaches to Brussels, the Belgian
capital. With the French Seventh Army on their left and the
French First Army on their right, their front was to be the
little river Dyle, about twenty kilometres outside the city,
along which—it was reported—the Belgians had prepared a
line of strongpoints and trenches into which the British could
conveniently move.

Before reaching the Dyle the Germans would need to cross
the flat lands of Belgium for one hundred kilometres. This
stretch of country, with its waterways and its fortress strongpoints, was manned by the static units of the Belgian Army:
not first-class troops, maybe, but average soldiers fighting in
defence of their homeland. In the end the Germans would
break through. That was inevitable, the penalty that the Belgians would have to pay for their failure to cooperate with the
Allies. But the breakthrough would take time, two or three
weeks at least, and meanwhile the British could get themselves stoutly dug in to meet the advance when it came. The
British allowed three days for their forward units to get into
place along the Dyle. Up to ten more days were allowed for
consolidating the prepared Belgian defensive works, laying
out a telephone system, registering the guns, and all the other
necessary preliminaries to meeting the German advance.

Soon the British advance started to go wrong. Fuel was
short because of the bombing. The Belgians insisted that
Brussels, to preserve its population from German bombing,
should be declared a demilitarised "open city," out of bounds
to army traffic. The first British troops followed the short
route to their destination, riding through the centre of the
capital. The photographers arranged for some men to march
through on foot. Women were persuaded to hand up flowers
to their country's new allies. But soon the British trucks were

shunted off into the suburbs, where they wandered around in frustration. When they asked to be put on the right way the interpreters found, to their dismay, that many Belgians answered in strange, guttural Flemish, and did not respond at all to classroom French. The hand of the German "fifth column" was seen at work.

When the advance parties reached the Dyle they had a nasty shock. The river, so significant on the map, is in fact not much more than a large ditch. The opening of the downstream sluices, to flood the fields towards Antwerp and defend the Belgian front line, had emptied the river even of its usual sluggish flow. The advertised defensive positions did not exist. All the work of digging and entrenching was yet to be done. The troops whom the British had moved forward first were fighting men, not pioneers with spades.

It was just as well that the advance parties were trained fighting units. Instead of fifteen days, it took the Germans four to reach the Dyle. On May 14th, while the British heavy guns were still making their way forward by rail, scouting parties of motorcyclists and armoured cars were seen approaching from the east, in German grey uniforms. At 6 p.m. the leading British units were ordered to withdraw their listening posts from the east bank of the Dyle, and consolidate. The retreat had begun.

Neither at headquarters nor at the fighting front did the British know what had hit them. Lord Gort's headquarters, which moved forward into Belgium on May 11th, had left behind its intelligence staff. Gort liked to keep a trim ship, without too many hangers-on, and he had ordered his director of military intelligence, Major-General Mason-Macfarlane, to bring only two staff officers with him. This was a catastrophic mistake.

Mason-Macfarlane, without a proper intelligence staff, got what news he could mainly from the British Embassy in Brussels. The embassy's main source was the same as the ordinary soldier's, the news bulletins of the BBC. They in turn reflected, as they had to, the fatuous optimism of the official military communiqués put out by the French high command in Paris. Rumour piled upon rumour. Any sign of defeat was blamed on German treachery and the fifth column. The main truth to which the fighting soldiers could bear witness was

that large numbers of raggle-taggle Belgian troops were retreating in front of them, and trying to pass rearwards through
the British lines. On May 15th it was the turn of the British
to shoot up their new allies, when the Grenadier Guards inflicted fairly heavy casualties on elements of the Belgian Tenth
Division who suddenly began to approach their front.

By May 15th the BEF's forward troops were engaged in
serious skirmishes with German scouting parties. On their
right the French First Army was facing a full-scale attack,
with support from German aircraft. From the First Army's
right again came rumours—soon confirmed—that the French
Ninth Army was smashed and on the run before the unexpected German attack through the Ardennes and across the
Meuse. To guard its own right flank, the First Army began
to retreat. The BEF, next evening, was ordered to do the
same. Otherwise it too would be outflanked.

The British were furious. They had not been seriously
shelled, or bombed from the air, or faced with enemy tanks.
They were told to run away before they had properly begun
to fight. They could have no idea of the furious onslaught that
had driven their allies back. They saw unshaven, disarmed,
leaderless Belgians falling back towards them. They were
confirmed in every prejudice they had about the weakness of
the foreigners with whom they were involved in disaster.

Ordered off the Dyle line, without firm orders, deprived by
their commander-in-chief's choice of the intelligence staff that
might have helped work out a concerted plan with their allies,
they now fell short in the one resource in which they had
been superior to the French. The BEF had enough motor
transport to carry its troops in relays on a planned advance.
They had too little for an impromptu retreat on roads
crammed with refugees and menaced from the air. Fuel ran
out almost completely. The soldiers had been told they were
in an army that would no longer have to walk. Now they were
walking. The marching columns made movement more difficult yet for the motor vehicles that were still in service.

Communication between mobile units became impossible.
The BEF in France had relied mainly on the public telephone
system. There were few English-speaking operators in the
Belgian exchanges, and anyway Belgium's telephone network
was highly unreliable. Throughout the phoney war the BEF

had kept wireless silence to preserve security. Practically untested, the radio network now proved almost useless. Arrangements for charging the heavy batteries of the day broke down. The wireless truck in each battalion became a mere encumbrance. As for the field telephones, the signal linesmen had followed up the advancing troops, laying cables as they went. In the hurry of retreat the lines could usually not be recovered. The telephones became useless. Maps were withdrawn from all infantry units below battalion level, since if captured they might betray secrets to the Germans.

Nobody knew what was going on. Orders and messages from unit to unit had to be conveyed by officers in cars, or by motorcycle despatch riders sweating in their leather jerkins, whose spectacular smashes became a memorable feature of the campaign. The roads on which they had to move were packed with marching men, refugees, horse-drawn French and Belgian guns, wrecks, staff cars trying to exercise their authority by passing on the wrong side. Messages failed to arrive, orders were garbled, the confusion thickened. An anti-aircraft battery sent this note to its brigade headquarters on May 18th: "No telephone in building, but Public Cabinet across the road. I have arranged for the Manageress to send to Battery Headquarters if the battery is asked for."

A great many British units were not even equipped for fighting. Eight divisions of the BEF, with their supporting artillery, engineers, headquarters troops and supply organisation, had moved forward into Belgium after May 10th. One more Scottish division was serving separately on the Maginot Line. But these nine fighting divisions and the units in direct support of them made up only about half of the BEF. There were four more divisions, half trained, half equipped, lacking artillery, lacking ammunition, lacking any signals organisation save the French telephone system. There were even more men in supply units, trench-digging parties, mobile bath teams, chemical-warfare groups, embryo transport formations along the BEF's lines of communications, which ran right back three hundred kilometres to the ports of Brittany through which the British army received its supplies.

The German panzer army, striking across northern France behind the Allied front in Belgium, fell right on these forces. Rapidly, and by improvisation that was often brilliant, they were scrambled together into fighting formations temporarily christened after elderly generals sent off from desk jobs to take command—Frankforce, Usherforce, Macforce, and so on. That the forces held together at all was an achievement. That they fought back when put within range of the enemy was a miracle. The German General Rommel took the surrender of one such group, and praised the fact that they had fought although equipped only with half-power ammunition for a training exercise. Rommel's interrogators misunderstood what they were told, or were deceived. These British did not have training ammunition. They had no ammunition at all. And yet they had stood their ground. Often such forces delayed the German advance. But they could never stem it. And their morale was bound to crack. They could not know what was going on. They believed they had been betrayed.

The liveliest rumours, carefully fostered by advance German propaganda, concerned the "fifth column." This novel term had originated in the Spanish Civil War when one General Mola, advancing on Madrid in 1937 with four columns of rebel troops, claimed that the Francoist supporters within the city were his fifth column, ready to undermine the defence from the rear. The German variant of this was that, when advancing into a country with a German-speaking minority (as in Czechoslovakia or Poland), their forces could rely for help on Nazi sympathisers among the population. The retreating British pressed through country in which this theory almost held good.

Brussels and its suburbs are mainly French-speaking. But in the province of Brabant, all around it, Flemish is the people's language. As you move west towards the Channel you pass rapidly into Flemish-speaking Flanders; to the south lies French-speaking Hainault. There has always been, and still is, tension between the two language groups in Belgium. In the 1930s a fair number of Flemings, speaking a Germanic language and resenting what they historically felt was unfair treatment by their Francophone co-nationals, were attracted by the racial fantasies of Nazism. In a few places the Germans had placed in advance of their invasion, or dropped in by parachute, Nazi activists and infiltrators. With some cunning they also dropped dummies on parachutes into woods and wastelands, thus diverting the energies of retreating Allied troops into fruitless manhunts.

The extent of this fifth-column activity was then, and has since remained, unclear. It seems to have been tiny. What mattered at the time was that the British and French armies believed it was widespread, and found in the alleged successes of the fifth column a welcome excuse for their own failure to match the conventional German Army. To the confusion the British added the muddle of their own racial fantasies. Gordon Beckles, in his account of the retreat published in 1940, records his suspicions of a farmer on whom he was billeted, based exclusively on the fact that the man had two pretty, buxom, Germanic daughters.

Flemish farmers, it was believed, had instructions to lay out arrows on the ground to point out British positions to German aircraft. In some accounts these arrows were ploughed by horses, in others mown with a scythe in hay. A correspondent has assured this writer that he saw such an arrow mown on the overgrown lawn of the château at Rosendael, pointing towards a vital canal bridge. Mr. H. J. Dibbens, then a lieutenant of military police on secondment from Scotland Yard, saw a brigadier in uniform personally remove the offending sign with a hand lawn-mower.

In the confusion of the retreat, the soldiers saw spies everywhere. At St.-Venant it was a French unit that arrested a rather beautiful young woman, who, under questioning, readily admitted to being an *espionne parachutiste*. She was sent for summary execution. Before the firing squad could do its work Commandant Bourlet had her searched for incriminating documents. In a pocket of her dress they found an evacuation form issued by the local madhouse.

Near Armentières about this time Lieutenant-General Alan Brooke was also bothered by escaped lunatics:

> With catastrophe on all sides, bombarded by rumours of every description, flooded by refugees and a demoralised French army, bombed from a low altitude, and now on top of it all lunatics in brown corduroy suits standing at the side of the road, grinning at one with an inane smile, a flow of saliva running from the corner of their mouths, and dripping noses! Had it not been that one's senses

were numbed by the magnitude of the catastrophe that surrounded one, the situation would have been unbearable.

Brooke's nightmare vision betrays his deep contempt for
the French Army and the French people. The general prided
himself, like many Anglo-Irish grandees, on his command of
the French language. But he never tried to understand the
French Army. The best French fighting units were organised
in *divisions légères mécanisées*, DLM—light mechanised divisions. Brooke always thought they were called *divisions
lourdes motorisées*, heavy motorised divisions, and equipped
for a role they were never meant to perform.

If the general's morale was low, that of the ordinary troops
was at rock bottom, especially in the many units that were
not trained for fighting and had not expected to fight. Many
of them split up into small groups, looking avidly for orders
and desperately for food and drink. Looting was common.
Lieutenant James Langley of the Second Battalion, Coldstream Guards, remembers entering a brewery manager's office where he found a captain of another unit trying to shoot
the lock off the brewery manager's desk with his revolver.
Langley summoned the military police. '' 'What will happen
now?' I asked the sergeant. 'My orders are explicit. Shoot
looters on the spot. But there are some officers over there,'
he replied, pointing to a group nearby. 'And I shall request
the senior to confirm these orders.' ''

Stealing from civilians soon became official policy. After
May 20th, when the Germans cut the British supply lines,
food began to run short. There were only three days' rations
in reserve. General Montgomery, resourceful as always, ordered his divisional headquarters to drive a herd of cattle with
them in case of emergency. The official history of the Coldstream Guards, published in 1951, provides a laconic but vivid
account of a well-disciplined British unit's conduct towards
civilian life and property. It was written, incidentally, by two
officers of the regiment who later became leading Oxford
intellectuals, Warden John Sparrow of All Souls' and Professor Michael Howard of the same college:

May 22nd was likewise quiet, the only excitement being
provided by fifth columnists among the local inhabitants,

a number of whom had to be arrested and shot. "To add interest to life," in the words of the Commanding Officer (Lieutenant-Colonel A. de L. Cazenove), "we were told that the B.E.F. was not cut off from its normal supplies, and we were to collect all the local produce we could and to live on the country. By the time we had left, our cooks' lorries were groaning with beef and pork, chickens and ducks, not to mention fresh eggs and milk. It is safe to say that from this day on the Battalion was never better fed."

The British army used its power to commandeer without payment and to execute without trial. The Grenadier Guards, about the same time, recorded the shooting of seventeen suspected "fifth columnists" at Helchin. This was how British— and other—soldiers had behaved in the Low Countries in the days of Edward III, or Cromwell, or Marlborough, or Wellington. It is small wonder if local civilians were anxious only to see the back of them—even if the replacement was to be the German army, whose propaganda had plenty of material to work with.

On occasion the army achieved miracles of improvised bravery. Here a platoon, there a single gun, now and then a company or a whole battalion in organised action, harried and delayed the German advance to win time for its own retreat. But too often the British, like the French, collapsed. Peter Hadley's frank account of his retreat to Dunkirk, published in 1944, described a "disorderly mob" of British soldiers running from a false report that the German tanks were just behind them: "They hurried on, looking (if the truth be told) very much like the popular conception of the Italian army." In a cooler moment Hadley wrote an assessment that has the ring of truth:

The BEF of 1940 started the Flanders campaign full of a self-confidence due principally to newspaper and other propaganda emphasising the strength and preparedness of the Allied armies: but with the rapid German advance it became gradually and increasingly clear that the Allies were in fact inferior and that self-confidence had been

born of delusion. Blasted from this stronghold, therefore, morale fell back to the alternative position where
it became dependent on discipline alone.

Discipline itself became increasingly hard to enforce as
officers were killed or separated from their units. The only
protection against air attack was to travel in open order, and
marching companies soon became scattered along the roads.
Attempts to close formations up could have catastrophic effects, and caused the only serious loss of life suffered by the
British from air attack. It was at Leuze, near Tournai. The
145th Brigade was travelling in trucks. A Royal Engineers
major, in charge of movement control, ordered the vehicles
to close up and move in a more soldierly fashion. As they
obeyed, nine Heinkels appeared and swooped on the tight-
packed convoy. The Gloucestershire Regiment lost 194 men
killed and wounded, the Oxfordshire and Buckinghamshire
Light Infantry lost 48. Vehicles were smashed across the road.
The survivors marched on afoot; most of the wounded were
left behind to await such transport as might appear.

But on the whole the British were lucky. They were not in
the line of a main German advance, and the weight of the
dive-bombing and machine-gunning was reserved for the
French and the Belgians. This was just as well. Outside its
specialised anti-aircraft units the BEF had no protection
against air attack. The big water-cooled Vickers guns of the
machine-gun regiments could not be elevated to fire into the
air. The infantry's Bren guns with their twenty-eight-round
magazines could shoot off their whole charge in less than four
seconds, and the attacking plane was gone before you could
get a new magazine on; the Bren tripods were cumbersome,
and rarely available when planes attacked. The only infantry
weapons useful against aircraft were the outdated Lewis guns,
issued to reserve units. They at least had drum magazines
holding forty-seven or ninety-seven rounds, and a tripod suitable for firing upwards.

In the early days they used to fire off rifles at aircraft; there
was even a special drill for this, when sections stood in rows
and blazed away into the air on the word of command. There
seems to be no proof that rifle fire ever shot down a plane,

and after a while the riflemen were instructed simply to lie down and make themselves small when a plane came over.

James Langley remembers a pep-talk from the commander of the First Guards Brigade on how to deal with Stukas. This was Brigadier Beckwith-Smith's advice: "Stand up to them. Shoot at them with a Bren gun from the shoulder. Take them like a high pheasant. Give them plenty of lead. Remember, five pounds to any man who brings one down. I have already paid out ten pounds." The brigadier, no doubt, had more experience of high pheasants than most of his Bren gunners. But he might have known that if you try to fire a Bren from the shoulder like a shotgun, the red-hot cartridge cases will give your left arm a nasty burn.

In the back of men's minds was the fear of being captured. They supposed that the enemy's orders would be the same as their own. Unarmed captives are a drag on a retreating army, especially when food is short. British fighting units had orders to take no prisoners, except when specifically ordered to take in captive Germans for interrogation. Patrick Turnbull had better grounds for worry. "With my revolver I had eight rounds, two of them soft-nosed, justification I was told with relish for my instant execution were I captured with them in my possession." Soft-nosed dumdum bullets were banned by the Geneva convention on the rules of war.

There are, moreover, two well-authenticated cases of mass murder by German soldiers of British prisoners of war. At Wormhoudt, on May 28th, over eighty men, mostly of the Warwickshire Regiment, were slaughtered after surrendering to troops of the SS Adolf Hitler Regiment. Ninety prisoners of the Norfolk Regiment were similarly slaughtered at the little village of Le Cornet Malo on May 27th. Their murderers were also SS men, this time of the Totenkopf, or Death's Head, Division, which the German Army much disliked.

The massacre of May 27th was discovered on the following day by an elderly and well-born German officer from Sixth Army headquarters. Major Freiherr von Riederer's job was to act as gas security officer. As such he had not much to do other than to wander around and see how things were going. He was horrified by what he found behind a farmstead wall at Le Cornet Malo. He counted the bodies of eighty-nine men in British uniform. "These people had almost all suffered head wounds from shots that must have been fired at very close range. Some had their whole skull smashed in, an injury that can almost only be caused by a blow from a gun butt or similar means.'' Promptly he put in a report to army headquarters, having taken the precaution of identifying as an additional witness Signalman Tenius, a radio operator on press and propaganda duties.

At army headquarters the regular officers pursued their inquiries with speed and energy; on May 29th a medical officer, Staff Doctor Wilhelm Haddenhorst from Army Corps headquarters, was also sent to the scene, where he counted about ninety corpses in British uniforms and found five more in a pond and four in a nearby field. As usual the regulars were keen to bring the despised SS troops under closer control. A stern message was sent to the SS division commander asking for an explanation.

The reply, signed by *SS Gruppenführer und Generalleutnant* Eicke, is a curious and almost hysterical document. It does not deny that the British prisoners were killed. Indeed, it seeks deviously to justify the action. The British, said Eicke's letter, had been using soft-nosed dumdum bullets, contrary to the Geneva Convention. Moreover, they had hung out a swastika flag to draw the SS troops into a position, and had then fired upon them from the rear. Four German officers and 153 other ranks had been killed, 18 officers and 483 other ranks wounded, 53 Germans were missing, unaccounted for. It is clear that he was not referring to the engagement at Le Cornet, after which the British prisoners were killed, but to an event a few days previously. The SS commander's explanation ends with this peculiar passage whose grammar is a problem for translators: ''The sneaking, rascally methods of combat of the English had to be expunged by the shooting, under military law, of the rest of those concerned in this cowardly ambush, in the interest of our own troops.''*

The German Army's investigation, of course, led nowhere. The SS troops were soon moved to another command for the

*''Die hinterhältige, schurkische Kampfesweise de Engländer musste mit der standrechtliche Erschiessung der Reste der am feigen Überfall beteiligten im Interesse der eigenen Truppe gesühnt werden.'' The evidence behind this SS allegation that they were avenging previous murders is examined on pages 83–84.

assault on Paris, and the matter was conveniently forgotten in the military bureaucracy. After the war two British privates, Messrs. Pooley and O'Callaghan, who had providentially escaped murder and been tended by other German soldiers, were able to prove that the event had really happened. A former SS company commander was hanged.

By the time of the massacres, anyway, the British army was heading out of France as fast as it could go. In retrospect, its reputation was saved by the carefully fostered belief that it was the French and the Belgians, and not the British, who were beaten. But the men of the BEF knew perfectly well that they were defeated, and longed for a miracle. Even the Coldstream Guards, a regiment whose morale one would not normally dare to question, had abandoned their early hopes of victory in Europe. At Roubaix, ninety kilometres from Dunkirk, Lieutenant-Colonel L. Bootle-Wilbraham of the Second Battalion assembled his company officers on May 27th, to tell them that orders had come to break off the fight and march back fifty-five miles for embarkation and England. Their regimental history records one captain's reaction to the colonel's words, as though he spoke for all:

No one had expected this. We had vague ideas of falling back as the armies of 1914 had fallen back until, somehow, we too should stand and fight our victorious battle of the Marne. But this! There was a sudden loosening of the tension we had been living in for so long. We felt a surge of contentment beneath our anxiety about the war news in general and our own immediate prospects in particular. Then we thought again of the 55 miles, and wondered.

The previous day the Admiralty in London had issued the order that Operation Dynamo, the sea evacuation from Dunkirk, was to commence. The entire British army was on its way home, if it could get there. Mr Churchill was, even at this late stage, full of suggestions for offensive action. On May 27th he proposed to Lord Gort that he should send a column to the relief of Calais, although that town had in reality surrendered to the Germans the previous evening. But his final words were finely judged to the mood of Gort's weary soldiers: "Presume troops know they are fighting their way home to Blighty.* Never was there such a spur to fighting." From now on the task of the BEF was plain, and sanctioned by the highest authority: get home, via Dunkirk. As the Prime Minister's message passed over the cable, Belgian generals were still trying to persuade their reluctant King that surrender was inevitable, and French generals were mustering their troops for a long defence of the northernmost port of their homeland, Dunkirk.

Between the start of the German attack on May 10th and the embarkation of the final British soldiers from Dunkirk on June 2nd, the BEF fought just one concerted offensive action, at Arras on May 21st. That little engagement involved just two battalions of British infantry and two of tanks. But they received the highest praise that soldiers can be given, in the admiration of their enemies. The story shows the British army at its best and at its worst. It deserves a chapter to itself.

---

*"Blighty" was a First World War term for home. A Blighty wound, in the British army, is still a wound bad enough to get a soldier repatriated, but not bad enough to cripple him for life.

6

THE FIGHT AT ARRAS

When the war was over the commander of German Army Group A, General von Rundstedt, described his forces' triumphant drive from Germany to the Channel coast. He paid the finest of compliments to the British, who were now his captors:

> A critical moment in the drive came just as my forces had reached the Channel. It was caused by a British counter-strike southwards from Arras on May 21st. For a short time it was feared that our armoured divisions would be cut off before the infantry divisions could come up to support them. None of the French counter-attacks carried any threat such as this one did.

The Germans in their blitzkrieg had broken all the rules of the staff colleges. Their tanks had dashed across France, covering an average of fifty kilometres a day. By the evening of May 19th their scouts were looking out over the English Channel. They had cut a swathe that divided the Allied armies of the northern front from the main body of the forces defending France. But the strip they held was narrow and its flanks were undefended. As their reinforcements and supplies moved up to consolidate the victory of the spearhead, the German high command grew increasingly aware that at any time the Allies might attack from the flank at this perilous lifeline, from north, from south, or from both at once. The fighting commanders had staked their reputations, and their lives, on the inability of the Allies to bring off such a counter-stroke.

The French high command, meanwhile, were trying to or-ganise exactly the manoeuvre that the Germans feared. Speed was essential. With every hour that passed, the German-held corridor grew wider and stronger. The only force the Allies could muster in time was tiny. It consisted of two battalions of British tanks, supported by two battalions of half-trained British infantry. They were repelled with heavy losses. But the threat they presented caused the Germans to pause and ponder, and contributed to the delay which enabled the Brit-ish and the French to establish their defences round Dunkirk.

The British Expeditionary Force had only two battalions of tanks, the Fourth and Seventh of the Royal Tank Regiment (4 and 7 RTR). When the BEF was ordered into Belgium they had gone up the line by train. Soon after their arrival they were ordered back again to meet the German panzer drive across the Allied rear. A train was marshalled to take them back, but German bombing prevented them from using it. False reports were received that a German panzer attack was imminent; the British tanks rolled pointlessly round the landscape, looking for non-existent enemy tanks, wasting fuel and wearing out their tracks. Eventually they rolled under their own power back to where they had started from, the permanent headquarters in France of the BEF in the old town of Arras.

The British tanks were designed to cover a mere ten miles a day between overhauls. By May 18th, when they arrived back at Arras, they had travelled 120 miles without access to workshops. A quarter of the original 100 tanks were out of action. The operating force now consisted of 58 Mark I tanks, heavily armoured but with a single machine gun as their only weapon, and 16 Mark II (Matilda) tanks, carrying as well as their machine gun a two-pounder (37-mm.) gun, equivalent to the standard armament of a German battle tank.

The tanks arrived at Arras just as the support units of the BEF were being organised into improvised fighting teams, each named after a deskbound general suddenly transformed into a fighting commander. The tanks joined Frankforce, named after Major-General Franklyn. Lord Gort, the BEF's commander, had for some days been pressed by the Allied high command (that is to say, by the French) to mount a joint Anglo-French counter-attack southwards against the advancing German columns. He had dismissed the idea as quite unrealistic. On Monday, May 20th, Prime Minister Churchill himself decided that such a counter-attack should be made. He so instructed the War Office, and the War Office gave Gort his orders. This time the orders were obeyed. Gort gave the job to Frankforce, because it had the tanks. To support the armoured battalions, Franklyn assigned two battalions of infantry, the Sixth and Eighth Durham Light Infantry (6 and 8 DLI).

These were Territorial Army battalions, recruited in the depressed mining and shipbuilding communities of north-east England. By tradition the maximum height for a light infantryman was five feet two inches (1.57 metres). County Durham, at the end of twenty years of catastrophic unemployment in the coal-pits and shipyards, had plenty of people small enough and willing to take a job as a soldier. But nobody had seriously expected them to have to fight. As miners, they had a reputation for building wonderful trenches, and they had spent the war so far employed as labourers. Every single platoon of both battalions was commanded by a second lieutenant—lads fresh from grammar school, or clerks in their forties who had seen service in the previous war. Most platoons had no sergeant, and practically all the non-commissioned officers were either First War veterans, in their forties, or new recruits themselves. The Durhams had half the official supply of Bren light-machine guns, no radios and no supporting artillery. These deficiencies should be remembered in the record of their conduct in battle.

General Franklyn's orders were to secure the defences of Arras, and then to move on to block the roads to the south of the town, "thus cutting off the German communications from the east." This was precisely the manoeuvre that the Germans most feared and half expected. It was also the manoeuvre that the French high command in Paris had ordered, and that the French commanders on the spot were trying to organise.

Franklyn, on receipt of his orders, went off to try to coordinate his intended operation with his French colleagues. He made contact with two officers senior to him: General Prioux, of the Cavalry Corps, and General Altmayer of the French Fifth Corps. At their meeting another French General was present, with gold leaf all round his képi. Franklyn was introduced to this officer, but did not recognise him or even identify his badges of rank. It was General Billotte, commanding the French First Group of Armies, the officer from whom Lord Gort himself was supposed to be taking orders. Franklyn had apparently never heard of him. Lord Gort's subordinates had not been briefed about the Allied chain of command, or told to take seriously the British government's order that they should cooperate with the French. Franklyn and Billotte shook hands, but did not speak. The impossibility of a major Allied combined counter-offensive was symbolised by that handshake.

This took place in the afternoon of May 20th. Franklyn patched up such arrangements as he might with Altmayer, and learned of Altmayer's plans for an attack southwards the following day by the French Third Light Mechanised Division, with about 250 heavy tanks. Later Altmayer told Franklyn the plan was postponed for a day, until May 22nd. The French troops were having trouble getting into position for an attack across the German lines of communication. The men were exhausted, and the tanks desperately short of fuel.

Franklyn too was having difficulty getting his troops into position in time. There were not enough trucks to transport the Durham Light Infantry. The inexperienced platoon officers had not ensured that the light infantrymen washed their feet and changed their socks regularly. Fair numbers of soldiers fell out of the march with blisters. But the British went ahead, without the French.

On May 21st in the morning the attack started. Led by motorcycle scouts, the tanks plunged ahead at 11 a.m. The infantry, who had spent the night beside the great Canadian war memorial at Vimy Ridge, near Arras, were supposed to march fifteen kilometres in two and a half hours, in order to take up position behind the tanks. They were late. (The day's war diary of 6 DLI began: "0730: Milked cows to provide tea for breakfast." 8 DLI had no food at all throughout the day.) The Durhams had no radios for communication with the tanks; anyway, the tanks had flat batteries, and their own radios failed to work. Moreover, Franklyn's orders were ambiguous, failing to make clear whether the tank officers or the infantry were in command of the operation.

The tanks' first target appeared near the village of Duisans. There was a brisk exchange of fire with some other tanks. Little damage was done. This was fortunate, since the tanks receiving and returning the British fire turned out to be French. This nonsense was sorted out, and the British continued their advance in the comforting knowledge that they had a strong French tank force behind them.

Just after 2 p.m. 7 RTR arrived at the road by Achicourt, on the southern fringe of Arras. It was an amazing piece of luck. The German tank spearhead had just passed along the road, going as fast as they could make it towards the west. Avoiding the centre of Arras, which was still in French hands, they were cutting round the byways to rejoin the main road to Le Touquet on the coast. Behind the tank spearhead were infantry in unarmoured trucks, offering a perfect target. The German anti-tank guns were powerless against the heavy armour-plating of the Matildas and Mark I's. "One tank showed as many as 14 direct hits and the only indication the crew had of being hit was a red glow for a few seconds on the inside of the armour plate": this note was made by a British tank officer after the fight. Soon both battalions of the Royal Tank Regiment were firing at will.

But tragedy soon struck. Lieutenant-Colonel Fitzmaurice, commanding 4 RTR, was operating from inside a fast but lightly armoured light tank, by preference to an unwieldy Mark I. It was hit by a shell from a field gun, and Fitzmaurice died instantly. Lieutenant-Colonel Heyland, commanding 7 RTR, was trying to get his tanks lined up correctly to take the Germans on the flank. His wireless did not work. He dismounted to make hand signals to his men. Exposed in the open, he was killed by machine-gun fire—friendly or hostile makes no difference—as he semaphored to his battalion.

In this phase of the battle the British did not lose many men, except for their battalion commanders. But twenty of the seventy-four tanks broke down. Travelling now off the roads, their worn-out tracks would not take the strain. Although their hulls were practically impervious to enemy fire, they carried outside a mass of necessary clutter—spare cans of scrounged fuel, baulks of timber for leverage in emergencies, pots of grease, soldiers' spare clothing. Several caught fire. Once out of their tanks, the men were useless: they carried only revolvers. ("The sooner sub-machine guns are provided for RTR personnel, the better," said the subsequent report.)

The Germans were doing even worse. Their soft-skinned vehicles were set alight, their men shot down as they ran. The unlucky German unit belonged not to the Army but to the Totenkopf Division of the SS. Despite their fierce name they were not trained soldiers, but young Nazis without proper officers. The "points of interest" in the British tank men's subsequent report noted as the first item "the poor fighting qualities of the German troops encountered. They were very young and large numbers were observed lying on the ground face downwards feigning dead, others ran up to the tanks surrendering."

By four o'clock in the afternoon the exhausted and practically untrained men of the DLI had caught up with the tanks and were at last in action. The anti-tank guns and the support platoon of 8 DLI had a nasty exchange of fire with some French tanks. There were casualties on both sides. There followed some incidents for which there is no satisfactory explanation. The official history of the DLI has this to say, in its account of the advance of the Eighth Battalion:

> "C" Company, in company with some French tanks, then attacked a cemetery near Duisans where some hundred Germans had taken refuge from the Royal Tank Regiment. When they occupied it, they found only eighteen alive and the French stripped them to the skin and made them lie face down on the road until it was time to take them away.

The war diary of the First Army Tank Brigade (composed of the two RTR battalions) notes more vaguely: "At one time a large number of prisoners were taken—these were handed over to the infantry." The war diary of 6 DLI records that "large numbers of prisoners were taken." On the only surviving copy of this document, in the Public Record Office at

Kew, the number of prisoners taken was recorded. In the process of clipping it into a file, the digit preceding the two zeros in the total has been cut out of the paper. Other sources, notably the semi-fictional *Return Via Dunkirk*, by Gun Buster, put the number of prisoners at four hundred. There is no subsequent trace of these prisoners.

An officer of 7 RTR on a scouting mission captured a German non-commissioned officer, and carried him back for interrogation. "I continued into Dainville and handed over the prisoner to a Captain of the DLI for conveyance to Provost personnel. The troops displayed great animosity towards the prisoner, and I was compelled to draw my revolver and order them off before I could reach their officer."* If the Germans had to rely on the Durhams' officers for their protection they were out of luck. By the evening of May 21st most of the DLI officers were dead, and every single one of the eight companies present was commanded by a second lieutenant.

The distasteful truth is that men of the Durham Light Infantry did murder an unknown number of Germans who had surrendered, and were legitimate prisoners of war. The DLI advanced, took prisoners and were then forced to retreat. They could not take the prisoners back with them, so they killed the SS men rather than set them free to fight again. That, at least, is how some surviving members of the DLI describe the event.

Other units of the British army paid the price in blood a week later, at the hands of SS men whose comrades had been killed in the fight at Arras. On May 27th at Le Cornet, and on May 28th at Wormhoudt, SS men murdered at least 170 British prisoners (see page 74). They claimed they were acting in retaliation for British war crimes. These murderers wore the death's-head badge of the Totenkopf Division. Back in England in mid-June the surviving other ranks of 8 DLI, in base camp at Rugeley, were "ordered to remove all unauthorised badges from clothing and equipment e.g. BEF on coloured shoulder-tabs, skull and cross-bones on steel helmets etc."

At the spearhead of the British tank advance, meanwhile, the

*This officer's report is quoted in the official history of the war in France and Flanders; the passage here extracted was, understandably, omitted by the official historian.

Germans were pulling themselves together. Their reaction was swift and deadly. The British had struck at the soft-skinned vehicles following up the tanks of the Seventh Panzer Division. Among the soldiers in this echelon was the divisional commander, General Erwin Rommel, accompanied as usual by his aide-de-camp, Lieutenant Most. Rommel's diary takes up the story:

> The enemy tank fire had created chaos and confusion among our troops in the village, and they were jamming up the roads and yards with their vehicles instead of going into action with every available weapon to fight off the oncoming enemy. . . . With Most's help I brought every available gun into action at top speed against the tanks . . . I personally gave every gun its target. With the enemy so perilously close, only rapid fire from every gun could save the situation. . . . Although we were under very heavy fire during this action, the gun crews worked magnificently. The worst seemed to be over and the attack beaten off, when suddenly Most sank to the ground behind a 20-mm. anti-aircraft gun close beside me. He was mortally wounded and blood gushed from his mouth. . . . The death of this brave man, a magnificent soldier, touched me deeply.

Rommel's ability to strike back fast and hard at his attackers was largely due to the most brilliant of German weapons, the 88-mm. anti-aircraft guns that travelled with the panzer spearhead and were designed for use against tanks as well as against aircraft. Even the armour of the Matildas, 70 mm. thick, could not withstand their high-velocity fire, as accurate as a rifle. (This first confrontation between British tanks and Rommel's 88s was to be repeated again and again, in the coming fight in the North African desert.) But above all Rommel, the front-line commander, had the authority to pull his disorganised soldiers into a brave and coherent defence, and the efficient radio to summon up the Luftwaffe. The Stukas came duly in and broke up the British infantry, who by now were plodding energetically after the tanks.

The British had not expected their success, nor the enemy's swift reaction to it. General Franklyn sought the help of the RAF, to keep off the Stukas and help the infantry hold onto the ground they had gained. But by now the Hurricanes of the BEF's air component had shifted their bases back across the Channel. The message summoning them would have had to pass through BEF headquarters, across to London by cable, then down to their airfield in Kent. It never arrived. The Luftwaffe had, as usual, the freedom of the skies. Under the bombs the British troops limped northwards away from the enemy, unencumbered by prisoners, but leaving more than half their tanks disabled on the field of battle.

The Germans pursued, and ran into an unscheduled trap. The French Third Light Mechanised Division was waiting to start the attack in which they hoped the British would be joining them the following morning. The French tanks, although slower and much less reliable than the German panzers, had much thicker armour and heavier guns. It was the only Allied tank victory of the campaign. All through the night the fighting continued, with the last isolated and exhausted group of Durhams being rescued by the unexpected arrival of French tanks at three the next morning.

At dawn on May 23rd, the Third Light Mechanised Division launched its own attack, on the line the British had already pioneered. They had three times as many tanks as the British. But they lacked the advantage of surprise. As the tanks moved off, the German light observation planes watched them. Soon the Stukas arrived and the German heavy guns opened up. That was the end of the French attack.

But the British action at Arras had important consequences. General Rommel noted in his diary that the day's fighting, including the encounter with the French tanks at the end, had cost his panzer division 89 men killed, 116 wounded and 173 missing. That was four times as many men as it had lost so far in the entire campaign since the division started across the German frontier eleven days before. (Total German casualties at Arras were much higher than this; Rommel counted only the men of his own division, not the SS and other troops engaged on the German side.) The British had struck at Rommel himself, who had seen his personal staff officer killed at his side. Generals do not often get that close to the carnage.

Rommel's excited reports of his adventures confirmed the fears of the German Army's top brass, and notably of three very senior generals—army commander von Kluge, panzer group leader von Kleist, and army group commander von Rundstedt. These Prussian grandees were cautious professional soldiers. They hated the whole business of advancing with their flanks unprotected. Rundstedt wrote later:

> Kluge was inclined to stop all movement of the advance westwards, until the situation in the Arras sector was stabilised. Kleist, for his part, became prudent almost to the point of nervousness. He at once ordered Guderian [commanding the Nineteenth Panzer Corps], who was moving northwards, not to move so fast on Boulogne and Calais.

In this sense the Arras adventure was a brilliant success. It powerfully influenced Rundstedt's decision to halt the panzer advance on the river Aa on May 24th—an order that Hitler himself confirmed, at the fateful meeting of the German supreme command in the airfield control tower at Charleville. Had the Germans not halted then, allowing the French to establish their line of defences on the west side of Dunkirk, the British army might well not have had its chance to escape.

But the Arras offensive also marked the end of the Anglo-French alliance as a working arrangement on the northern front. Lord Gort had not wanted to counter-attack; he had already decided that the battle in France was lost, and that the best thing to do with the British army was to get as much of it as possible over to England. Reluctantly, and under orders directly inspired by the Prime Minister, he had committed a small force to the attack at Arras. Despite the wishes of the French (who, after all, were supposed to exercise overall command of the Allied forces) he had let the attack go ahead without the much stronger French forces that would have become available on the following day. When the British attack of May 21st could be seen to have failed, his staff did not tell the French that there would be no British participation in the attack of May 22nd.

After Arras the British were clearly on the run. In a single action, with only two battalions of tanks and two of infantry, they had experienced and inflicted all the savagery of modern war. They had shown how the Germans could be shaken. But they had also convinced themselves that further battles were not worth fighting.

7

THE RUN FOR THE COAST

Even today there are mysteries concealed in the white cliffs of Dover, and not just symbolical ones either. On top of the port—completed in 1908 to hold the destroyers of the Channel fleet—stands the castle, whose earliest extant building is a Roman lighthouse of the first century. Below it, in the intervening years, the chalk has been dug as full of holes as a Swiss cheese, and the holes contain pieces of equipment that only the Royal Navy has known the uses of. One of the tunnels has an opening, giving a splendid view of ships and water across the twenty-one miles to the corresponding height behind Calais. In the First World War this well-ventilated chamber housed the generator for the Navy's command post in the Channel. In 1940 the generator had been moved and modernised, and the aperture in the cliff was transformed into a Spartan but efficient office. It was still called the Dynamo Room. From it was commanded the operation that, between May 26th and June 3rd, 1940, brought 220,000 British soldiers, 110,000 French and a few others across the Channel for a chance to fight again.

This escape had seemed impossible. The Germans certainly believed it so. By May 25th their Air Force had closed the port of Dunkirk, and the supreme commander, Field Marshal Goering, had promised that its quays could not be restored to use. The French had considered the evacuation of Dunkirk not merely impossible, but undesirable too. On May

25th General Blanchard, commanding all Allied forces on the northern front, issued a formal order to all units—French, Belgian, British—under his command around Dunkirk. "The bridgehead will be held with no thought of defeat," said Blanchard, and his subordinates did not demur.

Even the Royal Navy did not believe in miracles. With foresight, and without a word to the French, the Vice-Admiral, Dover—the Royal Navy officer in command of the narrow seas between Britain and the Continent—had been instructed to set up a skeleton staff to carry out an evacuation that might, in the case of catastrophe, become necessary. Admiral Bertram Ramsay stationed this staff in the Dynamo Room, gave their plan the name of Operation Dynamo, and carried it through. The initial target laid down by the Admiralty for Operation Dynamo was to evacuate 45,000 men in two days. The eventual achievement was to evacuate almost 340,000 in nine days. That is the full measure of the triumph of Dunkirk.

Military operations of this order of success are not achieved without ruthlessness, cheating, massive slaughter and gargantuan waste. In this case there was also a full measure of Allied heroism, German complacency, ideal weather—a host of fortunate chances exploited with dogged persistence, a series of unforeseen opportunities seized by individuals in the teeth of the odds. Nothing can detract from the amazing success of Admiral Ramsay and his sailors, or from the solid resistance put up by the soldiers who defended the perimeter around Dunkirk and allowed their fellow-countrymen and their allies to get safe to sea.

But, despite the legends, such things are not done without careful planning and preparation, carried out in secrecy. In this case secrecy was preserved not merely from the Germans, who could certainly have done more to prevent the evacuation if they had known the plans for it, but also from the French. That Operation Dynamo was an astonishing success is not in question. That it involved methodical deception of Britain's only ally is unfortunately just as true.

The first of the moves that were to determine the success of Dynamo was part of a more general precaution. On May 14th—the day after the Dutch Army stopped fighting—the Churchill government began to mobilise the British people.

The Secretary of State for War, Mr. Anthony Eden, announced the formation of a new force of Local Defence Volunteers (later renamed the Home Guard) for men too old, too young or too unfit to serve in the conventional forces.

The Royal Navy called for reserves too. That same day the BBC broadcast in its nine o'clock news this official announcement: ''The Admiralty have made an order requesting all owners of self-propelled pleasure craft between thirty and one hundred feet in length to send all particulars to the Admiralty within fourteen days from today, if they have not already been offered or requisitioned.'' Somebody in authority was looking ahead. It was as well to be prepared for some kind of operation in the shallow waters between Britain and the Continent.

A little bureaucracy was set up, jointly between the Ministry of Shipping and the Admiralty. At the Thames estuary port of Sheerness a semi-retired naval officer, Rear-Admiral Taylor, was empowered to collect, service and pay the crews of small craft that might be put temporarily at the disposition of the Royal Navy. In the ministry a civil servant, Mr. H. C. Riggs, was put in charge of the unorthodox arrangements. The Small Vessels Pool was established. It was the start of a pleasure-boating season in which boats could not be used for pleasure off the English coast. Many boat-owners were only too happy to register their craft, if only to give their engines a run. So, with the Germans still fighting their way across the Meuse, and with evacuation from France by the British army an undreamed-of disgrace, the Dunkirk rescue fleet began to be assembled.

Ample supplies were printed of Form T124, by signing which civilians became subject to Royal Navy discipline for one month, in exchange for three pounds in pay. Over ninety suitable boat-owners, mechanics, fishermen and other specialists were signed up for prompt service. In every port of southern England retired naval officers and petty officers were listed as suitable to take over registered civilian boats in an emergency. In yacht clubs and commercial moorings, casual berths and fishing harbours, middle-aged men shook the mothballs out of their naval caps and thought about going to sea in the springtime. But the shape of the emergency was unforeseen.

The first glimpse of the dangerous future was taken at an

altogether higher level. On May 16th the Prime Minister, Mr. Churchill, flew to Paris in response to messages of alarm from his French opposite number, Paul Reynaud. He took with him the Deputy Chief of the Imperial General Staff, Lieutenant-General Sir John Dill. They found the French government in a state of high alarm about the German breakthrough across the Meuse. The Supreme Commander, General Gamelin, was in despair.

The first thing Churchill did on his return next morning was to write a memorandum to the Lord President of the Council, Neville Chamberlain. The Prime Minister requested his predecessor to set up a small committee "to examine the consequences of the withdrawal of the French government from Paris in the event of the fall of that city, as well as the problems that would arise if it were necessary to withdraw the BEF from France, either along its communications or by the Belgian and Channel ports."

Chamberlain's colleagues on this most secret committee were three senior politicians. They concentrated on the political aspects of the weakness of France. But like the Prime Minister and the whole Cabinet they were hoping to maintain and strengthen the French alliance. General Dill was also a member of the committee. He and his staff had to concentrate on the military means of securing the safety of the only army Britain had, the BEF. Dill had until recently commanded a corps of the BEF in France, and had there learned to share his colleagues' lack of faith in the French Army. Now he was on the fast route to promotion, and on May 27th he was to succeed General Sir Edmund Ironside as Chief of the Imperial General Staff.

From across the Channel Dill and his staff officers were getting discouraging reports from BEF headquarters on the state of cooperation with the French. Lord Gort had disbanded his headquarters intelligence staff, and the British army's communications had practically broken down. Gort's communications with the French were in an even worse state. He had no idea what they were up to, but suspected it was no good.

Under the agreement of May 12th all Allied forces in the north—meaning Gort himself, the King of the Belgians and the French armies too—were meant to take orders from General Billotte, commanding the French First Group of Armies. Only five days later, on May 17th, Gort told his chief of staff, General Pownall, that he was not prepared to accept orders from Billotte. "I am not prepared to lose my force," said Gort. Later that day in a note handed to Billotte himself Gort formally declined to accept instructions to make a stand, together with the French, on the river Senne. "He [Gort] is not prepared to stay another night on the river Sennes [*sic*]. . . . This withdrawal tonight will be to the line of the river Dendre where he may be prepared to stand for two nights if not closely followed by the Germans." Gort formally refused to fight.

The first time the BEF headquarters war diary speaks of a retreat to the coast is two days later. At midnight on May 18–19th General Billotte was at the end of his tether. "*Je crève de fatigue, et contre ces panzers je ne peux rien faire*," he told his British liaison officer in the car on the way to the BEF headquarters—"I am completely done in, and I can't do a thing against these panzers." His supreme commander, the famous General Gamelin, had just been sacked. The headquarters of his Seventh Army had just been overrun. But he was trying to muster his forces for a counter-attack, to stop the Germans. He wanted the British to make a stand alongside the French First Army.

Gort would have none of it. The war diary notes: "His [Billotte's] proposals were not considered to have any good chance of becoming effective, and it became apparent that it might be necessary for the BEF to withdraw to the coast."

When Billotte was gone, Gort and his staff conferred. Three options were open to the BEF. They might mount a counter-attack against the Germans advancing through Belgium. Or they might counter-attack in the opposite direction against the Germans in France. Or they might run for the Channel ports of Boulogne, Calais and Dunkirk, in readiness to get out of France across the Channel as best they might. The first two options were risky, and feasible at best if there was full co-operation with the French high command, and if the French troops on the ground actually did the fighting their generals might agree to. On both counts the British were sceptical.

Gort reported this hard choice to London. He told his staff to draw up a preliminary plan for the third. Afterwards Gort

wrote: "I realised that this course was in theory a last alternative." In practice it seemed the only way. The staff officers
took this view. All along the British front the movement was
for "consolidation," which in military language means a first,
prudent preparation for defeat.

The war diary of the quartermaster's office at BEF headquarters appears to have been reconstructed from memory at
some later date—the original was presumably lost. It records
that on May 18th or 19th Lieutenant-Colonel Hewer, of the
quartermaster's staff, was "sent to War Office to discuss
maintenance and evacuation through Dunkirk." Also on May
19th all headquarters troops not required for fighting were
sent to Dunkirk by special train, for evacuation. This, be it
noted, was before the Germans had reached Abbeville at the
mouth of the Somme and cut off the Allied armies of the
north from the main forces in France.

This was the spirit, and these were the actions, at BEF
headquarters. Duly they were reported to the War Office in
London—perhaps through the arrival there of Colonel Hewer.
The politicians, and the political generals, were horrified.
The director of operations at the War Office got in touch
with the Chief of the Imperial General Staff, Sir Edmund
Ironside; he in turn raised the matter at the next meeting of
the War Cabinet, and told its members that even if the BEF
managed to assemble at Dunkirk "we could certainly never
evacuate the force completely."

Ironside, incidentally, was loyal to the Prime Minister's
view of the French alliance as vital to British war interests.
In the War Cabinet Mr. Arthur Greenwood, a Labour minister, spoke of the French as "these bloody Allies." Ironside
recalled in his published diaries: "I told him that we had
depended on the French Army. That we had made no Army
and that therefore it was not right to say 'these bloody Allies.'
It was for them to say that of us."

Mr. Churchill agreed fully with his chief military adviser.
Anyway, he said, at Dunkirk "the BEF would be closely
invested in a bomb-trap"—the same view as was taken, luckily, by Field Marshal Goering in command of the Luftwaffe.
Ironside was sent straight off to put some backbone into Gort;
he carried to France on May 20th an order that Gort was to
work with the French for a counter-attack south-westwards,

to re-establish the BEF's lines of communications into the French heartland. That same day, as we have seen, the Germans closed the gap to the south.

Ironside duly delivered his message. Gort defended himself by claiming that Billotte "had given the BEF no orders for some eight days." This was a plain lie. Gort, as we have seen, had received and refused Billotte's order to make a stand on May 17th, three days earlier. (Just for the record, Gort's friends defend him by claiming that Billotte was not "commander" but "coordinator" of the northern front.) Anyway it was Ironside's job to get the fight going against the Germans, not to arbitrate grievances. So he went off, together with Gort's chief of staff, General Pownall, to find Billotte. They found him with the First Army commander, General Blanchard. Both French generals, according to Pownall, were in "a proper dither." Ironside convinced them that the BEF would from now on work with them and accept their coordination of an Allied counter-attack.

The direct result of this visit by Ironside was indeed a counter-attack—or rather two such attacks, for the cooperation on which success depended did not happen. The British struck with two tank battalions and two infantry battalions towards Arras on May 21st. (This operation is described on pages 78–87.) Next day a similar but much more numerous French force tried to strike in the same direction. Both operations failed. Together they might conceivably have succeeded in cutting the German supply lines and stopping the panzers. But their failure was decisive. From now on the BEF was bound for Dunkirk, and the vague chance that some of its surviving men might get away by sea.

The officer put in charge of the Dunkirk advance planning was Lieutenant-Colonel the Viscount Bridgeman, who shared with his fellow viscount Gort a background in the Foot Guards. He started work promptly on May 19th, with great efficiency. At first he was working on a contingency plan. It soon became a scheme of operations. As soon as the Germans reached the mouth of the Somme, Dunkirk became the main channel of supply for both the French and the British armies in the north. Ships arriving full of stores do not, of course, need to return empty. The opportunity was taken to fill them with what became known as *les bouches inutiles*, the useless mouths who ate up provisions without contributing to the fight. Some were genuinely useless: railway specialists with no railways to run, gas warfare people whose proven presence might be of use for German propaganda. Others would have been valuable, like intelligence staff, map-making teams, bakers. Anyway, at a time when the defence of Dunkirk demanded, in French eyes, every man who could hold a rifle, their disappearance was a sign of defeatism. By the start of the formal evacuation of the BEF in Operation Dynamo, on May 26th, 27,936 men had already been safely carried to England from Dunkirk.

Gort's staff conference of May 19th, at which Bridgeman was instructed to prepare the army's contingency plan for an escape via Dunkirk, was matched by a naval conference in London the same day. It considered and decided on the evacuation of unwanted personnel as from the next day, at the rate of two thousand men a day. It laid contingency plans for a slightly more rapid and extensive evacuation starting on May 22nd, of up to fifteen thousand man. It discussed and dismissed as unlikely the "hazardous evacuation of very large forces." The French meanwhile were considering and dismissing the same possibility, and planning with some energy the organisation of supplies to the Dunkirk redoubt, by sea from the ports of Normandy and Brittany.

The following day, with the situation worsening all the time—and with more or less accurate accounts of reality at last getting through to Britain—Admiral Ramsay held another planning conference at Dover. The agenda included the sinister topic "Emergency evacuation across the Channel of very large forces." A full list of available shipping was drawn up, consisting mainly of the cross-Channel ferries specifically designed for this work; somebody also suggested the addition to the list of a fleet of Dutch coasters—flat-bottomed craft with a three-man crew, called *schuyts* (pronounced by the British as "skoots"). Forty of these craft, which had sailed across to the Thames estuary on the fall of the Netherlands, were requisitioned and manned by Royal Navy reservists. From this meeting on May 20th dates the formal organisation of Ramsay's Dynamo Room, under whose firm control the entire Dunkirk evacuation was carried to success.

And so the preparations went ahead. By May 26th, eighty

thousand gallons of drinking water in cans had been disposed in guarded dumps along the beaches to the east of Dunkirk. This piece of foresight, executed thanks to close co-operation between the Dynamo staff at Dover and Bridgeman's staff in France, was clearly decisive in preserving the chance of survival of the troops as they arrived among the dry dunes.

So far, though, all these preparations could be described as part of a contingency plan, not as a plan for action. In rare moments of optimism, senior officers tried to make themselves believe that the German advance could and would be stopped. On May 24th, for example, the British radio listening services intercepted the order, in the name of the Führer, stopping the panzer divisions on the line of the river Aa. Major-General Pownall, Lord Gort's chief of staff, noted in his diary: "Of course these Germans are about all in, that's certain."

The Allied armies in the north were cut off on May 20th when the Germans arrived at the mouth of the Somme. But they still had three open routes of communication with the outside world, through the highly efficient Channel ports of Boulogne, Calais and Dunkirk. Through them, if need be, the armies of the north could be supplied and reinforced, under the protection of the RAF from its bases in Kent. This, at any rate, was how it looked from London. The War Office, with the Prime Minister urging them on, rushed to send reinforcements to Boulogne and Calais. These two ports were garrisoned only by small contingents of second-grade French infantry, and by the French marines who manned the coastal batteries there. But the problem was that the British had practically no reinforcements to send. Moreover, Boulogne was at first badly served by its French defenders.

That this ancient port could ever be attacked by land had seemed inconceivable until the panzer divisions appeared across the landscape. The port defences were commanded by a retired naval officer in his seventies, *Capitaine de vaisseau* Dutfoy de Mont de Benque. Messages and rumours—and dive-bombers—arrived piecemeal. The orders were ambiguous. The old man panicked. On May 21st he ordered the evacuation of Boulogne. Two weeks later poor Captain Dutfoy, who had escaped by sea to Cherbourg, was sentenced to twenty years in prison for dereliction of duty. And anyway his orders were never carried out. Despite their commander, the French marines held on to their guns. Soon an infantry division—incomplete, disorganised, but willing to fight and commanded by the able General Lanquetot—arrived to stiffen the defences.

From Britain, in haste, the last reserves of combat troops were assembled. Two battalions of Foot Guards were taken off a night exercise on the heathland at Camberley, put onto ships and landed at Boulogne, together with a single battery of anti-tank gunners, on the morning of May 22nd. At 5 p.m. that day the Germans attacked. Twenty-four hours later the Royal Navy was ordered to clear the Guards out again, and by 2:45 a.m. on May 24th the British reinforcements had all gone—lifted off by Royal Navy destroyers, often under intense fire, in an operation that foreshadowed in miniature that which was to follow at Dunkirk.

The Navy's part in this evacuation was brilliantly and gallantly played. But the British Army came out of it with less credit. In Boulogne were large numbers of noncombatant British troops of the BEF's supply lines—notably a battalion of pioneers, elderly trench-diggers and bricklayers, many of whom had barely handled a loaded rifle since 1918. Their commanding officer, Lieutenant-Colonel Dean, had won the Victoria Cross in the previous war against the Germans. Proudly he led his token soldiers into the line alongside the splendid giants of the Irish and Welsh Guards, and could fairly claim the rare honour of covering the Guards' retreat.

The pioneers can hardly be blamed if they failed to live up to their commanders' soldierly standards. When the destroyer HMS *Whitshed* pulled alongside the quay in the late afternoon of May 23rd she found the port guarded by a party of sailors armed with rifles. These sailors had a nasty job. Admiral Ramsay reported later: "On the quay a panic-stricken rabble of Auxiliary Military Pioneer Corps tried to rush the ship but were driven back by the demolition party at the point of the bayonet. Many of them were drunk."

The officer in command of the naval shore party was more specific: "Many British and Allied soldiers were drunk, presumably having obtained their liquor from rifling wine shops and cafés in the town. . . . at least three officers (one British) were quite incapable of carrying out their duties."

The Guards, everyone agreed, were magnificent. But even they showed signs of panic when the big 4.7-inch (120-mm.) ship's guns fired straight over their heads at what the captains thought were Germans. In fact the ship's targets were French troops, trying to find out what the British were up to. In exchange the French killed several British soldiers by firing machine guns in retaliation.

The disgrace of Boulogne, however, was in the leaving of it. The Guards were pulled out when their commander reported that the port was untenable. No notice of this British departure was given to the more numerous French troops in town. They proved that it was not untenable, by resisting the German advance for over thirty hours after the British had left. Before finally going, the Royal Navy sank a blockship in the harbour mouth, thus ensuring that the French defenders who fought so gallantly on could be neither supplied nor rescued by sea.

Naturally enough the French were furious, and protested bitterly to the War Office. The protest had its repercussions at Calais, to which British troops were also sent on May 22nd. The infantry units sent to Calais were the next smartest in the British Army after the Guards: a brigade of Green Jackets. They had been trained specifically for mobile warfare, not for garrison work, and were accompanied by a battalion of tanks. The disembarkation was a terrible muddle: the ships had been loaded in the wrong order, and left Calais for fear of enemy air attack without unloading half of the stores and vehicles that the light infantrymen needed. Moreover, the force's orders had been drawn up in England in complete ignorance of the situation on the spot, and the tanks were immediately sent racing off to be lost in small actions against German panzers.

At two o'clock in the morning of May 24th, as the last guardsmen were getting out of Boulogne, Brigadier Nicholson in Calais was told to get ready to pull out, too. This order was confirmed in the evening, and he got his soldiers out of the fighting line ready for embarkation. By now the high-level French protest at the abandonment of Boulogne by the British had reached the War Office. The Prime Minister insisted that no further offence must be given to the French.

Some staff officer in London then sent to Brigadier Nicholson, in his dangerous situation, what may well be the most insulting message ever dispatched to a fighting commander:

In spite of policy of evacuation given to you this morning fact that British forces in your area now under Fagalde [the French general commanding all Channel port forces] who has ordered no repeat no evacuation means that you must comply for the sake of Allied Solidarity. Your role is therefore to hold on, harbour being of no importance to the BEF . . .

Nicholson, a gallant officer, was unfazed by this doom-laded missive, and went on to conduct a defence so stout that he won glowing tributes from the Germans. They particularly admired his reply to a German officer of terms for surrender: "The answer is no, as it is the British Army's duty to fight as well as it is the German's." The person most upset by the War Office's message was Mr. Churchill, who, on seeing it, flew into a rage, asked whether there were defeatists in the War Office, and ordered his disciple Anthony Eden, the Secretary of State for War, to sign a further message whose style betrays its Churchillian drafting: "Defence of Calais to the utmost is of highest importance to our country as symbolising our continued cooperation with France. The eyes of the Empire are on the defence of Calais, and HM Government are confident you and your gallant regiments will perform an exploit worthy of the British name."

Now, nobody—least of all Churchill himself, a soldier of many campaigns—could imagine that this sort of prose cuts much ice in a battle. The message was not really meant for its addressee, the brave Brigadier Nicholson. It was meant eventually for the newspapers. But before being published it was meant to be intercepted and decrypted not only by the enemy, but by the ally with whom continued cooperation was so warmly commended in it. In the afternoon of May 26th Brigadier Nicholson and his staff surrendered. The last French defenders—marines of the coastal defence forces—gave up the fight as dark fell. The Allies had gone down almost together. The alliance was preserved, Nicholson and his brigade were lost, and so were three times as many French soldiers.

The apparently rhetorical reference to ''the eyes of the Empire'' in Eden's Churchillian message had a real meaning. With the Guards in Boulogne and the Light Infantry in Calais, there was now literally only one battle-ready force left in England, and that was not British. It was the Canadian First Infantry Division, whose commander, Major-General McNaughton, was during the night of May 23rd visiting Calais and Dunkirk in a destroyer. At Dover his traffic policemen and other advance elements were already waiting aboard ship, ready to move the division across the Channel. But McNaughton lost no time in summing up the situation. He could not agree to send his country's first and best fighting men into a hopeless combat. The Canadian troops were disembarked without leaving port in England. The report sent from his destroyer helped conclude the argument in the War Office and the War Cabinet. The military decision was taken to get as many British soldiers as possible off the Continent, rather than to try to shore up an already hopeless situation.

But politically this awful truth could not be admitted, except in the privacy of discussions among the most senior British generals and politicians. Belgium was still in the war; there were Belgian soldiers killing Germans, therefore fewer Germans to kill British. This must be kept up as long as possible.

With France the game was bigger yet. Two-thirds of the gigantic French Army was not yet engaged in the conflict; the vast preponderance of the French national territory was untouched by war. Britain, above all, had a vital interest in keeping the powerful French Army on stand-by in the Mediterranean against the evil day when Hitler's jackal Mussolini would join the war and threaten Britain's lifeline to Suez and the Empire. More even than in ordinary wars, there was a gulf between the objectives of the grand strategists at home and of the fighting generals near the front.

Politically, Britain encouraged her friends to fight on. Meanwhile, her soldiers were disengaging from the fight. It was the policy of the patriotic lie, and it stuck in some Englishmen's throats. On May 21st, after setting in motion the plans for the retreat to Dunkirk, and ordering a token counterattack at Arras, Lord Gort went to Ypres for what was to have been a decisive inter-Allied planning conference. Gort arrived too late to meet the supreme commander, General Weygand, whose trip was therefore wasted. But he did have a quick conversation with the King of the Belgians. Leopold was accompanied by a most distinguished Englishman, Admiral of the Fleet Sir Roger Keyes, Member of Parliament for Portsmouth.

Keyes was senior in rank to Gort, and although the Victoria Cross was almost the only medal missing from his famous seven rows of ribbons, he was reputed to be equally brave. Now he was serving Winston Churchill as the British Prime Minister's personal representative at the Belgian court and high command. He had been a close friend of the King's late father, and genuinely loved Belgium, where in the First World War he had led the legendary naval exploit of the Zeebrugge Raid. Now, together with Gort, it was Keyes's job to persuade the Belgian King to keep his beaten Army in the field for a few more days. He knew the British were planning the opposite course to that which they were recommending to their ally. As they left the meeting Gort had a quiet word with the admiral. "Do the Belgians really think us awful dirty dogs?" asked the commander-in-chief of the BEF. His superior officer did not reply.

Next day Weygand gave his orders to all Allied forces on the northern front: "Try to form as wide a bridgehead as possible covering Dunkirk, indispensable for supplying the battle." This was certainly vague, and the staff of the BEF thought it was quite unrealistic. But it was the best Weygand could do to pull his forces together and sustain their morale. In response, the French tried to rally themselves for a long defensive struggle based on the port. The Belgians stayed in the fight, which was no longer intended to save any of their national territory from occupation, for five more days. The British got ready to leave.

Documentary evidence of this British deception is scarce. For security almost all the BEF's communications with the War Office in London were conducted by telephone, and few notes of the conversations are available or have survived. Lord Gort's headquarters moved from exchange to exchange towards the coast down the cross-Channel buried telephone cable, and right up to Gort's departure for England BEF headquarters was maintained in the little Belgian resort town of La Panne, just across the border from Dunkirk, where the cross-Channel cable terminated in a special exchange serving old King Albert's summer villa by the sea. They could talk in full security in London, without fear of interception by either their enemies or their allies. By contrast, from the German capture of Abbeville on May 20th onwards all French communications with their government and general headquarters in Paris had to be by courier, or by radio signals which the Germans were of course regularly intercepting and decrypting.

Despite the precautions of the British command, the French came within an ace of finding out the truth about their allies' intention to quit. One British officer committed a grave breach of security. Major Archdale, a cheery and optimistic man, had served as British liaison officer at the headquarters of the First Group of Armies throughout the winter. As was his duty, he had made good friends with his opposite number on the French staff, Commandant Fauvelle. On May 23rd in the evening Archdale paid an unexpected call on Fauvelle. It was more a personal than a business call, said Archdale: he had come to say goodbye. He was going home, with the rest of the BEF. Archdale knew the British move was still a secret. But quite soon the news would be officially notified to the French, and he did not want to go without leaving his good wishes.

Fauvelle was touched. He was also alarmed. This was serious news, even if given in a spirit of friendship. By now it was almost midnight, but Fauvelle woke up his chief of staff, Colonel Humbert, and passed his information on. Humbert was even more deeply concerned. First thing next morning he took Fauvelle to see the Army Group commander, General Blanchard (who, following the death of General Billotte in a motor accident, had just taken over command). Blanchard was desperately tired, but he was sufficiently disturbed by the news to rush straight off in search of Lord Gort, to try to check up on the rumour.

When Blanchard arrived at Gort's headquarters, he was told the British commander was out visiting his troops. Major-General Pownall, Gort's chief of staff, was however available. Pownall asserted that the British had no intention of quitting. But something in his manner led Blanchard to disbelieve him. It seemed vital to get the question straight: misunderstandings between the British and French commands were of benefit mainly to the Germans. Fauvelle was therefore sent straight off to Paris, to inform the commander-in-chief of the rumour and to sort the matter out at the highest level.

Fauvelle rushed to Dunkirk, where he thought he would find an aircraft to take him across the German lines to Paris. But the Mardyck airstrip had been made useless by bombing. On his own initiative he took a fast torpedo boat to Dover, from there went by train to London, and the following morning, May 25th, caught the liaison flight from Croydon airport to Paris. He reached his destination just thirty hours after first hearing Archdale's friendly words of farewell.

Fauvelle reached the Ministry of War just in time for the daily meeting of the *Comité de Guerre*, at which the supreme commander, General Weygand, and his staff were joined by Prime Minister Reynaud to hear the reports and assess the strategic position. There was not time for Fauvelle to explain his full story to the generalissimo. But he was a senior intelligence officer, and the first direct witness of events in Flanders to arrive in Paris since Weygand's own visit of May 21st. So Weygand told Fauvelle to come into the meeting in person, and to tell his story there.

Fauvelle was exhausted after his journey, still in his combat uniform, exceedingly nervous at having to deliver his delicate report direct to the two most powerful—and anxious—men in France, Reynaud and Weygand. On entering the meeting he found there a visitor whose presence made his task even harder. Reynaud was in friendly conversation with an officer in the red lapel tabs of a British major-general. This was the redoubtable Edward Louis Spears, Conservative Member of Parliament for Lincoln, Winston Churchill's personal liaison officer with the French government.

Spears had arrived on his mission that very morning, bearing an effusive letter of recommendation from Mr. Churchill to M. Reynaud. He needed no such introduction. He was a personal friend of Reynaud, who knew him as Churchill's close political ally. He was so known to almost everyone who was anyone in French political life, through his chairmanship of the Anglo-French parliamentary association. Spears was perfectly bilingual—he was, indeed, French born, having anglicised his name early in life from its original Spier. He let it be understood that he was Alsatian; many people assumed he was Jewish. Since 1915, when he became chief British liaison officer with the French general staff in Paris, he had been closely associated with British military intelligence. In front of him, and amid the distractions of a meeting interrupted by irrelevant telephone calls, Fauvelle—a mere major—had to unveil his suspicion that the British were in secret preparing to leave the French army in the lurch.

It is not clear whether Spears himself had full knowledge of the extent of Lord Gort's preparations for departure. But his brief from Mr. Churchill was to put some stuffing into the French leadership, to scotch any defeatist nonsense. Fauvelle's story, if believed, would have precisely the opposite effect. Spears' memoirs, although written long after the event, give a taste of the scorn that the elegant general poured on the unkempt major: "I have in my time seen broken men, but never before one deliquescent, that is, in a state where he was fit only to be scraped up with a spoon or mopped up." It was quite possible, the British general conceded, that his colleagues might have vaguely studied a scheme for evacuation, in case the situation got worse. But it could not be put into effect without orders from His Majesty's Government, and no such orders existed. The British, Spears insisted, would fight on.

Reynaud chose to believe his friend, Churchill's spokesman. But it was Major Fauvelle who told the truth. Fauvelle, whom Spears described as a coward, completed his report and at once set out via Cherbourg and Dover to return to his duties on the military staff at Dunkirk, probably the only officer of any army to re-enter of his own free will the doomed bridgehead. Four days later, realising that the French had by now realised the truth about the evacuation, Mr. Churchill instructed General Spears formally to notify the French government of it. The following morning, when Spears duly delivered the message, he asked the British Ambassador, Sir Ronald Campbell, to accompany him to the meeting. It was Campbell, not Spears, who on May 30th informed the French government that the British army had been evacuating from Dunkirk since the late afternoon of May 26th.

So the British put off the moment when their ally would

learn of their desertion. It was not only the politicians and intelligence officers who joined in this deliberate deception. One exchange of telegrams of May 25th, the day of Fauvelle's humiliation by Spears, confirms that deceit was Britain's official policy. At 6:30 p.m. that day Lord Gort gave the firm order that his troops must break off all hope of making a stand and run for the coast. He so informed the Secretary of State for War by cable, but without mentioning the intention to evacuate. Mr. Eden's reply accepted that "the only course open to you may be to fight your way back to the west, where all beaches and ports east of Gravelines will be used for embarkation." The following day, said Mr. Eden, Mr. Churchill would be meeting with his opposite number, M. Reynaud, to clarify the French attitude to the possible move (a move, incidentally, which Gort said was not just possible, but under way). The final words were telling: "In the meantime it is obvious that you should not discuss the possibility of the move with the French or the Belgians."

Whatever his personal wishes, Gort was thus formally ordered to deceive his allies about the British army's intentions. On May 26th he received orders from his French superior Blanchard to co-operate in a new counter-attack southwards. Almost simultaneously Gort received a direct order from Eden in London to get as fast as possible towards the beaches "to the east of Gravelines"—that is, round Dunkirk—and embark. Gort ignored the French order and awaited the result of his Prime Minister's meeting with Paul Reynaud, at which—Gort had been told—the politicians would sort out their differences, so that the soldiers could get on with planning the evacuation as allies.

Churchill, in London that Sunday, first received the exiled Prime Minister of Belgium, who complained that his King was on the point of surrender. Then there was a great service at Westminster Abbey, at which prayers were offered for God's help to England. King George and Queen Elizabeth were present, and emotion ran high. Then Churchill lunched with M. Reynaud, who had just arrived by plane, and after lunch the formal meeting of their Council of War began. Reynaud was most deeply concerned about reports that Italy was about to declare war on France. He asked for more British reinforcements, particularly for more of the RAF's as yet uninvolved fighters. He then reported that there were those in his Cabinet who thought France would have to seek a separate peace if things went on as they were.

Churchill was acutely embarrassed at having to refuse further RAF support; on this he had been definitely outvoted by his own Cabinet. Moreover, he had to give full support to Reynaud in the latter's own argument against the defeatists in Paris. Churchill assured Reynaud of Britain's absolute commitment to victory. The fact that British troops were even now starting to move out of Dunkirk was not mentioned.

Reynaud went home unsuspecting. As soon as he left, Churchill confirmed that the Admiralty was to give the order "Operation Dynamo is to commence." Admiral Ramsay's work had begun.

On May 27th, the day after Dynamo began and Churchill had omitted to mention it to Reynaud, Gort again received instructions that his "sole duty is now to evacuate to England the greater part of your forces." There was no mention even of defending the perimeter around Dunkirk, to make the escape possible. That same morning, May 27th, the pro-French Chief of the Imperial General Staff, General Ironside, was moved out of his job as head of the British Army and put in command of the ground forces in Britian. General Dill, no lover of the French, was made CIGS in his place.

Weygand meanwhile made signal to all forces under his command in the Dunkirk area: "Resistance to the limit, behind lines covering not only Dunkirk but the other Channel ports. Every day of struggle adds to the respite that the French Army needs to prepare the battlefields of the Somme and the Aisne." Thus the French Army was instructed to defend the port that the British Army was abandoning.

In Dover, the same day, a Dynamo planning session took place. The British Admirals Ramsay and Somerville had invited two French admirals, Odend'hal and Leclerc—naval operations in the Channel were coordinated as a matter of routine, and there was nothing unusual about this. The Frenchmen were amazed to find that the British had been preparing the evacuation for a week, but were consoled by the information that everything had been determined at the highest political level, and there was nothing naval men could do about it save get on with the job. And so they did. A combined operation was agreed between the two navies. It was agreed in principle that both countries should take an equal share in the operation, although the French had fewer warships under command.

Another French officer at the Dover meeting took a less matter-of-fact view of the circumstances. *Capitaine de vaisseau* Auphan, staff officer in charge of coordination at the French Admiralty, left Dover by destroyer for Cherbourg, and thence flew next morning to Paris to report to the naval commander-in-chief, Admiral Darlan. Together they went to see General Weygand, who by now was perforce becoming accustomed to receiving exhausted messengers bearing tales of British perfidy. This time there was no Spears to deny the facts. And Auphan's information came not from a friendly chat, but from a formal inter-allied naval conference. Thus the French high command at last gained confirmation of what it had suspected about the British plans to pull out. Formal notification of the British move still did not come until May 30th, when as we have seen Spears took along Ambassador Campbell to help him break the news.

But on May 28th, when Auphan brought his message from Dover, the headquarters office in Paris had no way of informing Admiral Abrial in Dunkirk, except by radio which meant informing the Germans too. Abrial was left in the dark. On the spot, in Dunkirk, the confusion continued. The British and French seamen, of the two navies and the two Channel fleets of passenger ferries, worked closely together as usual. But when the ships—British and French ferries, with British and French warships on escort—arrived at Dunkirk, no French troops were allowed to embark. The British in Dunkirk insisted that this was a purely British operation.

By May 29th, 72,000 British soldiers had been carried across the Channel under Operation Dynamo. The number of French who had arrived in England was recorded as 655. Somehow a rumour had spread among the French troops that an evacuation was going on—maybe they had used their eyes and seen it—and Frenchmen were claiming places, especially on the French Channel ferries. Lord Gort was told of this, and became most indignant. He went to complain to the French officer commanding Dunkirk, Admiral Abrial. The admiral was astonished—not that Frenchmen were claiming equal treatment with the British, but that the British were evacuating at all. This was the first he had heard of it. Operation Dynamo had been under way for three days, and a third of the BEF had been evacuated, without either of the two officers in command on the spot understanding the other's position.

Abrial and Gort sensibly went off to telegraph to their own higher authorities. At this point, finally, the political and the military direction of the operation was aligned between the Allies. Lord Gort received clear orders that French troops were to be embarked in equal numbers with British. Since the French were organised to man the defences of the perimeter, while the British were queuing up for boats along the beach, this did not have much effect. In practice, whatever the orders, the British sailed first. After Gort was ordered to sail for home on May 31st the order for equal shares had to be firmly repeated to his successor, General Alexander. But at least on the political level the great escape became a joint operation.

In the end, despite what the French saw as the great British betrayal of their allies, the vast majority of both armies got away to England. Well before the end the Germans had given up their attempts to take the town by main force, or to frustrate the evacuation. Their best soldiers, and their entire modern Air Force, were transferred to the more important operation of advancing on Paris and bringing all France to its knees. Dunkirk became a sideshow. The rescue of the last tens of thousands of French soldiers proved pointless, since none of them got back into the fighting before being ordered by their government to surrender.

Yet the political consequences have lingered on even until today, as powerfully in the minds of many Frenchmen as the Dunkirk legend lingers in the collective conscience of the British. If the British ever have to choose between Europe and the ocean, said the greatest of twentieth-century Frenchmen, General de Gaulle, *"ils choisiront toujours le grand large,"* they will always choose the open sea. Winston Churchill spotted at the time the danger of having encouraged the French in this belief. He did his best to remedy it, in so far as it could be remedied by a politician. The occasion was the next meeting between British and French prime ministers, on May 31st.

This was the day when three-quarters of the BEF was known to be safe in England, and Lord Gort, his task of controlling the evacuation well on the way to completion, was ordered to leave France for home with his men. The political leaders met in Paris, and it was a full Council of War. Mr. Churchill was seconded by his Labour Party deputy, Major Attlee; M. Reynaud by his rather more imposing deputy, Marshal Pétain. The Marshal, as everyone present knew, was in despair. He believed—rightly, as it turned out—that the war was already lost for France. He largely blamed the English for that, with their pathetic expeditionary force of nine combat divisions, and their air force that stayed at home. Early in the proceedings, after a review of the gloomy prospect for the defence of Paris, the evacuation of Dunkirk was considered. Pétain took the opportunity to ask Churchill for the numbers of men evacuated in this great operation to save the Allied armies of the north.

Churchill had to send out for the figures. He received them back with surprising promptness and efficiency from Admiral Ramsay's Dynamo Room in Dover. As he reported them to the meeting, his French opposite numbers thought him visibly embarrassed. The midday score was 150,000 British soldiers landed in Britain, and 15,000 French. A ratio of ten to one did not look like fair shares. With these statistics in mind, the Council of War drafted a formal signal for the senior Allied officer in Dunkirk, Admiral Abrial. As a naval man, he was to receive his orders through the commander-in-chief of the French Navy, Admiral Darlan—than whom nobody present was by now more suspicious of British intentions. Darlan's draft text did not much more than tell Abrial to carry on with what he was already doing:

A bridgehead will be maintained round Dunkirk, including the divisions under your command and those under British command, to permit the embarkation of the Allied forces. As soon as it is confirmed that there are no troops outside the bridgehead who can reach the embarkation point, the perimeter defence units will embark in their turn, starting with the British forces.

More was to follow, but Churchill broke in with a roar: "Never! I refuse to accept that the British should embark first!" Then, in his awful French, *"Nong! Partage! Bras-dessus, bras-dessous!"* He twirled his arms around his body, to signify the comradeship of suffering. In place of Darlan's last sentence, Churchill wrote in his own hand on the English text: "The British troops will remain as a rear-guard, for as long as possible."

The text was sent off. Of course it changed nothing. The British departed. Then the French got away as best they might, leaving forty thousand men—including the last, stubborn defenders of the Dunkirk perimeter—behind them to be taken prisoner in the morning. Mr. Churchill believed to the end of his honoured life that his impassioned gesture had helped to persuade the French that Britain is no perfidious nation.

Part Three
OPERATION DYNAMO

8

THE DYNAMO TURNS: MAY 26TH

"I must not conceal from you that a great part of the BEF and its equipment will inevitably be lost even in best circumstances."
  —Cable, LORD GORT to Secretary of State of War, May 26th

"Only fishing boats can get over now. Let's hope the Tommies are good swimmers."
        —FIELD MARSHAL HERMANN GOERING,
          Commander-in-Chief, Luftwaffe, May 26th

The British army in France was beaten and exhausted, sick of the Continent, longing for home. As the shadows lengthened towards evening, at three minutes to seven o'clock on May 26th, the Admiralty in London formally made signal to the flag officer commanding, Dover, Vice-Admiral Bertram Ramsay: "Operation Dynamo is to commence." The Royal Navy was coming to the rescue. Indeed, it was already on its way. Ramsay's staff, in the bunker overlooking Dover harbour where once the generators had hummed, had acted four hours before they got their orders. They had sent the ferry-boats out across the Channel to Dunkirk. It was a run of thirty-nine miles, straight over to the buoy off Calais harbour mouth, then due east along the coast, between the sandbars and the sloping strand, in the tide-rip to Dunkirk.

The Germans were already in Calais. All day from the Dynamo Room itself the British naval staff had watched the bombers swoop like flies into the smoke over the town, just twenty-one miles across the glittering Channel. With the evening the last of its defenders gave up the struggle. In Ramsay's first flotilla sailed the Isle of Man packet-boat *Mona's Queen*, brought round early in the war from her home port of Liverpool to run shuttle across to France, servicing the British Army. She sailed straight into a battle. The Germans were advancing into the Calais citadel to capture its last French defenders. Two British destroyers were lying off the town, providing supporting fire for its defence. Captain R. Duggan of the *Mona's Queen* reported the dangerous situation off Calais buoy:

We were shelled from the shore by single guns and also by salvos from shore batteries. Shells were flying all round us, the first salvo went over us, the second, astern of us. I thought the next salvo would hit us but fortunately it dropped short, right under our stern. The ship was riddled with shrapnel, mostly all on the boat and promenade decks. Then we were attacked from the air. A Junkers bomber made a power dive towards us and dropped five bombs, but he was off the mark too, I should say about 150 feet from us. All this while we were still being shelled, although we were getting out of range. The Junkers that bombed us was shot down and crashed into the water in front of us (no survivors). Then another Junkers attacked us, but before he reached us he was brought down in flames.

Several of the passenger ships bound for Dunkirk turned back. *Mona's Queen* sailed on. The Germans, thinking perhaps that she was intended for the relief of the Calais garrison, and had sheered off, left her alone. Mr. Duggan could see ahead the terrible pall of smoke over the harbour he was sailing for:

Owing to the bombardment, I could see that the nerves of some of my men were badly shaken. I did not feel too well myself, but I mustered the crew and told them that Dunkirk was being bombed and was on fire. On being asked if they would volunteer to go in they did so to a man and I am glad to say we took off as many as *Mona's Queen* could carry. Coming back from Dunkirk, I made a route for myself and am glad to say we arrived safely at Dover in the early hours of Monday morning.

The worst of the eventualities provided for by the Admiralty a week before had come about: "the hazardous evacuation of very large forces." Then, on May 19th, the naval planners had assumed that there would be three ports—Calais and Boulogne as well as Dunkirk—to lift the soldiers out of, and that the sea approaches to France would be free of gunfire. The operation that now began was infinitely more hazardous than anyone could have predicted.

Mr. Duggan's account gives, right at the start, indications of why it was to prove successful. He and his crew, in full knowledge of the risk they ran, freely decided to go ahead. And on the run back to England Mr. Duggan "made a route" by skill and seamanship across the treacherous sandbanks off the French coast. The British seamen had begun to volunteer, and to improvise. That was how they won their battle.

The conventional route across the Channel by Calais was now under fire from enemy guns, as well as liable to raids by enemy planes. The port of Dunkirk itself was ablaze, subject to regular air raids, and likely to be blocked by a wreck at any moment. The harbour consisted of a chain of basins in which the water, normally, was maintained at navigable level by locks; on May 26th the main lock gate, immobilised by bombing, was removed and the docks were opened to the rise and fall of the tide, a full five metres (sixteen feet) at this season. One by one ships were being sunk or set ablaze in the narrow approaches to the port. The British tanker *Spinel*, afire, was blocking the inner harbour. Ships from Britain could now enter the outer harbour, load and turn away, only while the tide stayed high. It was obvious that this could not go on for long—unless there was another way.

But so far nobody could see a way to bring the soldiers out

other than in conventional passenger ships, from the quays of Dunkirk's outer harbour, at high tide. Nobody expected the operation to last long or many men to be rescued. Late on Sunday evening, May 26th, Admiral Ramsay received firm instructions from the Admiralty: ''. . . it is imperative for 'Dynamo' to be implemented with the greatest vigour, with a view to lifting up to 45,000 of the British Expeditionary Force within two days, at the end of which it is probable that evacuation will be terminated by enemy action.''

There were known to be over 200,000 British troops on shore over there; nobody even thought about how many French there might be. These early expectations give some idea of how immense was to be the achievement, before the end, of Operation Dynamo. In the next nine days it was to lift almost 340,000 men to safety.

Now, at the start, the ships available to Admiral Ramsay were thirty-five conventional passenger vessels, twenty-two coasters and barges, and forty of the Dutch *schuyts* which had taken refuge in Britain at the fall of the Netherlands, and which were now manned with crews from the Royal Navy Volunteer Reserve. There was also a miscellany of cargo ships that had already been at work taking ammunition and stores to Dunkirk, and returning with the so-called ''useless mouths'' of the BEF. By midnight on May 26th none of the ships despatched from Britain under Dynamo orders had returned: they were still loading or in transit. But the total number of men of the BEF evacuated to England since May 20th reached 28,000. Now, with formal orders for wholesale evacuation issued from Whitehall, the pretence could be abandoned that this was only a partial and selective retreat. The British and French navies, and the available merchant and passenger ships of both nations, set out to do their best. The problem was that the soldiers whose escape was planned were still scattered across the plain where France and Belgium meet, some as far as a hundred kilometres from Dunkirk.

On shore, in Dunkirk and around it, the main task was to organise a defensive perimeter. The French, as we have seen, wished to establish their defences for a long stand against the Germans. The British wanted only to make a stand for as long as it took to get as many as possible of their soldiers away. But whatever their final objective, both wanted to keep the Germans away from the town and to bring into the perimeter as many as possible of the soldiers of both armies still fighting, or retreating, far inland.

The area of land held by the Allies, after the fall of Calais at dusk on May 26th, had its base on the sea from Gravelines, halfway between Calais and Dunkirk, at the mouth of the river Aa, to Ostend, well inside Belgium. On that coastal base, about seventy kilometres long, an unevenly shaped triangle extended inland for a hundred kilometres to just beyond Lille. The main battle was around Lille itself, where the French First Army had settled down to a slogging defensive fight. The French at Lille—who included many African soldiers—were to keep a superior German force busy until June 1st.

On the western face of the triangle within which the Allies were contained was the line formed by the river Aa. Here, as we have seen, the panzer forces of German Army Group A had been stopped for two days by order of the Führer himself. When they restarted their attack on May 26th it was without heavy tanks and most of their guns, which had been withdrawn to refit for the campaign southwards into France. Given two days of relative respite to organise their defences, the French on this front were well able to hold the Aa line, and to retreat in good order to the even stronger position on the Canal de Mardyck on the outskirts of Dunkirk on May 27th in the evening.

The main threat to the Allies came from the slower-moving forces of General von Bock's Army Group B, advancing through Belgium. The fear of the British commanders was that these troops would push forward into the triangle, cutting off the retreat to the coast by the British forces who had disengaged from the flank of the French First Army. The British rushed back to the coast near La Panne, marching all day, driving all night in unlit convoys. As a transport exercise it was brilliant.

In the words of Sir Arthur Bryant, biographer and admirer of Lieutenant-General Alan Brooke, this retreat was the manoeuvre that saved the British army. It did much to establish the reputations of two of Brooke's subordinates, Major-Generals Montgomery and Alexander; as Field Marshals Brooke, Montgomery and Alexander were all to play crucial parts in later Allied victories. But their escape on this occasion involved little fighting. The Germans advanced slower than the British retreated. German Army Group B, plodding with its horse-drawn guns down the Belgian plain, was held up in some places by the desperate last resistance of the Belgian Army, in others by the administrative complexities caused by mass Belgian surrenders to forward German units not numerous enough, or well enough supplied, suddenly to take in charge thousands of reluctant if unbelligerent captives.

But, as the British started the formal phase of their evacuation, it was by no means clear who would be keeping the Germans off while the BEF got away. Lord Gort and his staff had no confidence at all in the ability or the willingness of the French to do so. They knew that the Belgians were on their way down to surrender. The British could not both defend their bridgehead and get out from it. Yet to get the British army out was the absolute priority. At 5:25 in the afternoon of May 26th Lord Gort made a strange request of the War Office in London. He asked that a Canadian brigade be sent over to France, followed soon by another, drawn from the Canadian First Division, which was the only combat-ready force left in Britain. The purpose, he said, was "to enable offensive mobile operations to be undertaken on Belgian front by other troops in order to safeguard security of withdrawal." In other words, he wanted the Canadians to cover the British retreat, drawing them into the holocaust from which the BEF was trying to escape. Major-General McNaughton, the Canadian commander-in-chief, got in touch at once with his friends on the Imperial General Staff, which promptly vetoed Gort's request for what McNaughton described as "this rather theatrical sacrifice."

But the Dunkirk bridgehead was granted one protection that had been withheld from the Allied armies in the campaign leading to their defeat. The Royal Air Force had its fighter bases in Kent, within eighty kilometres of Dunkirk, while the Luftwaffe's bombers had to fly from Germany, three times as far away. Fine mornings on the English Channel are misty mornings, and the mists were thickened to smog by the burning houses and oil tanks of the Channel ports. Both the RAF and the climate afforded some protection against air attack to the defenders of Dunkirk, and the German army commanders knew it.

Field Marshal Goering, for whom the Luftwaffe was the pinnacle of National Socialist achievement, kept promising that it would smash whatever Allied forces lay below it. The soldiers on the ground complained that the British were sneaking away. "It is very bitter to see this . . . we do not want to find these men, newly equipped, up against us later," they said prophetically. The Luftwaffe high command replied haughtily: "The attack is being conducted in such a manner as to make further embarkations impossible."

Marching soldiers habitually despise their more glamorous flying friends, and the German Army's criticisms of the Luftwaffe were sharpened by the political airs its leaders put on. But the British Army too, at Dunkirk, was to question with some reason the claims of the "Brylcreem boys" of the RAF over Dunkirk. The boasts and counter-boasts of the rival air forces were to prove one of the wonders of the evacuation. Its second day, May 27th, saw the war in the air grow cruel, as the men of the British Expeditionary Force crowded into the perimeter that might be a trap, and might be an escape route.

9

THE DAY OF THE FIREBOMBS: MAY 27TH

"Port continuously bombed all day and on fire.
Embarkation possible only from beaches East of
harbour. Send all ships there."
—CAPTAIN W. G. TENNANT, Senior Naval Officer,
   Dunkirk, 2005 hours, May 27th

The German air force had blocked the port. Now, on the second day of the British evacuation, they smashed the town behind it. Two thousand tons of high-explosive bombs threw buildings across the streets and ripped open the roofs of houses. Into the rubble dropped thirty thousand incendiary bombs, little flaming horrors weighing just one kilogramme each, designed to lodge in the rafters and set a fire where the inhabitants could not quench it. The water mains had burst the previous day. There was nothing the fire brigade could do. On this day died one thousand of the three thousand civilians killed during the evacuation of the miserable city. (For comparison, a total of some 5,000 men were killed on the voyage across the Channel.) There was nobody to bury the dead.

Uncertainly, the plans for the evacuation continued. Captain W. G. Tennant, RN, sent down the previous evening from the Admiralty in London to join Admiral Ramsay's Dy-

Dover Castle on the White Cliffs: operational headquarters for the Dunkirk evacuation.

The road to safety: British troops retreating through Dunkirk.

French sailors run to the anti-aircraft guns as the alert is signaled at Dunkirk.

The East Mole, the precarious escape route for most of the BEF. Up to 6,000 men an hour embarked by the narrow walkway, protected by a few machine-guns.

The view from a Clyde steamer—a famous Dunkirk photograph, probably faked, since no ship could have approached the beach as close as this appears to be.

The laborious ferries: two lifeboats towed by a launch to a waiting destroyer.

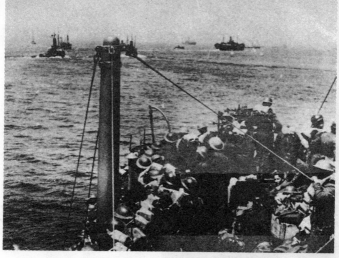

The crowded decks: in the Channel.

Some ships did not make it: the French destroyer *Bourrasque*, sunk and grounded off Nieuport.

General Weygand, Commander-in-Chief, leaves headquarters at Bastion 32 on 21 May.

The defender of Dunkirk: Admiral Jean Abrial (left, smoking) in London on 5 June, with Admiral Odend'hal of the French Embassy.

The man who organised the rescue: Admiral Ramsay, Vice-Admiral, Dover—photographed here later in the war, when he commanded Allied naval forces in the invasion of Normandy.

The royal Commander-in-Chief: King Leopold III of the Belgians with his Minister of Defence, General Denis (left), and Chief of Staff, General Vandenberghen.

The bitter end: French prisoners of war at Dunkirk, waiting to be organised by their German captors.

NEW YORK TIMES

The collaborators: in a Belgian town near the German frontier, the Nazi invaders get a warm welcome.

namo staff at Dover, arrived at Dunkirk at 6 p.m. with twelve
officers and 160 ratings to take control of the evacuation on
shore in France. He was appalled. The lock gates of the inner
harbour were gone. The outer harbour seemed blocked by
wrecks, and any ship trying to enter was pounced upon by
dive-bombers. Even the route to the port through the town
seemed unusable, blocked by rubble or licked by flames, and
crammed with leaderless men. Soldiers of the British, French
and Belgian armies—headquarters people belonging to no organised fighting unit, or stragglers separated from their companions by mischance, indiscipline or cowardice—were
converging on the town, finding no way through the bombardment, and taking refuge where they might.

Anthony Rhodes, a second lieutenant in the Royal Engineers, took to a cellar to shelter from the bombs:

> By midday the cellar was becoming rather smelly, it
> held sixty men only with difficulty. Many of them did
> not bother to come up for air during the intervals [be-
> tween the air raids], and it soon took on that musty,
> military smell, so much part of an army. It was not im-
> proved by a well-intentioned soldier who had given some
> foie-gras to one of the stray dogs which had taken refuge
> with us; it promptly vomited in the corner on somebody's
> gas mask. . . .
>
> By four in the afternoon our nerves were becoming a
> little frayed. One of the NCOs (wearing last-war ribbons)
> was crying quietly in the corner and several men began
> to make queer little animal noises—rather like homesick
> dogs. This was understandable because, as the raids re-
> peated, they seemed to have a sort of cumulative effect
> on one's system; after a while the mere thought of a raid
> was worse than its reality.

Half an hour later Rhodes heard shouts in the street for
officers, and was encouraged to see a Royal Navy liaison man
in process of gathering a group around him. The sailor was
from one of Captain Tennant's shore parties. He announced
that the Navy had given up hope of any evacuation from Dunkirk harbour. The smoke from the burning town by now gave
some protection from sighting by enemy aircraft. The army

officers, under cover of the smoke, were advised to gather as many British soldiers as possible and move onto the beaches to the east of the town, whence the navy would try to take off as many people as possible by small boats.

And so the evacuation from the beaches began. It was not a success. There were too few small boats, and those that were available were mostly ships' lifeboats or naval power boats, solid wooden craft designed to ride out a storm on the open sea. It was hoped to employ them in ferrying troops out to passenger ferries offshore. The big ships could not come close to the shelving beach. In the shallows, where they could manoeuvre only at slow speed in the fast tidal stream, the risk of running aground was redoubled by the risk of being dive-bombed.

The idea was to select groups of about a dozen men, organise them to row out in a small boat the necessary half-mile to a parent ship, unload the weary dozen up the ships' ladders, find volunteers to row back half a mile, and start all over again. It was desperately slow. Along at La Panne, at the other end of the fifteen-kilometre stretch of open beach, Lord Gort and his headquarters staff reckoned that only about two hundred men had got away when full darkness fell about 10 p.m. This was an underestimate. The total lifted onto ships may have been as high as 2,500. But certainly the numbers were hopelessly inadequate to provide any chance of getting significant British forces home to carry on the fight.

There was trouble on the sea route too. Most of the vessels sent out from Dover arrived at the marker-buoy off Calais, saw the German batteries' fire strike fountains from the water in their path, and turned back. The Manx ferry *Mona's Isle* had been in Dunkirk overnight, and had loaded 1,400 troops. At dawn she was off Calais, in full view of the German gunners. Their shells splashed around her, but she sailed through. Then the dive-bombers arrived. Their machine guns were more effective than their bombs. She limped into Dover with twenty-three corpses aboard and sixty wounded men. The word soon spread in the English port.

From anchorage off Ramsgate the motor vessel *Sequacity* sailed for Dunkirk. Her captain, Mr. J. MacDonald, saw shells strike the water ahead of his ship, but could not believe that they were meant for him. Then a shell went right through his ship's main hold, at the waterline, in on the port side and out to starboard:

I sent my mate down into the hold with some of the crew to try and patch the hole up. The next shot came through the port side of the engine room and smashed up the auxiliary engines that drove our dynamo, etc., put our switchboard out of action, and went out the starboard side.

This put our pumps entirely out of action for pumping out of the hold.

Another shot came through the wheelhouse and went through the hatches, down the forehold, and right through the ship's bottom.

We then shaped our course away from the shore, and the *Yewdale* which was outside of us did likewise.

In the meantime eleven German planes appeared overhead and bombed both the *Yewdale* and ourselves. Another shell burst over our fiddley and put the Bren gun out of action, and wounded the chief engineer.

Meanwhile the wind increased and caused a nasty chop on the sea, which allowed a lot of water to come through the hole in our side, and as we were unable to pump our hold out the ship began to take a nasty list.

I blew for the *Yewdale* to stand by us, but he did not appear to notice our signal. A British plane then appeared and saw the trouble we were in, and flew ahead to the *Yewdale* and dropped some red flares.

The *Yewdale* then returned to us, and we launched our lifeboat, and then after we had got aboard the *Yewdale* she [the *Sequacity*] went down by the head and sunk.

I should add that in addition to the two soldiers that worked our Bren gun, before we left the Downs we took on a young naval rating named Evans with Lewis guns. We had to fix these on the open bridge, and all the time we were being attacked by the planes he kept up incessant fire with the Lewis guns and stuck to his job manfully.

The lesson was plain. To plan a course past the German guns and air observation points at Calais was madness. There

were two other possible routes through the line of sandbanks
thrown up on the seabed by the rush of the tide through the
Channel (see sketch map, page 126). In heavy seas both the
Ruytingen and Zuydcoote "passes" were impassable at any
state of the tide, by any ship. In fair weather large ships can
clear these routes through the shoals, but only at high tide.

In May 1940 there were two additional hazards. One came
from the French-laid fixed minefields blocking the approach
to Dunkirk through the Ruytingen pass. The other, more dangerous yet, consisted of the new German "magnetic mines,"
activated by the electrical field of a metal ship's hull. They
were dropped from aircraft and their exact location could not
be known. Against magnetic mines the Royal Navy had just
developed a counter-measure called "degaussing": it involved enveloping a ship's hull in an artificially polarised
magnetic field to counteract the ship's built-in polarity.

The degaussing procedure was highly ingenious, but not
yet reliably proven. But the naval command in Dover decided
to risk it. From all over the North Sea minesweepers were
summoned to clear the fixed French mines from the Ruytingen channel, called Route X. Meanwhile ships were despatched to risk the magnetic mines via the northern
Zuydcoote channel, called Route Y. The conventional route
to Dunkirk, Route Z via Calais, was thirty-nine sea miles.
Route X was fifty-five sea miles. Route Y, the only one immediately available, entailed a journey of eighty-seven sea
miles. The sailing time was more than doubled; the lifting
capacity of the available ships from Dover was halved.

The great escape, at the end of its first full day, was giving
tragically feeble results. The figures for measuring its success
were, for obvious reasons, collected only at the British end
of the operation, when the disembarking soldiers were
counted. They show that 7,669 men arrived in Britain on May
27th; most of them, obviously, had embarked during the previous night, from the outer harbour of Dunkirk. No arrivals
from the beaches are recorded for this first full day, although—as we have seen—Captain Tennant had decided that
the only safe route out was by the beaches.

In France, meanwhile, the Allies were trying to organise
the defence of the bridgehead. At 7 a.m. General Fagalde,
nominally in command of all Allied troops in the Channel

ports, had called a conference at Cassel, thirty kilometres inland from Dunkirk. There it was decided that the Allies would form a defensive line to the west of Dunkirk town, along the wide canals that ring it; the French sector would run from the great naval fortress at Mardyck inland along the Canal de Mardyck, then eastwards along the Canal de la Haute-Colme to the fortress town of Bergues, perched on its odd little hill amid the plain.

From Bergues eastwards the British would take up the defence of the line of the Canal de la Basse-Colme, which runs out to the sea at Nieuport, ten kilometres inside Belgium. This line had the advantage of protecting the British front behind the reclaimed sea marsh known as Les Moëres, the marshes—De Moeren in Flemish. The sea dykes had been opened as a precaution on May 20th, and the water was gradually backing up to turn this area into a shallow lake, with only the roads standing clear of the water. Although retreating Allied troops could safely pass on the roads, no enemy without amphibious transport would dare to attack here.

The British had only two short sectors that really needed defending. One was the canal bank for three or four kilometres to the east of Bergues—a particularly nasty place to defend, since there were rows of houses on the south bank of the canal, giving good cover for advancing German troops. The other possible route for an attack on the British lines was along the dry sand dunes that form a strip up to one kilometre wide behind the beach.

The French, although they by now had no confidence in the fighting spirit of the British, thought it safe to leave them these small strips of front; especially as the Germans had not yet arrived there. For their part, the French retreated in the evening in good order to their defences along the western canals, and started to plan a counter-attack towards Calais, according to the orders radioed overnight from General Weygand, the supreme commander in Paris. The British knew that the French had orders to stand, fight, and counter-attack if they could. The French did not know that the British had orders to get out as fast as possible.

Neither British nor French knew about the Belgians. During the day the Belgian Army gradually gave up the fight. The Germans broke through in three places, and were almost

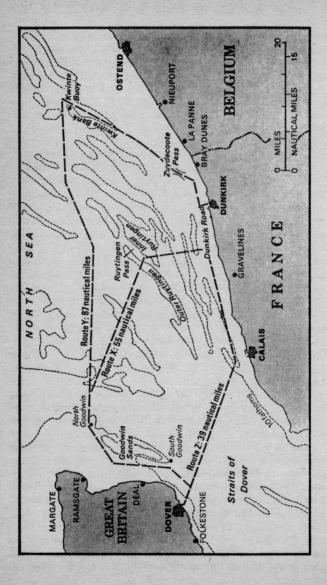

in Bruges, where lay the Belgian high command and the King, the commander-in-chief of the Army. Just after midday the King telephoned Lord Gort and warned him that the Belgian Army could take no more, and must soon surrender. He postponed the final step as long as he dared; it was five o'clock in the afternoon when he sent a messenger under a white flag to meet the German Fourth Army. They arranged for the surrender to take effect at four o'clock the following morning. There were no conditions.

It has passed into British mythology that the surrender of the Belgian Army was accomplished without notice to their allies. Sir Arthur Bryant, in his admiring account of the campaigns of General Alan Brooke, describes Brooke's conduct in command of the British Second Corps at Dunkirk in these terms: "During the four days between the Belgian collapse and the beginning of the evacuation Alan Brooke, with the four divisions of his Corps, covered the long exposed flank opened by King Leopold's surrender." In fact the British evacuation started twenty-four hours before the Belgians began the process of surrender; and the Belgians scrupulously told the British of their intentions to surrender, while the British carefully guarded the secret of their intention to get out.

So, as the day ended, the Allies were in desperate straits. The Belgians were out of the war. The port of Dunkirk was blocked, and the town rendered almost impassable. Evacuating troops from the beach had been shown—with the means available—to be too slow a process. And the Royal Air Force had been shown to be incapable of defending the troops on the ground from continuing attack from the air in fine weather.

The RAF's aim had been to maintain continuous air cover over Dunkirk, from their fighter bases eighty kilometres away in Kent. For most of the day that meant having a single squadron on patrol over the town. The Germans, on the other hand, sent their aircraft from their more distant bases in great waves, too numerous for the RAF's small teams to deal with effectively. On May 27th the RAF lost fourteen fighters over Dunkirk. The RAF's pilots, and the British anti-aircraft gunners on the ground in France, claimed thirty-eight German planes shot down. If true this would have been a victory, although

scarcely an impressive one: the Germans were mostly flying
slow bombers, while the RAF were flying modern fighters.

In fact the RAF suffered a bad defeat. The Luftwaffe's records show that on May 27th the total of German planes lost
on all operations was thirty-five, of which twenty-five went
down in districts of France and Belgium far removed from
the Channel coast. At Dunkirk the British lost fourteen aircraft in exchange for ten German planes. But even these losses
were too heavy for the Luftwaffe. Their pilots had been flying
missions without interruption for seventeen days. Half of their
fighter force was out of action or under repair. There was a
shortage of bombs. Moreover, their air reconnaissance pho-
tographs showed clearly that Dunkirk port was out of action
for large ships. Dunkirk town, for its part, was a blazing
inferno. Airmen are always reluctant to believe that their
bombs may not kill. The German incendiaries had made a
blaze in which it looked from the air as if nobody could
survive. The observers could not have known about Anthony
Rhodes and his sixty companions in that squalid cellar, surviving. The over-confident reports of the Luftwaffe's air crews
persuaded their commander to give them a rest.

As evening drew on, the air raids at the town and port
stopped. It was two days before they began again in full
strength. Beneath the cloud of smoke that hung over the town
Captain Tennant and his naval shore parties decided on a
desperate experiment. That they managed to communicate
with ships at sea at all is a wonder. They had no shore-to-
ship radio, and only one Aldiss signalling lamp which they
got to function off the batteries of a commandeered civilian
car. But somehow they worked the trick. It calls for a short
technical explanation, since this was the discovery that saved
the bulk of the British Expeditionary Force.

Dunkirk harbour is an artificial creation on what was once
a little river-mouth breaking twenty kilometres of sandy shore.
Its inner basins, with lock gates to keep the water always at
a level to float a sizeable ship, were dredged to keep them
deep. (On May 26th, as we have seen, the lock gates were
removed following bomb damage, and the basins were rendered useless.) To seaward of the dredged basins runs a
deep-water channel, whose depth is maintained not only by

dredging but also by the rush of tidal water along a course directed by artificial barriers set on the seabed.

These barriers served also as breakwaters to shelter the harbour entrance from wind and tide. In French they were called *jetées*; because a jetty is something smaller in English the merchant seamen who used the port called them the Moles. In 1940 the West Mole was relatively stubby and built of solid stone. The East Mole stretched for sixteen hundred metres (almost exactly an English mile) straight out to sea from the actual entrance of the harbour. Its inner section was of solid stone, but most of its length consisted of open-work concrete piles through which the sea flowed, surmounted by a wooden walkway wide enough for four men to walk abreast. At intervals along the walkway were large stanchions for ships' hawsers, set there to facilitate building and maintenance work.

The East Mole was never intended for vessels to moor at; indeed, it was thoroughly unsuitable for mooring, since the tide ripped along and through the piling, and the water level rose and fell for over five metres (sixteen feet) when the tides were at the springs—as they were on June 1st, 1940. The deck of a sizeable ship—a destroyer, say—was at the level of the walkway at high tide, but five metres below when the tide was out. In any weather this rise and fall made continual adjustments necessary to a ship's moorings; in windy weather any vessel risked having its sides stove in against the concrete and rubble of the foundations. Warships, naturally enough, do not have reinforced sides designed to let them rub against a pier. Bringing destroyers alongside the East Mole was a sensationally risky procedure.

But this is what Captain Tennant decided must be done. The base of the East Mole runs right in to the sandy beach at the town limits of Dunkirk, where the holiday resort of Malo-les-Bains begins. Tennant saw that troops could be mustered on the sands of Malo, and marched out in disciplined groups straight onto the Mole and along the walkway on its top. There was no need for the men to enter Dunkirk town at all. Under their own officers, and with the instructions of the Royal Navy's shore parties, they could move directly from slit trenches on the beach into the ships.

The name of the first ship to undertake the tricky manoeuvre of tying up at the Mole and loading passengers from it is not recorded. No doubt at the time it seemed just another experiment. It showed that, given superb seamanship and firm control of the men on shore, the trick could be done. For seamanship Tennant could rely on the skippers of the Channel ferries and the captains of the Royal and French navies. For control of the flow of troops he worked out a system of liaison between the piermaster, Commander Clouston, and the Royal Navy shore parties, who passed on instructions to the army officers.

As dark fell on May 27th the first ship edged in, tied up by her bows, and started to take men aboard. The escape route had been found. Along the East Mole almost 200,000 of the 338,000 British and French troops rescued from Dunkirk passed to England and safety.

10

CLOUD COVER: MAY 28TH

"There appeared to be a large wood close to the shore but on approaching nearer this was seen to be a mass of troops on the sand."
                    —Master's report, HMS Gossamer,
                    2115 hours, May 28th

"The beach was an extraordinary sight. As far as the eye could see it stretched away into the distance, the firm sand of the shore stretching farther back into dunes where the surface was no more than a thin yellow powder interspersed with parched tussocks of coarse grass. And covering this vast expanse, like some mighty antheap upturned by a giant's foot, were the remains of the British Expeditionary Force, some standing in black clusters at the water's edge, waiting for the boats that were to take them to the two or three ships lying off-shore, while others, whose turn had not yet come, or who were too tired to care whether it was their turn or not, lay huddled together in a disorderly and exhausted multitude."
                    —PETER HADLEY, Third Class to Dunkirk, 1944.

Now the weather changed. At dawn clouds began to blow up the Channel. At two o'clock in the afternoon the rain began, drifting gently in from the west. Dunkirk town was still burning, grey smoke from the rubble of the houses mixing with greasy black fumes from the fuel-oil tanks by the harbour. Impenetrable from the air, the damp smog shaded the beach for several kilometers to the east of the port. The main force of the Luftwaffe was grounded. Now and again fighter planes swooped down through the mist to machine-gun along the line of the water's edge. The bullets spent their force in the damp sand. The occasional bombs thudded harmlessly below the surface.

Under cover of the smoke and the gathering clouds, Captain Tennant's experiment with bringing ships into the East Mole was bearing fruit. There were no passenger ships waiting to take men off. But in the channel outside the port were waiting the destroyers of Dover command. Tennant ordered them to the Mole; they dashed in, tied up a single hawser from their bows, and loaded up. At most states of the tide their decks were well below the level of the walkway along the top of the Mole. They put ashore their ladders, their improvised gangplanks, their boarding nets designed for slinging overside to allow men from the water to climb to rescue. So the soldiers scrambled down to their decks.

Ashore, Tennant had appointed Commander J. C. Clouston as piermaster. He took army officers under his control, ordering them to prepare groups of men by fifties and twenties to dash at the word of command along the Mole and scramble aboard the destroyers. In twenty minutes it proved possible to pack up to six hundred men onto the cramped decks of the armed ships. Once loaded, the destroyers backed off in the narrow channel, turned, raced for Dover, and came back for more. It was an almost unbelievable feat both of improvised organisation and of seamanship.

In the afternoon the flow of troops from the Mole was disappointingly slow. Three big passenger ships—*Prague*, a Channel ferry, *Manxman* from the Irish Sea, and *Paris*, a hospital ship—ran aground when trying to cross the Zuydcoote channel through the shoals at low tide; there they waited until the water rose in the evening and they could proceed. It was not the ships' masters' fault: they had no charts for these waters, which no large vessel would try to cross in peacetime. But the danger was terrible. With their capture of the ports of Holland, the Germans were moving into position to strike at the evacuation with their E-boats, the fast torpedo boats that sped over the surface and ran no risk from shoals in calm weather. On the morning of May 28th the passenger ship *Aboukir*, sailing from Ostend with the last British refugees from Belgium, was sunk by an E-boat. The northern passage by Route Y was under threat.

But overnight the minesweepers had been at work on the central Route X, clearing the French minefields from the approach to Dunkirk over the Ruytingen channel. As they finished their work the minesweepers were directed to Dunkirk. For the most part these were civilian trawlers and other fishing boats, converted from dragging nets to their wartime duty of dragging mine sweeps. Their captains, although bearing due rank in the naval reserve or volunteer reserve, were their peacetime skippers, and there was nothing they did not know about navigation in confined waters. The minesweepers, with their shallow draught and easy manoeuverability, could work well off the beaches where the Navy's deep-keeled fighting ships could not enter, and there they were mostly sent.

Now, too, the smaller boats of the south coast were going over to Dunkirk. The preparations of the Small Vessels Pool, the signing-on of boat owners and mechanics into the Royal Naval Volunteer Reserve, began to bear fruit. Here is a report from Deal on the Kent Coast:

> I am writing this letter on behalf of myself, Harry Brown and Fred Hook who were the crew of the *Gipsy King*, a small motor-boat. We went to Dunkirk on May 28th. We stayed there about forty-eight hours. We were under shell-fire and machine-gun fire. We stayed there until every British soldier was off the beach. I should like to mention Harry Brown who did a brave action. We just loaded boat with troops. We saw a pontoon with soldiers in, being swamped with waves. Brown, being the swimmer, decided to go over the side with a rope, he tied it to the pontoon and saved the soldiers from

being drowned. I am writing this letter as Fred Hook
and Harry Brown are in the minesweepers.
    If this letter is satisfactory would you give me a reply.

                                                    A. BETTS

The same Mr. Harry Brown, still at work with his nets on
the Deal foreshore in the spring of 1980, did not want to talk
about the brave action recorded here. But he vividly described the sound of the *Gipsy King*'s oars as they came down
on the fingers of soldiers grasping in panic at the gunwales
to get aboard, and threatening to overset the boat. Mr. Brown
and his two companions were the only Deal fishermen, out
of about two hundred in the little town, who volunteered for
Dunkirk in 1940. Throughout the evacuation there was a desperate shortage of small craft to work off the beaches.
    The small fishing boats, few as they were, proved far more
handy in shallow water than the big ships' lifeboats that were
all that had been available the previous day. The minesweepers too could get far closer to the shore than the big vessels
had been able to. A regular drill developed ashore, with officers and NCOs mustering small groups of men in the dunes,
where they could lie in scrapes in the sand as protection
against air attack. The theory was that these groups could
then be brought forward to the water's edge in manageable
numbers, for detailing off into small boats as they arrived,
and then in turn for ferrying out to the minesweepers. The
reality was very different.
    Peter Hadley's description at the head of this chapter may
give an impression of what the beaches looked like. Anthony
Rhodes was standing waiting in one of the queues at the water's edge; a naval officer with a drawn pistol was marshalling
the queue, now and again threatening to shoot anyone who
got out of line:

    Once I saw a man suddenly rush past him out of turn.
    Immediately a determined shout went up from the other
    men who were in front of him in the queue. "Get out.
    Get back, you bastard. Have him back. Have him back,
    the swine." There was no mistaking their tone. The man
    failed to reach the boat which was now putting out to

sea. He shrank back, immediately forgotten and unob-
served, into the queue. . . . In our urgency we forgot
things as quickly as animals, we had the memories of
monkeys.

Imminent chaos on the beaches was controlled by the discipline of fear. The naval officers' revolvers had to be used.
It was essential to avoid a rush on the incoming boat that
would surely upset it. But forming an orderly queue at the
water's edge was not so easy. The water margin itself might
shift by a hundred meters within an hour, inwards or out-
wards as the tide ran and the beach shelved. The slope of the
sand was uneven, dropping now and then to a deep pool
scooped by the tide, or rising to form a sandbar further out
that prevented the approach of even a light rowing-boat.

Lines of troops facing the tide would feel it rise to their
knees, their stomachs, their shoulders even. Those who had
reached the head of a queue were unwilling to break off in
face of the rising water and go to the rear. The risk of drowning might be less than the risk of waiting: the cloud might
lift, the dive-bombers return, and a man's wait could be eter-
nal.

When a boat arrived it faced a rush of men trying to climb
in over the side, where they could easily upset it. Ropes and
floating debris, oil-scummed overcoats and corpses were
caught in the screws and the rudders of the power boats.
Engines and propellers gave way under the strain. Rowing-
boats did good service; but it was one thing to row out to a
waiting ship for rescue, quite another to row back again for
a new load. An empty boat was brought in by the tide within
the grasp of soldiers who with luck might manage to row it
out to a waiting ship—then turn it loose again to await the
next inflowing tide. Each boat needed a disciplined crew to
take it back and forth, back and forth.

The Navy, and the rare civilian crewmen, showed an interminable, humdrum heroism. They came to hate the weary,
sodden men they were saving. They hated the ones carrying
rifles, which cluttered up the boats and made it harder to
clamber aboard. They hated the ones without rifles, regarding
them as cowards. The sea was calm. But now and again a
fast naval destroyer would speed past on an errand. The speed

that was the soldiers' salvation made them throw up great wakes, casting cold spray on the chilled waiting men, and threatening to overset the tiny boats in which they clung like bees.

But on May 28th the great escape finally got under way. From the beaches six thousand men were landed in England this day; from the harbour twice as many men were rescued. From now on, every day would see those numbers rise, to be quadrupled three days later.*

Ashore, the German advance was held up on both fronts. Before moving away with his panzer forces to mount the attack on Paris, General Guderian, the ace tank commander, went up to visit Mardyck on the very outskirts of Dunkirk. His view of the ground convinced him that Hitler and Rundstedt had been right to order the halt on the Aa River: further tank attacks across this wet terrain would, he wrote, have involved "useless sacrifice of his best troops." On the eastern flank the Germans under General von Bock were preoccupied with organising the surrender of the Belgians. They moved slowly and cautiously, anxious above all not to alienate the civilian population of West Flanders, Flemish speakers all and—the Germans supposed—their natural friends. The Belgian officers too were anxious to spare the civilians as much as possible, and collaborated punctiliously with the Germans in the hand-over of military strongpoints and bridges, according to the rules of war.

During the night of May 27th–28th, as the Belgian Army prepared for surrender, it rendered one last service to the Allied cause. The Belgians provided enough trucks to transport an entire French infantry division out of reach of encirclement by the Germans. The division was set down on the French side of the frontier, at the point where the coastal strip of sand dunes behind the beach offered the enemy the only possible avenue of approach towards Dunkirk from the east. This division, the Sixtieth, manned the positions behind which the British finally retreated to safety within the Dunkirk perimeter. The British generals, and notably General Brooke, were meanwhile criticising the Belgians for surrendering and the French for not retreating.

*Some statistics of the evacuation are in Appendix I.

Communications between the British Expeditionary Force and the Allied high command had now completely broken down. The headquarters of the BEF was constantly on the move, and relied almost exclusively on the telephone for its links with the French. The telephone link from Paris to Belgium and the border areas of France passed through the exchange at Lille, and the British had smashed up the exchange when they abandoned the town to its French defenders on May 27th.

Communications within the BEF were almost as bad as British communications with the French. In the long fatigue of the night marches northwards, as the British columns tangled with French and Belgian units also moving frantically across what they thought was the line of the German advance, it was no wonder that unit commanders were out of touch with their headquarters; this was above all a manoeuvre in which subordinate commanders did the best they could, without the possibility of receiving orders from above.

Even General Brooke, commanding the British Second Corps on the extreme north-eastern flank, appears not to have known of the Belgian surrender until well into daylight on May 28th. His unit commanders did not hear of it until much later, and had no way of knowing that Belgian soldiers and civilians alike had been ordered by their King to make the necessary arrangements for a peaceful hand-over of authority to the Germans.

The mayor of the small Belgian commune of Oostduinkerke, between La Panne and Nieuport, feared naturally enough that if British troops continued to occupy his town the Germans might take reprisals against its citizens. He approached a British brigade headquarters to ask them to leave. The British did not have a Flemish interpreter, did not know Belgium was out of the war, and were apparently not sure that they were in Belgium. (East Dunkirk, after all, sounded like France.) They almost shot the mayor as a fifth columnist.

On the other bank of the canal running inland from Nieuport to Dixmude a British scouting party observed the progress of a German staff car flying a white flag, from which an officer descended in Nieuport to parley with the Belgian officer commanding the canal bridge. The British, suspecting treachery, grabbed a Belgian engineer officer up the canal at

Dixmude and forced him at gunpoint to blow up the canal bridge there, whose transfer to German control he had been ordered to arrange. Then the British patrol shot up the German staff car with its white flag, and settled down to defend the canal. One of the British officers involved was awarded the Distinguished Service Order for his part in this adventure although, contrary to every convention of war, he had fired on a truce party under the white flag. If the Germans had captured him they would have had every right to shoot him out of hand. But nobody had told him there was a truce on.

Soon the British were relieved of their awkward responsibility for guarding the eastern approaches to the Franco-Belgian frontier. The Frenchmen of the Sixtieth Infantry Division, brought in overnight in Belgian trucks, took over. Captain Tennant, much relieved, signalled at 10:45 p.m. to Dover: "French have taken over Belgian lines in the vicinity of Nieuport." The small boats, under cover of the dark, were doing their best along the beaches. Better still, at the East Mole two thousand men an hour were doubling out along the walkway and climbing down into the ships. There was hope at last that a good part of the BEF would get away—if only the weather and the RAF could hold the Germans off in the air, and the French hold them off on the ground.

The French had their orders to gather their forces and supplies in Dunkirk, and to break out as soon as possible towards Calais, for the relief of the French armies of the south. For that hard fight they would need every gun, every vehicle they could muster in the Dunkirk perimeter. By contrast the British knew very well that, even if they managed to get aboard ships, they could not hope to take their guns and their vehicles with them. On the British sector of the perimeter defences, from Bergues eastwards, British detachments were stationed at the canal crossings to ensure that no unnecessary clutter was brought in to add to the confusion. The orders were formal. All vehicles other than those carrying necessary ammunition were to be destroyed before their occupants crossed the canal.

The French were furious. They had few enough vehicles as it was—they regarded the BEF's transport as lavish—and they wanted to conserve them for the fight to come. And of course there were misunderstandings, some purely linguistic, some national. The British military police and provost sergeants manning the checkpoints ordered the French, at pistol point, to smash up their trucks. A French gunner major came to Captain Jean Beaux, in the French headquarters bastion down by the port, and furiously explained how the British MPs had let his guns go across and then, failing to understand his explanations, put pickaxes through the engines of the trucks carrying their ammunition. On the British side almost everyone, from generals to privates, grew puzzled and contemptuous at the French reluctance to carry out British orders. Nobody realised that the two allies had quite different objectives.

The policy of destruction at the line of the Canal de la Basse-Colme had unfortunate effects for the British too. As usual the orders got muddled. Colonel Lord Bridgeman, the officer on Lord Gort's staff who had been preparing the evacuation for the past week, told a liaison officer from the Second Anti-Aircraft Brigade that his gunners were to stay in action as long as possible, that gunners without guns were to fight as infantry, and that those who could not fight at all were to go to the beaches in the hope of catching a boat. As the liaison officer returned to brigade headquarters they were bombed or shelled—which is not clear. The order was garbled. All the guns were destroyed at once. Mr. L. Smith, then attached to a pioneer unit of a division that had no artillery at all, recalls seeing the guns of an AA unit ''at the roadside with muzzles split open and resembling a row of aspidistras.''

So the BEF lost its most modern set of anti-aircraft artillery. The Second AA Brigade had been armed with the splendid new 3.7-inch (94-mm.) weapons that had a new and sophisticated fire control system. There was plenty of ammunition for them. Fortunately the Germans were not to learn that someone had blundered.

11

THE DEFENCES HOLD: MAY 29TH

"The French staff at Dunkirk feel strongly that they are defending Dunkirk for us to evacuate, which is largely true."
—CAPTAIN W. G. TENNANT, Senior Naval Officer, Dunkirk, May 29th

Not an hour had passed on May 29th before disaster struck. The destroyer *Wakeful* had loaded 640 British soldiers from the beaches. The navy men had used their pistols to keep the soldiers in order. Now the exhausted troops were asleep below decks while *Wakeful* raced homewards across the shallows of the northerly Route Y. She had left her lifeboats behind, to continue their work on the beaches. She was travelling fast, at twenty knots, her wake bright with phosphorescence in the water behind. She dashed up to the Kwinte buoy, the marker at the northern extremity of the sandbanks of the Flanders shore, where ships on this route turn west across the deep to meet the Goodwin Sands and the English coast.

Out of the dark *Wakeful*'s officer of the watch saw two torpedo tracks approaching, glimmering in the water like his own wake. He ordered the ship to turn. One torpedo went clear. The other struck amidships, and blew her in half. All the troops on board, save one, were killed. Only the sailors on deck survived. This was the worst single loss of the evacuation. But more were to come. The Kwinte buoy was the crossing point for all traffic on Route Y. Within half an hour the sea was full of ships; all of them stopped, or circled slowly, in the hunt for survivors from the *Wakeful*—the drifters *Nautilus* and *Comfort*, the minesweepers *Lydd* and *Gossamer*, the destroyer *Grafton*. It was a perfect target.

Another pair of torpedoes struck *Grafton*. The blast of the explosion keeled the smaller *Comfort* half over, throwing back into the sea Commander Fisher, of the sunken *Wakeful*, who had just been pulled on board. *Comfort* ran on at full speed, in a circle, to avoid further torpedoes. Both on *Lydd* and on the sinking *Grafton* the gunners thought they had spotted their target. They opened fire on a small, fast-moving vessel nearby. The small ship they had seen was the circling *Comfort*. As the shells struck, *Comfort* slowed down. *Lydd*, at full speed now, rammed her amidships. Men from *Comfort* tried to scramble aboard *Lydd*. They were shot down with rifles, mistaken for a German boarding party. *Lydd*, meanwhile, fired on another small ship sighted obscurely in the dark, and her gunners reported an explosion. They had sunk the victorious E-boat. Her commander can never have known that he achieved the most striking German triumph of the fight at sea, with the sinking within an hour of two British destroyers and one minesweeper, and the death of almost a thousand British soldiers and sailors.

The northern Route Y was now declared unsafe. British ships were no longer to use it, save in an emergency. (Unfortunately this decision was not properly communicated to the French Navy, who were to suffer loss there on the following day.) The southerly Route Z was also closed on the morning of May 29th. At midnight off Calais the destroyer *Montrose*, laden with home-bound troops, had her bows blown off by shore-based German guns. She was towed stern first into Dover. By dawn the Royal Navy had lost three of its precious destroyers, the indispensable guardians of her supplies by sea. From now on there was a new caution among senior naval staff about the use of the ships to rescue the army.

The danger on the sea routes grew intense. During the previous night a brisk wind had blown up, clearing the clouds. Until the evening the Luftwaffe made no serious attack on the port or beaches of Dunkirk. Instead they concentrated on attacking Allied shipping. The German airmen were cautious. They very rarely ventured more than ten kilometres out to sea, fearing a strong reaction from the nearby English-based RAF squadrons. But along the French coast small parties of bombers, with strong fighter support, pounced on the waiting ships.

The Royal Air Force too was playing for safety. On May 27th they had flown twenty-three sorties, mostly of a single squadron each, to maintain almost continuous fighter cover of the port and beaches. They had lost fourteen planes, and failed to protect the evacuation. On May 29th they flew only nine sorties, but each one in much greater strength with two or even three squadrons. They lost nineteen planes. They consoled themselves by reporting that they had in exchange shot down sixty-five German aircraft, plus four more brought down by ships' guns. In reality the Germans lost a total of eighteen planes in all operations over France that day. The British had begun to claim—and the claim is still widely accepted today—that the RAF over Dunkirk established its "qualitative superiority" over the Luftwaffe. This was eyewash, mere propaganda. But the important thing was that the RAF's pilots believed it, and the belief sustained their morale far ahead, through the long agony of the Battle of Britain that was to come.

Nevertheless the evacuation carried on. The breeze that cleared the sky for the attacking planes raised a sharp little surf along the shallow beach. It is simply impossible for a man in wet clothes to climb into a small boat while two-foot waves are running. The larger vessels stood off the beach, vainly waiting for men to be brought out to them in the small boats. The German aircraft concentrated on these vessels, a wide-open target. Meanwhile, the East Mole was almost free of attacks from the air. Two thousand men an hour were passing along the Mole. At 10 a.m. Captain Tennant radioed from his command destroyer to Dover: "Enemy is leaving us alone. . . . There is little food or water in Dunkirk. These should be sent as soon as possible, also a staid force for control of traffic. Armies are unable to help or organise anything.''

During the day this army incompetence grew less. Tennant's naval shore parties were bringing the soldiers under discipline. And the soldiers themselves were men of better quality. Almost all the British headquarters units, stragglers and non-combatants had been taken away. Disciplined fighting soldiers were now arriving in large numbers in the perimeter. Morale improved; so did military behaviour. The soldiers and sailors began to work closely together, in an organised chain of command.

But relations between the British and the French were reaching the point of crisis. French troops were arriving on the perimeter canal with all their fighting gear, eager to use it again. The guards in the British sector were still insisting that all vehicles and unnecessary impedimenta should be destroyed, to avoid congestion within the perimeter. The British troops complied with these orders, although some resented them. Major-General John Carpenter, then a second-lieutenant in the Royal Army Service Corps, remembers his men weeping as they smashed up their beloved trucks, in which they had carried ammunition to combat units throughout the campaign. Lieutenant-Colonel H. S. Thuillier, DSO, then a captain of Royal Artillery, refused to destroy his 3.7-inch anti-aircraft guns, and got them down into action to defend the Mole from air attack.

The French were less able to resist the orders of the British military police. During the night there had been a few small shooting matches between British and French troops on the perimeter. In the morning official complaints began to come in. At Admiral Abrial's headquarters in Bastion 32 they recorded this memorandum from the general commanding the Sixtieth Infantry Division, which was establishing its line of defences along the Franco-Belgian border:

> The units which arrived with their weapons on the English line of resistance were allowed to cross only on condition that they were disarmed, the English having received orders that they were to destroy the weapons of French soldiers crossing their line of defence.
>
> An officer of my motor transport section was stopped

by the English, who compelled him to leave his car and destroyed it together with two trucks and two anti-tank weapons which were following.

Squadron Leader Arnaud suffered a similar adventure: his vehicles were burned by the English.

Furthermore an officer of the division, having been given on the beach an authorisation from a British officer to embark in a rowing-boat, was thrown into four metres of water as soon as he arrived at the passenger ship. He owed his survival only to his excellence as a swimmer.

Signed,
TESSEIRES, GENERAL.

Jacques Lenglart, in 1980 an assistant mayor of Dunkirk, had marched forty kilometres out of Belgium with his infantry company. In the early afternoon they reached the canal bridge near Hondschoote, happy to be back in France. But on the bridge an armed British sentry refused the French soldiers passage. Then a car arrived carrying a French general, and following the car a tank. On the general's orders the tank swivelled its turret to point at the sentry, and under this protection Lenglart and his soldiers marched across to take up their defensive position in the dunes.

The Anglo-French incidents were always confused, sometimes comic, rarely deadly. But as they accumulated they threatened to become really dangerous. As a result of the naval planning meeting at Dover on May 27th, French naval and civilian craft were now playing a full part in the evacuation. Some French soldiers, observing the progress of the British evacuation, and no doubt talking to French seamen around the port, were demanding places on ships for themselves. The British were chasing them off, sometimes at gunpoint. This could not be allowed to continue.

On the morning of May 29th the BEF's general headquarters made its final move, to La Panne, just inside Belgium across the border from Dunkirk. This was the point on the coast at which the British troops retreating out of Belgium were mostly expected to arrive. But the little seaside resort had several other advantages for Gort and his staff. It was not in France, so French generals would not necessarily have seniority there. Above all, the undersea telephone cable from

Brussels to London passed through the town, with a modern exchange serving old King Albert's holiday villa by the sea. (The King had always insisted on keeping in close touch with the London Stock Exchange.) So Lord Gort could talk to the War Office in London with no trouble at all. But he could not communicate with the military supreme command in Paris. Nor could he switch into the French telephone system to talk to naval headquarters in Dunkirk.

At midday on May 29th, Captain Tennant went to La Panne to report, in his words, "on the difficult situation vis-à-vis the French over the evacuation." To put things right Lord Gort drove along to Dunkirk to call on Admiral Abrial, his French opposite number.

The French command post was in the immense steel-and-concrete bunker of Bastion 32, right in the heart of the harbour area, in the centre of the action. From the Bastion Admiral Abrial, the *amiral Nord*—a very senior officer, with responsibilities for all French coastal waters and ports right along to Normandy from the Belgian border—upheld his traditional primacy of command in Dunkirk and its surrounding fortified area. Under his direct authority the marine gunners of the coastal batteries, and the troops of the *Secteur Fortifié des Flandres*, provided the backbone of the French defensive force. Under Abrial's strategic authority, command of all French land forces had been delegated to General Fagalde, as senior army officer in the Channel ports of Boulogne, Calais and Dunkirk. Gort was due the special courtesies accorded to the commander-in-chief of a national contingent of the Allied force. But in Abrial's estimation Gort came below Fagalde in the hierarchy of command.

This was not how Gort saw it at all. As far as he knew the agreed structure of the inter-Allied command had been smashed by the surrender of the Belgians more than twenty-four hours previously. He had no specific instructions, and certainly no wish, to acknowledge the authority of his French superior officers. Moreover, Abrial and Gort had received very different instructions from their own governments. Neither of them knew this. Gort had been in constant communication with London on the Belgian cross-Channel telephone link. By that route he had prepared his plans for evacuation, and received confirmation that his only duty was to withdraw.

Abrial's communications were in a far worse state. He had no telephone links with Paris or anywhere else. His radio link was unreliable, quite apart from the fact that it was rightly assumed that the German code-breakers were intercepting all signals. Abrial knew nothing at all of any plans for an evacuation, even though they had been discussed two days previously by his fellow-admirals Odend'hal and Leclerc with their British opposite number Admiral Ramsay at Dover.

Gort did not know that Abrial did not know about the evacuation. On arrival at Bastion 32, Gort breezily started discussing the details of the evacuation of the BEF, and in particular the division of responsibility for guarding the perimeter while they escaped. Abrial and his French colleagues were flabbergasted. They had been working to establish a fortified bridgehead around Dunkirk, a *camp retranché*. They had been inundated with complaints from incoming army units that the British were forcing them to destroy the equipment necessary to defend this bridgehead. Now they found out why. The British were leaving.

Both lots of senior officers at the meeting in Bastion 32 seem to have behaved with restraint and common sense. Both at once got in touch with their superiors to ask for firm orders. Gort had to drive along to La Panne to telephone to Mr. Eden, the Secretary of State for War in London. Abrial had less of a journey, but it took him longer to get through to Paris. In the interval Mr. Churchill had rushed a note to M. Reynaud, via his emissary General Spears in Paris, to tell the French government about the evacuation. This was the message delivered by Spears and Sir Ronald Campbell to Reynaud the following morning, May 30th (see page 104).

It was late evening before Gort and Abrial got their orders from London and Paris. The orders were that, from now on, the evacuation should truly be a joint operation. French and British troops should be embarked in equal numbers. British and French soldiers should play an equal part in the defence of the Dunkirk perimeter, to make the evacuation possible. This was not how Lord Gort had seen it at all. And for the British it was easier said than done. Gort's staff cursed what they saw as "political interference." Most of the British troops were already waiting on the beach or in the relative safety of the sand dunes for transport to England. The morale of those in the fighting line—or what would become the fighting line when the slow-moving troops of German Army Group B arrived—was sustained explicitly by the thought that (as Mr. Churchill had said) they were "fighting their way home to Blighty." The British generals were vividly aware that their soldiers were keener to escape than to fight.

The French, by contrast, were already in contact with the Germans along their front to the west of the town, with only a canal and no expanse of flooded marshes to keep the attackers off. And they were defending their homeland. To speak of retreat across the sea would sap, not strengthen, their morale. The two staffs agreed on a compromise, a token of co-operation. The following morning five thousand places would be reserved for French soldiers on French ships of the rescue fleet. This was not much, but it was a big increase. On May 29th, 47,301 Allied soldiers arrived in Britain from France. Of them, only 655 were French.

This was not for lack of Frenchmen trying to leave. When French troops tried to board boats on the beach, the Royal Navy shore parties organised squads of British soldiers with fixed bayonets to keep them back. On at least one occasion a British platoon laid down rifle fire against French soldiers seeking to embark. Luckily the French did not shoot back.

Whatever the wrangling on land, there was heroism at sea. The old paddle-driven Clyde steamer *Oriole* was serving in the Navy as a minesweeper, under the command of Lieutenant E. L. Davies of the Royal Naval Volunteer Reserve. He was a sailor of the old school, holding an Extra Master's Square-Rigged Certificate from the Board of Trade, and proud of it. In the morning Mr. Davies saw that with the surf running *Oriole* would get no troops aboard. So, with the tide falling, he ran her very gently aground and signalled to the soldiers to wade out. There was a rush of men, a disorderly fracas likely to endanger the ship. Mr. Davies reversed paddles and pulled off. He reported later: "Ship was taken to a more sparsely populated portion of beach, army officers were posted with revolvers to keep order and ship was beached again. Ship was again rushed by such numbers as to imperil her chances and chances of all aboard."

In another report Mr. Davies explained what then happened. "The troops at first had to be held off at revolver point, but we soon initiated a modicum of organisation and then distribution went with a swing.'' *Oriole* had turned herself into a temporary jetty. Three thousand men passed over her decks to safety in other vessels in deeper water at her stern. As the tide rose she floated off, and in two trips carried 2,591 soldiers herself to England. On his safe return to his home Mr. Davies reported himself to the Admiralty for the offence of knowingly endangering his command by running his ship ashore. He was quickly exonerated of this naval crime.

About noon the choppy sea grew calm again. Despite the Luftwaffe the rescues from the beaches gathered speed. Ships' captains, in the deadly narrows of the channel between the beach and the sandbanks, discovered a new technique for dodging bombs. As the planes approached, the ships put on speed and ran a straight course, to allow the enemy to line up and make a bombing run from dead astern. Then, as the bombs were seen to leave the attacking aircraft, the ship's captain ordered the rudder over as hard as it would go. The explosives fell harmlessly into the sea just off the beam. It took nerves of steel, and depended crucially on the ships' machine-gunners maintaining a steady rate of anti-aircraft fire to keep the attacking planes high.

In Dunkirk harbour ships could not dodge. Shells rather than bombs were the main danger inside the port entrance. The German guns were firing from just beyond the French-held Mardyck fort, less than ten kilometres from the port. They had the range precisely—too precisely. The shells fell in a steady stream right into the centre of the harbour. They missed the Mole again and again. For the ships' masters it was a formidable test of nerves. At any moment the gunners might alter their range.

At four in the afternoon the wind shifted into the north, and blew the smoke clear from over the port. At this moment the Luftwaffe arrived. Eight destroyers (three of them French), one passenger ferry, two troop-carrying passenger vessels of the Thames Local Defence Flotilla, six trawlers—all these were laid against the quayside in some part of the harbour, immobile, perfect targets from the air. The bombers struck. The first wave sank one of the destroyers, HMS *Grenade*, one of the troop transports, *Fenella*, and two trawlers.

Two more destroyers and the Channel passenger ferry *Canterbury* were badly damaged. The second Thames steamer, the old *Crested Eagle* from Southend, picked up some survivors from her sister ship and thrashed out clear of the Mole. Then she too was hit. Her wooden hull and upper works caught fire, but her master skilfully ran her aground in the shallows before the men had to jump for safety.

Fenella and *Crested Eagle* at the time of their destruction were flying neither the white ensign of the Royal Navy nor the red ensign of the British merchant fleet. Their ensign was blue, to signify their status as ships of the naval reserve. In peacetime they had carried pleasure-trippers on happy holidays. In wartime, with no more day-trippers to carry, they and their masters were commissioned for full-time naval service. Their usual crews, wearing often eccentric derivatives of Royal Navy uniforms, continued to sail them, and were supplemented by machine-gunners from local naval bases or Territorial Army units to man their improvised armament. For the Navy's administrative convenience they were classified as minesweepers, placing them in the same category as the fishing vessels that, also with their skippers and crews, were recruited specifically to clear mines.

These ships and their crews—there were many like them—were as much part of His Majesty's armed forces as any peacetime civilian recruited for the duration of hostilities. They had put on uniforms, picked up their guns and gone to war. It was natural, though, that the loss of one of these familiar craft with their peaceable names should strike a chord of special sympathy with the British public.

The author J. B. Priestley, in the first of the powerful propaganda broadcasts that he inaugurated on June 5th—the day after Dunkirk surrendered to the Germans—had a special memory of the minesweeper HMS *Gracie Fields*. Named after Britain's most popular singer, in pre-war days this comfortable paddle steamer had worked the passenger run between Portsmouth and the Isle of Wight, where Priestley had his home:

> I tell you, we were proud of the ''Gracie Fields,'' for she was the glittering queen of our local line, and, instead of taking an hour over her voyage, used to do it,

churning like mad, in forty-five minutes. And now never again will we board her at Cowes and go down into her dining saloon for a fine breakfast of bacon and eggs. She has paddled and churned away—for ever. But now—look—this little steamer, like all her brave and battered sisters, is immortal. She'll go sailing down the years in the epic of Dunkirk. And our great-grandchildren, when they learn how we began this War by snatching glory out of defeat, and then swept on to victory, may also learn how the little holiday steamers made an excursion to hell and came back glorious.

In Priestley's dark Yorkshire voice the story was irresistible. No wonder the legend spread of the fleet of civilian ships that volunteered for the Dunkirk rescue. Towards evening on May 29th His Majesty's minesweeper *Gracie Fields* was under orders in the shallow water off La Panne, waiting to receive the troops who were being so slowly ferried out from the sands. After their deadly strike on the port, the aircraft of the Luftwaffe transferred their attention to the other end of the beach.

Gracie Fields had 750 men on board when they hit her. Her engine room exploded. Steam from the pipes powering her paddles swept across her upper deck. Several men were poached to death. One paddle stopped turning, and the rudder jammed. As she circled, two Dutch *schuyts*, with their crews of the Royal Naval Volunteer Reserve—peacetime sailors, like the crew of the *Gracie Fields*—came alongside. With them was another passenger boat turned minesweeper, HMS *Pangbourne*. The survivors were taken off. Most were unharmed, some terribly scalded. *Pangbourne* took *Gracie Fields* in tow. She sank before reaching England.

But even if *Fenella*, *Crested Eagle* and *Gracie Fields* were full members of the Royal Navy, the ships that carried the largest number of soldiers out of Dunkirk were entirely civilian, with civilian crews and only a hastily mounted old Lewis machine gun or two to mark their warlike purpose. They were the passenger ferries that in time of peace linked Britain with the Continent and with the other British islands. One was the fast mailboat *Scotia*, property of the London, Midland and Scottish Railway Company, and employed in peacetime on passenger service between Holyhead in Wales and Dun Laoghaire in Ireland. (It was aboard her, or one of her identical sister ships, that this author as a baby suffered his first seasickness.) Early in the morning of May 29th *Scotia* made the run from Dover. Perhaps because she was fast—as famous for her speed as for her discomfort—she tried the short sea route by Calais Roads. Off Mardyck she was hit by shellfire. But she ran into the harbour of Dunkirk, and loaded about three thousand troops. She was built for eight hundred tight-packed Irish passengers. "The troops were exhausted and could hardly walk along the pier," wrote her master. *Scotia* was to be sunk by a bomb straight down her funnel three days later, but this time she made it home safe. *Mona's Queen*, another Irish Sea ferry serving now as a troop transport, had been the very first ship of the Dunkirk armada. Her fate was briefly recorded by her master, Mr. A. Holkam:

> I joined the *Mona's Queen* on May 28th. On the evening of that date I received orders to leave Dover on the early morning of the 29th to carry fresh water to Dunkirk and return with troops. Everything was uneventful until we reached to within about half a mile of Dunkirk, when the ship was mined and sank within two minutes, the survivors being rescued by the destroyer *Vanquisher*.

The Southern Railway steamer *Normannia* had a glorious end. She was holed below the waterline by a shell off Mardyck, and her master ran her aground on an even keel in shallow water, her bows pointed towards the port as though she were in the act of entering it. Nothing above her upper decks showed that she was not floating. Her bottom sank into the sand. Time and again the German planes swooped on this sitting target, vainly expending their bombs on a beached vessel that no explosive could have sunk. She saved as a decoy many ships and maybe hundreds of lives.

But whatever the achievements of ships and sailors, the concentrated German air attack of May 29th had its desired effect. The destroyer HMS *Greyhound* was crippled by shellfire shortly after midday when leaving Dunkirk harbour. This brought to four the number of Royal Navy destroyers put out of action during the day. The Admiralty decided that enough was enough: if Britain was to defend herself, in the long term warships were more important than soldiers. The Royal Navy's most modern destroyers were withdrawn from the action and sent to hunt E-boats off the coast of Holland. Next day Admiral Ramsay was to have only fifteen old destroyers for rescuing troops. It had by now been established that destroyers, with their own anti-aircraft defences and their very high speed, were indispensable for the rescue operation under air attack.

It had also been proven that evacuation from the beaches was too slow, and too vulnerable to the slightest rough weather, to give any chance of a safe return for most of the BEF. But bad news travels fast. After the massed Luftwaffe attack on Dunkirk harbour in the afternoon of May 29th grim reports of the destruction there passed rapidly to La Panne. A commander on Royal Navy shore patrol duties took the initiative of telephoning Dover with the mistaken information that Dunkirk harbour was blocked to shipping. This false news naturally strengthened Ramsay's determination to keep the modern destroyers out of the battle, since it was too risky to keep them standing off the beach for the hours necessary to load them by relays from small boats. Commander Dove's over-excited telephone call had potentially disastrous results. At 9:30 p.m. Ramsay ordered that no Royal Navy ships should enter Dunkirk harbour until further notice. In reality the Moles were undamaged and the approaches were miraculously not blocked. Admiral Wake-Walker, who arrived next day to speed up the evacuation, commented harshly on the commander's mistake: "Dover was, therefore, sending all ships to beaches and none to Dunkerque: it took two days to overcome the results of this indiscretion, which had considerable temporary effect on the plans."

Ashore there were horrors. Jean Beaux saw files of British troops marching past Bastion 32, on their way to the East Mole and safety. There was a little French square, a British military policeman directing the traffic. The bombs were falling, near-misses from the port. Beside the policeman lay the corpses of four of his predecessors, who had kept at their work until they were killed. And nearby there was a still more dreadful sight:

> In the middle of the road you could not help seeing the corpse of an Englishman, hacked about, but somehow all in one piece and upright, so that he seemed to have been planted like a tree in an imaginary hole. Both tragic and ridiculous, he seemed to be directing the traffic, with his face the colour of clay, his eyes dead, and his ears hanging partly off.
>
> From the start of the Dunkirk crisis, as though by a magical word of command, not a single body was buried. . . . Who could have taken responsibility for such a task?

The man who should have taken charge of such necessary chores was Abrial's second-in-command, *Contre-amiral* Platon. He was given the title of military governor of Dunkirk, and charged with organising its civilian services. When the water mains were cut by bombs, he ordered casks of wine to be put out in the streets, for the soldiers to drink at. And he tried to raise the morale of the civilian population, by putting up notices about the preservation of public order. His bulletin for May 29th ended with these statements: ''Dunkirk is suffering cruelly, but it will hold. French communiqués have for several days been reporting our advance beyond the Siegfried Line. America is sending us massive quantities of bomber aircraft, weapons and tanks. Signed, Admiral and Governor of Dunkirk, Platon.'' These specific lies were all, unfortunately, derived from French official announcements.

That afternoon, in the control tower of the airfield at Cambrai, 110 kilometres from Dunkirk, Hitler called a conference of his senior fighting commanders. He cautioned them against over-optimism, warned them that the French could yet mount an attack against the southern flank of their over-extended advance and appointed General Guderian to command a new armoured group including the four best panzer divisions. Guderian could call at will for full air support. This new group was to assemble as soon as possible, back at a new jumping-off point at Charleville near Sedan, 250 kilometres from Dunkirk. His job was to sweep down the rear of the

Maginot Line and finish the destruction of the French Army. The fate of France was sealed. Cutting off the British Expeditionary Force from its escape route through Dunkirk was no longer a main objective for the German Army and Air Force.

12

THE HAUL OFF THE BEACHES: MAY 30TH

"I was inshore as close as I dare. 'Stop shouting and save your breath, and bail out with your steel helmets,' was the only command suitable for the occasion. Scores offered me cash and personal belongings which I refused, saying, 'My name is Barrell, Canvey Island, send me a postcard if you get home all right.' They have all forgotten—no wonder!"

—Statement by Mr. Allan Barrell, owner, motorboat *Shamrock*, May 30th

This was the day when the beach boats did their best. For the first and only time during the evacuation the number lifted off the beaches was greater than that taken out of Dunkirk harbour: 29,500 off the beaches, 24,300 from the harbour. It was a tragic waste of lives and effort. The previous day, under bitter attack from the air, the number lifted from the harbour was 33,500. On May 30th, believing the port to be definitely closed, the Luftwaffe barely attacked it. Commander Dove of the Royal Navy had made the same mistake the previous evening. His excited report to Dover that the port was closed had led Admiral Ramsay to divert his ships to the beaches.

All through the morning of May 30th the port of Dunkirk

155

lay ready to receive the rescue ships. The mist was thick, the sea flat calm, the German air force absent, the German guns silent for lack of shells. Only one British vessel entered before noon. She was carrying food from England. The hungry, waiting troops mobbed the men unloading her. She carried no water, and water was what they craved.

Along the beach the ships waited a full kilometre out to sea, where they had water enough under their keels. With agonising slowness their boats by relays ferried out their load of men. There was still a desperate shortage of small craft suitable for working off the beach. Nobody had realised— they could not have realised—the problems that would be caused by the gentle slope of the sand into the tidal waters.

Motorboats and rowing-boats would pull in, grounding their bows in knee-deep water. Over the bows a dozen soldiers would clamber wearily aboard in their sodden battle dress. The extra weight would dig the keel into the sand, and before the boat could get off they would have to get out, push off, holding the boat steady against the tide, and start all over again. It was infuriating for the soldiers, who cursed what they saw as the incompetence of the seamen. It was agonising for the masters of the bigger ships offshore, as they waited for the arrival of the next load—or for the arrival of the bombers.

The evacuation from Dunkirk was still a secret in England. No civilians had volunteered specifically for the job; the potential volunteers had not been told about it. The small craft available, except for ships' lifeboats and naval whalers, were those that had previously registered with the officials of the Small Vessels Pool, at Sheerness in the mouth of the Thames estuary. Most of them were from nearby harbours; none of their owners or crews had any information about the adventure they were being asked to join.

Four of these small craft had sailed across the previous evening from Southend, on the north bank of the Thames estuary. In normal times they were for hire to pleasure fishermen in the summer months. One, the *Queen of England*, was run down and sunk by a Dutch coaster on the way to France. *Canvey Queen*'s engine broke down, but she was taken in tow by *Shamrock* and put to rights. *Princess Maud*

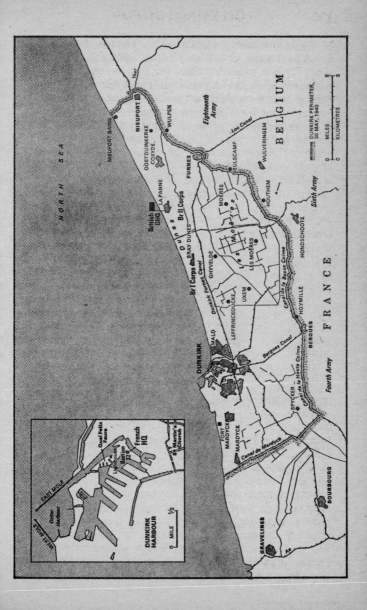

NORTH SEA

NIEUPORT
NIEUPORT-BAINS
OOSTDUINKERKE
COXYDE
WULPEN
Yser

BELGIUM

Eighteenth Army

Loo Canal

BULSCAMP
WULVERINGEM

DUNKIRK PERIMETER,
30 MAY, 1940

MILES
KILOMETRES

FURNES

LA PANNE
British GHQ
BRAY DUNES

Br I Corps
Br II Corps

D u n e s

MOERES
L e s M o e r e s
HOUTHEM

Sixth Army

GHYVELDE
LES MOÈRES
HONDSCHOOTE
Dunkirk Furnes Canal

LEFFRINCKOUCKE
UXEM
Canal de Basse Colme

MALO

DUNKIRK
HOYMILLE
Bergues Canal

FORT MARDYCK
BERGUES
Canal de la Haute Colme

MARDYCK
SPYCKER

Canal de Mardyck

FRANCE

Fourth Army

BOURBOURG

GRAVELINES
Aa

DUNKIRK HARBOUR

EAST MÔLE
Quai Felix Faure
St Martin's Church
French HQ
Lighthouse
Bastion 32
Outer Harbour
WEST MÔLE

DUNKIRK HARBOUR

MILE

got across without accident. The author David Divine recorded their story, as told by Allan Barrell of *Shamrock*:

Dawn soon came, we stared and stared at what looked like thousands of sticks on the beach and were amazed to see them turn into moving masses of humanity. I thought quickly of going on and picking up seventy to eighty and clearing off, with the sun behind me I calculated I should find some East Coast town. We got our freight, so did the *Canvey Queen*, when I realised it would be selfish to clear off when several destroyers and large vessels were waiting in deep water to be fed by small craft, so I decided what our job was to be.

We could seat sixty men and with those standing we had about eighty weary and starving British troops, some without boots, some only in their pants, but enough life left in them to clamber on board the destroyers with the kind hand of every available seaman. Again and again we brought our cargo to this ship until she was full. . . .

Navigation was extremely difficult owing to the various wreckage, upturned boats, floating torpedoes, and soldiers in the water trying to be sailors for the first time, they paddled their collapsible little boats out to me with the butts of their rifles, and many shouted that they were sinking, I could not help them. I was inshore as close as I dare. . . .

Later I took in two or three large Carley floats one behind the other. These were filled to capacity, about fifty men in each standing up to their waists in water in the net inside. My craft was well loaded too, we were just making for our destroyer when I was brought to a standstill; my engine stopped, we had fouled, I believe a human obstruction. There were many in the shallow water. . . . I was too weak to dive under the thick black oil which surrounded us, so rather than be left sitting on our useless craft I asked to be taken on HM ship. This was the last straw, having to leave my vessel which constituted my life savings . . .

Commander Richardson, in charge of the naval shore parties at Bray-Dunes, had a brilliant idea. Lorries were being abandoned and smashed up in the dunes, to prevent them from falling into the hands of the Germans. Richardson suggested that they be manhandled across the soft sand above high-tide level, then shoved out into the water in line ahead, and linked by planks to form piers. Several hundred men were thus enabled to board boats in deeper water. But as the tide swirled back in, the lorries began to float and rock, spilling junk into the surf to catch the propellers of the motorboats. No expedient, however ingenious, could overcome the natural deficiencies of the beaches as a place of embarkation. But at least the work of preparing the lorry piers gave the men ashore something to do.

Commander Richardson was depressed by the low morale of the troops, although he agreed with their "bitter words" at the apparent lack of air cover by the RAF. He criticised the Army's usual drill in an air raid, which was to lie down and wait until the attackers had gone away: "I consider that if one lies over on one's face during an air raid, one gets the impression that the bombs when falling with very horrid shrieking noises are each and all coming to land right in the small of one's back." He suggested that the men be told to stand up and shoot at the planes, however unlikely it was that they could hit one with a rifle. He had instructed his sailors to watch the bombers as they came. "I saw no sign, except in one very isolated case, of any of the Naval ratings being at all genuinely upset by the bombing. Machine-gunning, though, was quite embarrassing."

The soldiers on the shore were now suffering badly from shortages of food and water, as well as from terror, cold and boredom. During the night of May 29th–30th several big lighters loaded with supplies were towed across the Channel and shoved inshore at the top of the tide, to be unloaded as the water receded from around them. The stranded barges then did good service as makeshift piers when the tide came back in, and the tugs went off to other dangerous work.

The cross-Channel passenger ferry *Prague* had a deeper keel than most. On May 28th she had already run aground at low tide when crossing the Zuydcoote Pass. Now she bumped her way once more across the sandbanks of the central Route Y, avoiding the fresh wrecks as well as the more normal hazards of the shallows. Late in the afternoon of May 30th

she sailed into Dunkirk harbour and experimented with a new
berth far inside the entrance, whose attraction was mainly
that the smoke clouds were thick there, providing cover
against aircraft. As the tide flowed out a thousand men or
more clambered aboard. *Prague* stuck fast aground. Then the
German guns opened up, firing blind through the smoke, but
accurately ranged on the centre of the outer harbour. The tugs
Lady Brassey and *Foremost 87* pulled the *Prague* off the sand,
through the shellfire, and out on her route home.

As the day wore on the Royal Navy's shore control officers
became convinced that the beaches were not the best way
out. Early in the morning of May 30th Captain Tennant and
his hard-worked naval staff ashore got powerful reinforcements. Tennant's official designation remained unchanged as
senior naval officer ashore at Dunkirk. On the evening of May
29th—when the Dynamo Room staff supposed that Dunkirk
port was no longer useable—Rear-Admiral W. F. Wake-
Walker had been appointed "for command of sea-going ships
and vessels off the Belgian coast"—a formula apparently designed to avert any suspicion that he would undermine Tennant's authority, or conflict with that of the French Channel
command in Bastion 32.

Wake-Walker sailed over on the morning of May 30th, as-
sisted by two commodores (senior Royal Navy captains) and
two beach parties of eighty officers and men each. He was
determined to get things ship-shape ashore. As he wrote later,
one of his beach parties "was for disciplinary purposes on
the beaches. In the earlier stages the troops were completely
disorganised, discarding their rifles, lying down on the
beaches and refusing to get into the boats: it was intended
that men would not be taken off unless they had their rifles."

The admiral's day was energetic. He sailed across from
Dover in a destroyer. On arrival off Dunkirk he transferred
to a minesweeper, which was handier, and took her in to the
Mole. As he went ashore a crowd of soldiers who had been
vainly awaiting passage crammed aboard his ship. The admiral sent the minesweeper off with seven hundred men to
Dover, and transferred to a fast motor torpedo boat. She ran
short of fuel. So the admiral shifted into another minesweeper for a trip along the beach to La Panne, and there back into
a fresh destroyer to use her powerful radio, linked to the

Admiralty in London. This destroyer slowly filled up with troops from the beach, so just after midnight Wake-Walker wound up his working day by transferring into yet another destroyer. Thus he flew his admiral's flag from six ships within twenty-four hours, and laid claim to a record for any navy.

Wake-Walker's trips ashore were instructive. He visited Captain Tennant, and made contact with the French as well as the British army. His visit to the East Mole revealed that, despite the previous evening's bombing, it was still perfectly useable. His evening at La Panne proved to him that embarkation from the beaches, involving one and often two transhipments for the exhausted soldiers, was far too slow and exposed the waiting ships offshore to far too much danger from the air.

His first signal to Admiral Ramsay in Dover secured the services of all available destroyers for the Dunkirk Mole. He thus persuaded Ramsay to countermand the previous day's decision that this work was too risky. Unfortunately Ramsay's best and biggest modern destroyers had been sent off after German fast torpedo boats off Holland, and were not available for a day more. Wake-Walker ended his day with a visit to Lord Gort's headquarters at La Panne, where he strongly urged the soldiers to start moving westwards within reach of the Mole and safe access to the destroyers that would take them home.

The morning had been wasted in gallant efforts to get people off the beach. In the afternoon the mist and smoke lifted from over the port, and the Luftwaffe came back. After a heavy raid Captain Tennant left for Dover, where he could get the rest he desperately needed. On departure he signalled: "I consider Dunkirk will be untenable by Friday morning [May 31st]. Embarkation will be continued until last moment but depend upon large ships and destroyers at Pier tonight." But the soldiers were still scattered along the fifteen kilometres of beach as far as La Panne, and even beyond. It was the Navy's job to persuade them to move to where the ships could pick them up, at the Mole.

The soldiers were reluctant to accept that they should move along the beaches into France. There was a fairly bitter argument between Wake-Walker and the staff of the BEF. After dinner with Lord Gort and his colleagues at La Panne, Wake-Walker overheard Brigadier Sir Oliver Leese, the deputy chief of Gort's staff, mutter something about "the ineptitude of the Navy." In Wake-Walker's muted description, "I could not let this pass and told him he had no business or justification to talk like that." It was a lively little inter-service incident. As usual the Navy won in the end.

There were military as well as naval reasons for moving the BEF westwards towards Dunkirk. The by now rapidly diminishing British army was spread out along the beach. There were no more stragglers to come into the perimeter. But there was no agreement between the Allies about where the perimeter ended at its eastern extremity—and the Germans were arriving there in strength. Eastward from the Franco-Belgian frontier the British were occupying a strip of coast some ten kilometres long and at its extremity only four kilometres wide between the canal and the seashore.

This far end was under Lieutenant-General Alan Brooke, commanding the British Second Corps. His men were in a dangerously exposed position: accurate German artillery fire from the flank could have massacred them, and they had practically no ammunition for their own guns. Luckily the Germans too were short of ammunition. They did not press the British. And the French provided what was so desperately needed, a firm defensive line for the British to withdraw behind.

On May 30th the headquarters and two almost complete divisions of the French Third Corps withdrew into the British sector of the perimeter. The corps commander was General de la Laurencie, a friendly man who spoke excellent English and whose troops had already been seen by the British to be stout fighters. The general was amazed to find that the British had not troubled to man the existing strong defensive positions along the French border with Belgium. He decided to put his own men in there. Since this was on paper in the British sector he politely offered to put his corps under Lord Gort's command, so long as it could man the frontier line.

The French offer was gladly accepted. Now the British could break off the fight and march for Dunkirk, knowing that they had a firm line of defence to retire behind. In gratitude Lord Gort ordered that five thousand places should be reserved on British ships on May 31st, specifically for de la Laurencie's men if they decided to pull out. In fact they held on right until June 3rd, until well after the last British troops had left.

In general, relations between British and French on the beaches were far from harmonious. Lieutenant G. W. Vavasour, in charge of a Royal Navy beach party, reported on the confusion caused when the Frenchmen tried to join British queues for boats at the waterside. "A few wholesome lies to the French soldiers as to the position of their own ships soon cleared the area. They formed to the Eastward of our sections."

But at least it was now accepted that the French had the right to join the evacuation. Over 8,500 French soldiers arrived in Britain on May 30th. In all fairness it is possible that the French totals are understated in the British records—the French records were mostly destroyed after their surrender, and some reports may have been wrongly translated. (A Royal Navy list from Ramsgate pleasantly records the arrival of a French trawler under the name *Cul de Dieu*, "God's Backside"—her name was in reality *Ciel de Dieu*, "God's Heaven.")

Accurate records of numbers of Frenchmen arriving in Britain were not always made, because they were sent back to France as soon as possible, sometimes within twenty-four hours. As soon as landed they were disarmed, put onto trains for Southampton or Weymouth, and sailed across to Brest or Cherbourg to re-form into proper military units. Some sailed direct from Dunkirk to their home ports without stopping in England at all.

The story of the French share in the Dunkirk evacuation, although still incomplete, has been pieced together by the French naval historian Jacques Mordal. In May 1940 he was a navy doctor: his real name was Hervé Cras. His ship, the destroyer *Jaguar*, was sunk off Dunkirk harbour mouth on May 23rd by a German torpedo-boat. He served as a doctor throughout the evacuation, while his ship's crew were employed as soldiers to defend the port. In the night of June 3rd, well after the last British troops had departed, he sailed for England. He was sunk again (by a magnetic mine this time) just off the English coast. So he had good reason to be

interested in Dunkirk. The following stories, culled from his
research, may serve as examples of others that went unre-
corded, and help explain why British reports of the French
role in the evacuation are often incomplete.

One little French convoy was commanded by Sub-
Lieutenant (*Enseigne de vaisseau*) Aguttes. There were the
Marie, the *Pierre* and the *Sainte-Isabelle*, fishing drifters from
Brittany. They carried shells, mostly for anti-aircraft guns.
Their job was to sneak in and supply the Dunkirk garrison.
Aguttes sailed across to the English shore, coasted along to
Folkestone—maximum speed, seven knots—and took the
central route across the sandbanks to Dunkirk. There he ar-
rived in the morning mist, at 7:20 a.m. on May 30th. He had
no wireless, and had no idea about any evacuation. Still less
did he know that Dunkirk port was officially closed, after the
Luftwaffe's raids of the previous night. As he entered the
harbour he heard aircraft and saw British destroyers firing
into the sky. He tied up, according to the orders received
from Cherbourg three days before, at the base of the West
Mole.

There was nobody to welcome his ammunition. Indeed,
there were no Frenchmen to be seen at all. A few German
shells were lobbing into the water. A British officer came up.
Aguttes said he had ammunition aboard; the officer ordered
him away from the quay, as a danger to his men in case the
ammunition blew up. Aguttes found a few French soldiers
among the British on the quay, so he got them aboard and
moved further up the harbour. There by chance he met another French fishing boat, the *Bernadette*. Her master told
him about Bastion 32 and the French command post, so
Aguttes went off to report. A truck and an unloading party
were got together. At long last the precious load could be
delivered. But at 10:20, as the *Pierre* was discharging, a stray
German shell set her dangerous cargo afire. The little convoy
hurriedly left the quay. The three fishing boats had got about
a hundred people aboard, including four women and two children. And so they went over to Ramsgate.

Sub-Lieutenant Royer, on a similar trip with three French
and four Belgian trawlers loaded with shells, arrived in Dunkirk from Normandy on May 31st. They could not find anyone at all to accept their cargo, so they took the ammunition

over to Ramsgate, unloaded it, and returned to Dunkirk on the night of June 2nd and again on June 3rd to pick up French soldiers.

Meanwhile, away to the south, the French Army made its final desperate attempt to break through northwards to the relief of the armies locked into the Dunkirk perimeter. Already on May 28th the French Fourth Armoured Division had punched the Germans off the little hill overlooking from the south the bridges that cross the Somme at Abbeville. The hill is surmounted by an earthwork known as Caesar's Camp. By tradition it was the command post for the successful invasion of Britain in August 55 B.C.

The French had desperately little ammunition. On May 28th their tanks had used up all the available fuel. But their fighting spirit was up, and on May 30th they set off again northwards. The Germans, in defence, had sited their anti-aircraft guns in front of their lines. The leading French tanks were split open by the 88-mm. shells, fired from a range that the tanks' guns could not match. Dive-bombing squadrons diverted from Dunkirk completed the failure of the French attack. But by it the commander of the French division proved his worth as a fighter. He was a colonel, acting brigadier-general, by the name of Charles de Gaulle.

13

ARM IN ARM!: MAY 31ST

"Political pressure was now being brought on the C.-in-C. that the evacuation must be on a fifty-fifty basis with the French."
> —CAPTAIN TENNANT, Senior Naval Officer, Dunkirk, May 31st

"Got barge alongside and steamed in to 2 fathoms, a small boat took barge and beached her. Jerry bombing beach and ships anchored off. Left Dunkirk 6 p.m. 7 p.m. bombed by Jerry, two incendiary close to tug, one drifter went up. Tug Contest picked up crew. 7.30 passed Sun XV, VIII and IV going in, sorry for them, glad to get out."
> —Report of MR. J. R. LUKES, master, tug *Sun XI*, May 31st

The French authorities were now fully informed about the evacuation. The British public too were allowed to hear something of it. The London morning newspapers, after four and a half days of silence, were permitted by the censors to reveal that ''BEF forces returning from France were stated to be arriving yesterday in thousands at a South Coast port.''

166

The Germans also now had a clear chance to see what was going on, for the weather turned against the British.

At dawn a sweet south-westerly breeze sprang up over the Channel, bringing a summer day of fresh splendour. The haze along the Flemish coastline cleared. Little waves spanked against the beach. In Dunkirk town the great oily fires were burning low, and the smoke blew out across the Channel. The ruined town lay open to the sky and to the Luftwaffe.

As the early sun warmed the sand the air raids began. The German gunners got their opportunity, too. A little spotter aircraft hovered over Mardyck, and from beyond the French defences shells ranged accurately in upon the harbour. Over Nieuport, far away at the Belgian extremity of the beach, a balloon rose into the sky carrying in its basket a German artillery observer. From all sides there was danger to the Allied bridgehead.

At Dover, as dawn came, Admiral Ramsay received his reports from the ships' radios off Dunkirk and the beaches. They told him of the air raids and the shelling. They told him, too, that the waves were oversetting the small boats working the beaches, and of the consequent delays to the larger vessels waiting offshore for a load of soldiers, in constant peril of air attack. Ramsay could not afford to waste ships. In mid-morning he ordered sailings from England to be suspended.

After the morning radio signals the overnight departures from France began to check in at Dover. The results were highly encouraging. The night had been calm, both on sea and in the air. The ships had hovered close offshore until first light, packing men slowly but steadily aboard. Among the early comers were two of the three corps commanders of the BEF, Lieutenant-Generals Alan Brooke of Brookeborough and Sir Ronald Adam. After a wash, a shave and a good breakfast the two generals went to the Dynamo Room to call on Admiral Ramsay, their saviour.

Brooke was alarmed by Ramsay's mood. Bertie Ramsay—Brooke describes him as an old friend—seemed in doubt about continuing the evacuation. The general, by his own account, put this right: "He was planning for one more superhuman effort during the coming twenty-four hours and then to close down. I told him that this would not cater for all that still had

to be moved, that he would have to carry on with the endeavour for several more days . . . Providence was indeed
kind that we should have known each other so well before
this critical interview on which so much depended.'' Whether
or not it was Brooke who changed Ramsay's opinion, the
sailings soon resumed in strength.

The achievement of this day was splendid. More than a
fifth of all the soldiers evacuated from Dunkirk arrived in
England on May 31st—68,014 men, by the Royal Navy's careful reckoning. It was the highest total of any day of the evacuation. It was also the last day of large-scale evacuation from
the beaches. Almost 30,000 men arrived in England from the
beaches on May 30th, 23,000 on May 31st, only 17,350 on
June 1st. From Dunkirk harbour the numbers moved the other
way: 24,000 on May 30th, 45,000 on May 31st, 47,000 on
June 1st. In part this reflects the fact that the French were
now leaving in large numbers. Since the main body of their
force was in Dunkirk itself, or in the fighting area due inland
from the town, there was no need to put them through the
hazardous business of transshipment across the sand. But
the British too abandoned their plan to take people off the
beaches, because it was a failure.

Sea-going boats, however small, could not get close enough
to the shelving beach to get men aboard without making them
swim, or without an even smaller boat to ferry them the first
few hundred yards. Even the little fishing craft that habitually
worked off the English beaches proved unsuitable. From
Leigh-on-Sea in Essex there departed early in the morning of
May 31st a little flotilla of ''bawley-boats,'' ancient wooden
craft fitted with makeshift engines. Their usual prey was
shrimps and cockles, tiny shellfish to make treats for Cock-
neys. The Royal Navy men were full of admiration for the
skill and discipline of the fishermen, only one of whom had
ever been further out to sea than the mouth of the Thames
estuary at Ramsgate.

But the old boats, built of oak and elm, were useless off the
beaches. They drew too much water. As soon as a few soldiers
climbed in over their bows they grounded on the sand. Even the
smallest wave then lifted their floating sterns and threatened to
swing them round. The soldiers had to get out again, with great
reluctance, while the boats put more water under their keels.

The bawley-boats were taken off beach work after a few attempts, and put onto the job of acting as ferries to larger ships within Dunkirk harbour itself. Just after midnight they loaded up for the last time and sailed for Ramsgate, where they all arrived damaged and unfit for further service.

A greater failure was that of the "special tows" that left Ramsgate at 1 p.m. A large number of tiny craft had been assembled by the Small Vessels Pool, based on Sheerness. Some were motorboats, some had only oars. They came from all along the south-east coast of England, and from right up the Thames. The Sheerness organisation had roughly inspected and fitted them up, and assigned seamen to each craft. Then they were tied in strings behind larger ships, to be towed across the Channel. The intention was that there they would be fully manned by soldiers. Their owners stayed behind.

Very few of the little boats made it across. The upriver boats, in particular, were useless. They were built for lazy days on the quiet river. At sea, towed at speeds forbidden on the Thames, the tug of the ropes ripped off their stanchions. Several times the towing ships stopped and tried to attach new ropes to the sterns of the small craft. The sterns pulled right out of the hulls. A few motorboats from upriver did get across. As soon as their engines were started for the run in to the beach, rubbish was sucked into their cooling systems, and they stopped for good.*

There were some successes. From Ramsgate itself a little fleet of pleasure-fishing launches went across. From Southampton the Royal Air Force mustered the launches used for plying out to the flying boats that took off from the sheltered waters of the Solent. They all did their best. Others declined to cross the Channel. The local fishing fleet of Rye in Sussex collectively refused to go. The official registers of small craft included large numbers of fishing and pleasure boats from the Devon ports of Brixham and Dartmouth, with their civilian owners and crews. None of them volunteered. The Royal Navy commandeered the boats and tried to find naval mechanics to run their engines. But the engines were mostly

*Small craft with outboard motors would have been perfect for the job; but outboards, an American development, were very rare in Britain in 1940 and there is no record of their use at Dunkirk.

small diesels, which the available navy men had no experience with. There were constant breakdowns. As Admiral Ramsay commented afterwards: "These difficulties would never have arisen had the civilian crews, or even their drivers, been willing to take their boats across to Dunkirk."

The volunteer crews of the Royal National Life-Boat Institution from all around southern England were asked to take their boats across to France. The Ramsgate and Margate crews volunteered in their entirety; they were on the spot, and no doubt knew how important was the work. From Dover, the coxswain and the engineer of the lifeboat volunteered. The crew was completed by Royal Navy men. None of the other lifeboat crews volunteered when asked, and their boats sailed with complete naval crews. The lifeboatmen who declined to go were probably right. The lifeboats were built with deep and heavy keels, for stability in rough seas, and they were wholly unsuitable for work off the beaches of Dunkirk.

It is evident from the records that when civilian sailors were told the importance of the work being asked of them, they offered their services at once. But nobody can volunteer until he has been told there is something to volunteer for. Not until 6 p.m. on May 31st were the British people fully informed about the evacuation, on the BBC's early evening news. Until then it was a secret. Before the secret was lifted 72,000 soldiers left from the beaches, mostly in craft manned by the Royal Navy, or by the soldiers themselves. After the secret was lifted, when civilian volunteers began to come forward, 26,500 were rescued from the beaches. The contribution of civilian volunteers to the success of the Dunkirk evacuation was gallant and distinguished; but it was not significant in terms of numbers rescued.

The civilian contribution to the operation need not be judged solely in terms of the small number of men they brought home. The soldiers on the shore needed fresh water and food and ammunition. These were largely supplied by civilians in working boats. From the Thames above London the house-moving firm of Pickfords sent its lighters full of necessary stores. The London County Council contributed the hopper-barges that took household garbage out for dumping in the sea. They delivered cargoes and returned with men aboard.

From the pier opposite the Tate Gallery the London Fire
Brigade sent the fire tender *Massey Shaw*. Her job was at first
meant to be quenching the flames of Dunkirk port, but when
the signal came that the fires had burned out the crew kept
going. Some were regular firemen, some auxiliary volunteers—a lawyer, a city clerk. All went willingly, under discipline, knowing what they were in for. They may not,
however, have foreseen that the fire float with her big water
cannon on the foredeck would almost be sunk by a destroyer
who took her for a German gunboat.

Nine Port of London tugs of the Alexander Towing Company, all called *Sun* with different numbers, crossed towing
lighters and barges with food, water and ammunition. Even
the firm's general manager, Mr. Alexander, left his desk and
sailed in command of *Sun IV*. In their tows were a dozen
Thames barges, with names like *Ena, Doris, Pudge, Ethel
Everard*. These odd and highly specialised craft had flat bottoms, for running up tidal creeks and beaching on mud or
sand, carrying hay or potatoes or building sand to the towns
of the lower Thames. Now for the last time they spread their
ochre sails on the great sprit that also served as a crane, and
ran aground at Dunkirk.

Albert Barnes of Dagenham, then fourteen years old, was
galley boy on the tug *Sun XII*, and is almost certainly the
youngest surviving Dunkirk veteran. His main job was to
make tea for the tug's nine-man crew. They had been ordered
off a towing job in the King George V Dock, in London, and
sent round to Dover. There they took in tow a pair of Thames
barges full of ammunition. As they approached Dunkirk beach
the tug gathered speed, then cut her towing lines so that the
barges ran up the sand. Mr. Barnes remembers: "Then the
Stukas arrived. The barges went up bang like that. Nothing
left. Funny, one of the skippers, a real character with a long
white beard, he turned up again later, perfectly OK." *Sun
XII* went on to perform a string of rescues. It was fourteen
days before young Albert Barnes got home to his mother. She
was especially proud of his socks; they were so dirty they
stood up like Wellington boots. She showed them to all the
neighbours, the socks that had been to Dunkirk.

And so the commercial crewmen did their duty. The other
main source of civilian support for the Dunkirk operation

arose among the many naval and military veterans of southern England who were furious that their age had kept them out of the war. Captain R. Pim, an elderly member of the Royal Naval Volunteer Reserve, reported on the shore control party that he recruited among his superannuated contemporaries: "Several civilians at Deal desired to accompany the party, and five did in fact get to Dunkirk and were of the greatest possible use."

One of the most useful volunteers was an elderly army officer, Lieutenant-Colonel R. L. Hutchins, MC, of the Welsh Guards. He had an extremely boring job as army liaison officer at the Admiralty. Friday, May 31st, was his day off. By three o'clock that morning he had left Ramsgate in charge of a convoy of four War Office motor launches. In his own launch, the *Swallow*, he took more than seven hundred men from the beaches out to warships. He also helped in ironing out several points of confusion between the military and naval commands on the spot. Then he hitched a lift to England, leaving his launch behind, and was back at his desk in time for work on Saturday morning.

Mr. T. Towndrow sailed across to Dunkirk in the steam pinnace *Minotaur*:

> Of the whole of our operations this six hours' crossing was the worst as we had nothing to do but contemplate the job ahead of us and had been foolish enough to listen to the idle talk of naval ratings at Ramsgate before we left, who assured us that very few of the boats that had gone across had come back and that, now that Jerry had captured the harbour and had mounted machine-guns covering the beaches, our chances of coming through were very slender indeed. Of course, such was not the position. The whole of Dunkirk was still very much in our hands, but we did not know this.

Mr. Towndrow's calm recollection is in the best tradition of the Royal Navy, in which he had served as a young man. When he went to Dunkirk he was scoutmaster of the troop of Sea Scouts at Mortlake, up the Thames from London. *Minotaur* was the scouts' training barge, and her engineer was a Rover Scout.

The order had now gone out—under "political pressure," meaning orders from the Prime Minister—that French troops should be embarked in roughly equal numbers with the British. But the impromptu rescuers were there to save their own people. They could not speak French. They did not care about the French—not enough, anyway, to risk their lives and their ships on their behalf. They had no idea that the French too, all this long day, were fighting a tough fight in the Channel.

For some reason—perhaps because the British had not told them of the disaster two days previously when a thousand men were lost in the attack by a German torpedo boat near the Kwinte buoy—the French Navy was still using the northerly Route Y. On May 30th the destroyer *Bourrasque*, sailing out fully loaded past Nieuport, was driven off the channel between the minefields by shelling from the shore, hit a mine, and sank with the loss of about five hundred men. On May 31st the French suffered a similar disaster. Shortly after midnight the destroyer *Siroco*, commanded by *Capitaine de frégate* de Toulouse-Lautrec, was heading out toward the Kwinte buoy with 750 soldiers aboard for England. Most of the troops were French, from Dunkirk harbour. But she had stopped off La Panne and sent her whaler ashore to rescue some British soldiers as well. They included Major-General Montgomery's personal policeman, Sergeant Arthur Elkin. He was down in the galley, swapping his surplus cigarettes for sandwiches: "There was an almighty bang, all the lights went out and she started going down. I swam and got ashore, and she went down with the poor sods in who could not swim." A torpedo had struck home. *Siroco* ran aground, her decks still crammed with men, and was finished off by dive-bombers at dawn.

Near the Kwinte buoy her sister ship *Cyclone* was also torpedoed. Her bows were blown off, but she did not sink. The Polish escort destroyer *Blyskawica*—whose sister ship *Burza* had also had her bows blown off, by shellfire, three days before—chased and may have hit the attacking German submarine. But it was a grievous loss. The French Navy had been given a double task. They were taking men out of Dunkirk. They were also transporting men landed in England quickly back to France, to put them once more in the fighting line. For this purpose they had brought up some big ferries from the Mediterranean, where they usually ran between

Marseilles and Algiers. Many of their warships were diverted from the Dunkirk evacuation to act as escorts on this secondary route.

On May 31st the French managed to put about fifty vessels into the evacuation from Dunkirk. Most were small naval craft, or fishing boats commandeered by the Navy. Particularly good service was done by the trawlers of the Belgian fishing fleet. They had sailed south along the coast, often carrying refugees, when the Germans invaded the Belgian ports. Now they were back, with crews of the French Navy. Although small, they were ideally suited for the work.

By arrangement the British kept to the eastern side of Dunkirk and to the East Mole. The French used the West Mole and the harbour itself. It was piled up with wrecks. The water was shallow at low tide. German shells were pitching regularly in. But the fishing boats were perfectly well able to use it. In the evening of May 31st sixteen commandeered Belgian drifters arrived from Cherbourg, via Ramsgate, and sailed right into the Quai Félix-Faure, in the channel linking the inner and outer harbours. There they loaded forty or fifty men each in the space of two and a half hours. They turned round and arrived safely at Ramsgate at midday on June 1st. This brave little flotilla was commanded by a sub-lieutenant, *Enseigne de vaisseau* Le Coniat.

The French, now that they had been told to play a full part in the evacuation, were doing pretty well. But at midday the arrivals rescued so far in Operation Dynamo were counted up at Dover; the total was 150,000 British soldiers, 15,000 French. This score was no embarrassment to the British soldiers and seamen. But it was highly awkward for the politicians who were trying to hold the alliance together and keep France in the war. The figures were quickly reported to the Allied Council of War at its session in Paris that afternoon (see pages 109-110). Mr. Churchill made his famous claim that the two armies must henceforth fight in and depart from France arm in arm—*"Bras-dessus, bras-dessous."* True to his intention, the Prime Minister promptly caused a signal to be made to the remnant of the BEF, ordering that the British should henceforth play their full part in the defence of the Dunkirk perimeter, and that each British soldier embarked should be matched by a French one.

But things had changed at general headquarters of the BEF. Indeed, GHQ as such no longer existed. Lord Gort had received his marching orders the previous day: "You are to hand over and return as specified when your effective fighting force does not exceed the equivalent of three divisions. This is in accordance with correct military procedure, and no personal discretion is left to you in the matter. On political grounds it would be a needless triumph to the enemy to capture you when only a small force remained under your orders."

Early in the afternoon Gort carefully snipped the medal ribbons—Victoria Cross, Distinguished Service Order with two bars, Military Cross and all the rest—off his spare uniforms, left the clothes themselves and his private belongings to be collected by the Germans, and was ferried out taking only what he could stand up in to the destroyer *Hebe* off La Panne.

The previous day, as we have seen, two of the three corps commanders, Adam and Brooke, had gone over. In place of Brooke, Gort had nominated Major-General Montgomery to command the rump of II Corps. Now, with his own departure imminent, Gort had intended to nominate, as his successor in command of all remaining British forces, Lieutenant-General Barker of I Corps. Barker had already shown himself unreliable. Montgomery took Gort aside and told him so—a characteristic piece of impertinence from a relatively junior officer, which characteristically was right. Montgomery said that the best man was Major-General the Honourable H. R. L. G. Alexander, now commanding a division under poor General Barker. Gort accepted this view. The tough and imperturbable Alexander, a handsome Irish Guards officer, was put in charge.

Alexander's first duty was to call on Admiral Abrial in his bastion. There could be no ambiguity now. Abrial was the designated commander of Dunkirk. The latest telegram from the Council of War had specifically stated that position. Gort, a full general and commander-in-chief, might be expected to show a certain autonomy. A mere major-general was expected to obey orders.

But which orders? Captain Tennant explained the confusion that now arose:

I returned Dunkirk with General Alexander and discovered that totally different instructions had been given to General Alexander by Lord Gort and by Lord Gort in writing to Admiral Abrial and General Fagalde [the French commander, ground forces].

Lord Gort had told the French authorities that General Alexander would assist in holding the "Perimeter" for the French to embark and that he was to place himself and his division under General Fagalde's orders. General Alexander, however, was told by Lord Gort in my hearing that he was to do nothing to imperil his army and was ultimately responsible for their safety and evacuation.

Jean Beaux, then a staff captain in Bastion 32, described the scene from the French angle. According to him (and there is no difference of fact, only of perspective, between his account and Captain Tennant's), General Fagalde began the meeting by outlining the defensive role of the remaining three British divisions on the eastern sector of the perimeter. Alexander declared that he had no orders to defend the perimeter. Lord Gort, before leaving, had instructed him to withdraw as many troops as possible to the sea by midnight for embarkation. The British were not going to fight, whatever the French did.

Fagalde produced a letter which he had "taken the precaution of getting Gort to sign" on his farewell visit to Bastion 32 that morning. It specified that the BEF would play a full part in the continuing defence. Alexander waved it aside. According to Beaux, Alexander said, "I am sorry, but I shall disengage tonight. Anyway, the Germans are at the gates of Dunkirk and anyone who has not left tonight will be lost. Everything that could be saved has been saved." *Capitaine de frégate* de La Pérouse was far too junior an officer to be allowed to interrupt a general. But he interjected: *"Non, monsieur le général, il y reste l'honneur!*—No, General, there is still honour!"* Alexander looked at the table, wiped his forehead, and made no further comment.

The French tried to catch up with Lord Gort, to find out just which of his two contradictory orders was meant to apply. They were too late: they were told Gort had sailed. (But

he was still in a ship off La Panne at ten o'clock that night.)
Captain Tennant carries on the story:

> I suggested to General Alexander that he should at
> once return to La Panne before the telephone was cut off
> to telephone to the Secretary of State for War, and to get
> the matter cleared up. This he did. The Secretary of
> State instructed General Alexander to act on his own
> discretion and to proceed with the evacuation.

The formal telegram sent by Mr. Eden to Alexander an hour
later said something quite different: ''You should withdraw
your force on a 50-50 basis with the French Army, aiming at
completion night 1st/2nd. You should inform the French of
this Definite Instruction.'' Typically, the orders that the War
Office put in writing and showed to the French were different
from those transmitted by voice over the cross-Channel telephone, which the French could not tap.

There were still almost 200,000 French soldiers in the perimeter, and not much over 50,000 British. A withdrawal by
equal numbers meant leaving the French in the lurch. Abrial
tried to get in touch with his own government to let them
know of this. The radio was out of action.

What Alexander must have known, but could hardly have
admitted to the French, was that the British army could no
longer be relied upon to defend the perimeter. Some soldiers—by no means all, but enough—saw their comrades getting down to the port and safety, and were determined to get
away as well. In the afternoon of May 31st the Germans
mounted an attack on the British line beside Bergues. It was
an awkward sector: the houses on the German-held bank of
the canal gave good cover to the attackers, and the canal itself
was littered with debris and half-sunk barges, giving a basis
for a German crossing. It was also the only sector on which
the British were actually fighting.

Part of the line was held by a battalion of the Sherwood
Foresters, a Nottinghamshire regiment. It was numbered 2/5
Battalion, a half-trained Territorial unit that had lost many of
its officers and NCOs in the long confusion of the retreat to
the coasts. Under German fire the men simply stopped firing
back. Some crawled away, others just lay there. A single

company of the Royal Warwickshires was turned round at the
start of its march back to the beaches, and somehow held the
demolished canal bridge that their countrymen had abandoned.

All along the front, the British were falling back. For most
of the front it did not matter, since the floods in the fields
deterred the Germans from advancing. It is often not clear
from the records whether the British were withdrawing by
some plan or because they could hold on no longer. At the
eastern end of the line, though, the British withdrawal was
clearly deliberate. The German observation balloon in the sky
over Nieuport brought down an accurate artillery shoot on
the last British rearguard as it crept away along the dunes
towards the embarkation point by La Panne. In the afternoon
the Germans were seen to be massing for a new assault across
the canal. For the first and only time in France the RAF gave
close support to ground troops. Eighteen Blenheim bombers,
supported by a squadron of Royal Navy Albacore biplanes,
treated the Germans as the Luftwaffe had so often treated the
Allies. On the ground, the British soldiers cheered.

What they could not have known was that the Germans too
were at the end of their tether. The troops in the sandhills
were desperate for lack of water. The tanks had been diverted
southwards, the ammunition for the heavy guns was being
spared for the assault towards Paris, the wonderful 88-mm.
anti-aircraft guns had all been taken away for more important
targets. Only from the air could the Germans show their technical superiority. But that was to cost the Allies dear next
morning.

14

UNFINISHED BUSINESS: June 1ST

"Again there was a hold up and going on the bridge I hailed to enquire if there was a British Officer within hearing. At the third hail a man forced himself to the rail and replied, 'Don't be so windy. What do you want?' I replied, 'Damn you Sir, I am not windy or I would not be here. . . .' "
—Report by LIEUTENANT JOHN ANDERSON, RNR, commanding HM Minesweeper *Duchess of Fife*, Dunkirk, June 1st

Field Marshal Goering had assured his leader, at the start of the evacuation from Dunkirk, that his air force could prevent it. Many on the Allied side agreed. On June 1st he nearly brought off his boast. By early afternoon three Allied destroyers were sunk, three more were badly damaged, one big passenger ship was at the bottom of the sea and another was crippled.

Under a massive German raid George Benton, a sergeant in the Royal Army Medical Corps, was carrying wounded men on stretchers to a ship at the East Mole. A bomb blew a gap in the walkway. Benton put the stretchers over the gap and carried on with the evacuation.

On May 30th, May 31st and June 1st an average of 62,000

men a day arrived in England. On June 2nd, 3rd and 4th the
average was well under half that, just 26,400 men. For that
reduction the British blamed the Luftwaffe, while congratu-
lating their own sailors, with much justice, for their courage
in carrying on at all. But by midnight on June 1st practically
the whole of the British army was safe in England. On the
last two days of the evacuation the race was to save the French.
Inevitably the British did not commit their ships so whole-
heartedly to that cause.

All through the night of May 31st–June 1st the men had
crammed aboard from the port. All night the Germans kept
up their desultory shelling. Now and again a parachute flare
would fall from the sky, and a lone bomber plane would drop
its load on the harbour or the beaches. But that was, as always, an inaccurate and wasteful process: the sway and drift
of the flares as they drop creates deceptive targets, and the
result is more frightening than deadly to those below.

At five in the morning the sky was clear, the sun risen.
The German bombers arrived to a fair target. The RAF was
there to meet them. Again at 6 a.m. the British planes gave
cover against a raid. The RAF arrived again at 9 a.m. In the
interval between these British patrols the sky was wide open
for the Germans. They attacked in full force.

Among the many whose ships went down under them was
Admiral Wake-Walker. He was aboard the destroyer HMS
Keith. A near-miss jammed her rudder. She ran in circles and
was bombed again. This time a bomb went straight down her
funnel; she floated for a while, but could not move. Captain
Berthon dropped anchor, to allow rescue vessels to come
alongside in the run of the tide. Wake-Walker scrambled over
the side into a motor-torpedo boat and, after doing what he
could for the other survivors, sped across to Dover. There he
reported to Admiral Ramsay on the success of the German
air attack. Ramsay decided enough was enough: after one
supreme effort for the remainder of the day and night, there
should be no further attempt to take troops off by daylight.

Captain Berthon, commander of the stricken Keith, had a
terrible adventure. He went over the side into the tug St.
Abbs. She too in turn received a direct hit. Berthon and a few
survivors went overside again and swam to a drifting lighter.

By a miracle they were spotted almost eighteen hours later, still adrift, and were safely picked up.

The destroyer *Basilisk* was also sunk by bombs. *Ivanhoe*, *Whitehall* and *Worcester*, destroyers, were badly damaged in the morning raid. In the middle of the day, the French destroyer *Foudroyant* was smashed up by bombs, turned turtle and sank. Even greater loss of life was to be feared from the successful attacks on the passenger vessels *Prague* and *Scotia*. The rescue of their passengers is one of the most remarkable of the Dunkirk stories.

Prague, a Southern Railway ferryboat, sailed right in through the bombing to the base of the Mole and packed almost three thousand French soldiers aboard. On the way home, off Mardyck, she was ringed by shells from the guns on the shore; shortly afterwards she was dive-bombed. No shells or bombs actually hit her. But she had already run aground twice in the course of Operation Dynamo—on May 28th and on May 30th—and her plates were doubtless weakened. She began to leak. With her heavy human load the pumps could not cope with the water. But obviously she dared not stop. As she ran on at the best possible speed the destroyer *Shikari* came alongside, and five hundred French and African soldiers coolly transferred from ship to ship. Then the minesweeper *Queen of Thanet*, a converted fishing boat, did the same miraculous manoeuvre, taking on over fifteen hundred men. The little corvette *Shearwater* took two hundred more. Lightened of her load, *Prague* was able to make it home to Dover.

The Irish mailboat *Scotia* loaded about two thousand Frenchmen and slipped out of harbour straight into a heavy attack by dive-bombers. Two bombs on deck did light damage. A third bomb went straight down her after funnel. The engine-room crew were boiled in steam, and the ship began to sink by the stern. In answer to the captain's SOS the destroyer HMS *Esk* dashed out from Dunkirk, where she was on anti-aircraft duty at the harbour entrance.

As *Esk* came up, *Scotia* was tilting, her starboard boat deck half under water. The destroyer captain nosed his bow up to the steamer. Many soldiers leapt across the gap to safety; others scrambled aboard from the water. *Esk*, meanwhile, was keeping up anti-aircraft fire against a new wave of Ger-

man raiders, and her captain had to beware of being caught
and damaged by the *Scotia* as she sank. Nosing in from one
side and then the other, he enabled every single surviving
Frenchman to get aboard. By the end there were three men
clinging to the slimy, rounded keel of the mailboat. *Scotia's*
captain, Mr. W. H. Hughes, got a rope around each of them,
saw them hauled up onto the destroyer, and finally was hauled
up himself. Probably three hundred French soldiers died, and
thirty of *Scotia's* crew. Seventeen hundred men were saved.
It was a tremendous feat both of seamanship and of courage.

Such rescues from sinking ships were, again and again,
among the triumphs of Dunkirk. It was dangerous to stop in
the water. Few ships of the evacuation fleet had their full
complement of lifeboats and rafts, since so many had been
lent to ferry soldiers from the beaches to the vessels offshore.
Soldiers were packed on deck, between decks, into any
cranny that would take them, vulnerable if on deck to bombing and machine-gunning from the air, if between decks to
drowning. Of course any estimate of the numbers who died
on the crossing can only be an informed guess: captains and
masters did not keep an accurate tally of their passengers, for
obvious reasons. But in an operation that brought almost
340,000 men across the water, Admiral Ramsay at the time
reported only 2,000 men lost at sea. A fuller count brings
the total, including French and others, to about 5,000.

The rescues from *Scotia* and from *Prague* show how the
toll was kept down. It was a further, fortuitous advantage that
no really large ships could be used in the Dunkirk operation,
since the available sea routes and berths in the damaged port
were too shallow. At the subsequent evacuation of the last
relics of the British rearguard from St. Nazaire, on June 17th,
the great Cunard liner *Lancastria* was loaded with six thousand soldiers, packed below decks. She was bombed and
sank in half an hour. By the official figures of the time three
thousand of her passengers died; the real total was probably
more like five thousand. The disaster before dawn on May
29th, when almost one thousand men died in the multiple
sinkings off the Kwinte buoy, was the worst single fatality at
sea of the entire Dunkirk operation.

The result of the savage air raids of June 1st was an order
from Admiral Ramsay, insisting that all ships should be clear

of the French coast by dawn next morning, and that there should henceforth be no daylight sailings. Mr. Churchill, having maintained the previous day that British troops would fight on until the last Frenchman was clear, now telegraphed in a very different sense to his French counterpart, M. Reynaud. "It is desirable that the embarkation should cease this night. Up to the present, 225,000 men had been shipped. Abrial would like to prolong the embarkation, but he is perhaps not the best judge since he directs operations from a bunker. The generals on the spot should be left the responsibility of deciding when the embarkation should cease."

The previous day's telegram to Abrial, signed by both prime ministers, had specified: "The evacuation at Dunkirk will be carried out under your orders." General Spears, Churchill's conspiratorial special agent in Paris, called on M. Reynaud to discuss the new message. "I note," said Reynaud icily, "that the decision to have a united command only lasted twenty-four hours." If commanders on the spot should make the decision to stop the evacuation, why not rely on Abrial rather than on the British general? asked the French Prime Minister. Spears said that, although Abrial was on the spot, he did not often leave his bunker to see what was going on. He was not *l'amiral* Abrial, but *l'amiral Abri. Abri* means a bomb-proof shelter. "A poor pun," Spears admitted in his memoirs, "but it helped to lower the tension." Reynaud omitted to reply—he could not have known, and nor could Spears for that matter—that Abrial had on at least two occasions narrowly escaped when caught in the open by machine-gun fire.

The British leaders were, in fact, relying on the opinion of their own man on the spot in preference to that of his French superior. The man in question was General Alexander. He did not like or trust the French. He had been publicly humiliated the previous day at his meeting with Abrial, in the matter of Lord Gort's contradictory orders. He saw it as his first duty to get the remaining British out, whatever obstacles politicians like Mr. Churchill might put in his way. By the afternoon there were between six thousand and ten thousand British soldiers still in the Dunkirk perimeter. The eastward end of the beach, beyond the Belgian frontier, had been vacated by the British in the morning; about five thousand men got off, barely troubled by desultory shellfire. The chaplains were the last to leave.

The last men away from the defensive lines in Belgium were a company of Grenadier Guards from positions covering the canal crossing at Furnes, where the Germans had never attacked in strength. Mr. Ernest Couchman, then a guardsman, remembers the scene:

About midnight on May 31st we were told: "The beach is that way, it's every man for himself, stop for nobody." So we wrapped blankets round our boots for silence, the Navy fired a barrage over us, and we got out. It was dark on the beach and the Germans were shelling. At first light I could see the destroyers out to sea, but no small boats to get to them in. I hid my pack and rifle behind a wrecked vehicle and started to swim out. But a destroyer was hit by a bomb and they all left. So I swam back. By a miracle I found my pack and rifle. Then I started to walk along the beach to Dunkirk, it was all smoke, the beach is about ten miles long. I met up with a friend, Charlie Holyoake. Then we see a lot of men, about thirty, marching in step on the soft sand in column of three, with an officer at the front.

The officer says come on you two, fall in behind. So we do. It was all Grenadiers. But there was German planes overhead and all that, so we thought it best to drop back and let them march on. About 1 p.m. we got to the old stone jetty at Dunkirk, we saw a sailor putting men aboard the old *Ben-my-Chree*, the Isle of Man paddle-steamer. Four bombs fell alongside her, in the sea. Charlie says, "I'm not going in her, that's too dangerous." Then four more bombs fall alongside, right on the quay. The boat starts to move, so we jump aboard anyway.

When we got to Folkestone we got an orange, a twopenny bar of Cadbury's chocolate and a cup of tea. Then a staff officer came down, riding breeches and highly-polished boots. He said: "Come on you lot, you're back in England now, not a bloody rabble along the seashore." But people, civilians, they were wonderful. On the train as we slowed down in the stations they handed in cigarettes and quart bottles of beer.

The abandonment of the last strip of Belgian beach brought all but a very few of the British back within defensive lines either protected by flooding or guarded by the French. British troops were in contact with the enemy only along about four kilometres of the Canal de la Basse-Colme, from Bergues eastwards until the canal met the flooded fields beyond Hoymille. During the morning of June 1st they began to pull out. Some units quietly faded off the scene, back to the beaches near the town of Dunkirk.

The courage of the units that fought on was all the greater for the failure of their colleagues. James Langley describes a vicious defence of the canal line near Bergues by his company of the Coldstream Guards. He was ordered to shoot any British soldiers who retreated without orders. When the commander of the neighbouring company walked away down the road, Langley and a fellow Coldstreamer fired simultaneously, with sights at two hundred yards. The man fell into the ditch, and the soldiers he was leading returned to the firing line.

Langley's fight ended when a shell came through the roof of the farm building his platoon was defending. It smashed his arm. He was transported back to the beach:

> A grey life-boat lay at the water's edge with a man in a long dark blue naval overcoat standing by it. He came over. "Can you get off your stretcher?" "No, I do not think so." "Well, I am very sorry we cannot take you. Your stretcher would occupy the places of four men. Orders are only those who can stand or sit up."

Langley went into captivity, lost his arm, escaped, and became a chief organiser of the escape route maintained in France by the French resistance with British support.

It was not just the guards who showed gallantry in this last defence. Captain Ervine-Andrews of the First Battalion, East Lancashire Regiment, commanded a company. Most of its members faded from the scene. Ervine-Andrews, with about a dozen men and a Bren-gun carrier, went forward to a barn by the canal, climbed into the thatch and (the official accounts claim) shot seventeen Germans with a rifle. The Bren-gunner got a lot more. Then Ervine-Andrews sent his wounded back in the carrier and waded back himself through the floods with eight intact survivors. He was awarded the Victoria Cross.

But nobody had told the French about this British withdrawal. The Germans, seeing the British go, crossed the canal after them, and attacked the French on their flank at Bergues. Away on the eastern end of the perimeter the departure of the British brought the Germans right up against the French defences along the frontier; but there the French had known the British were going. The French fought back desperately and managed to establish a new, shorter defensive line behind the flood waters, while the British got away behind them.

As the perimeter shrank, the German artillery came into range of the towns within it. Malo-les-Bains began to suffer as Dunkirk had suffered. The residents held on as best they could in their threatened homes. There is an old saying in Flanders, so often the scene of war: *Sitôt partis, sitôt pillés*— as soon as you leave, you are looted. Few British soldiers were seen in the town—they only passed through on their way to the harbour, spending their waiting time out in the relative safety of the sand dunes. French troops did the stealing. The civilians could play that game, too. A man ran out of a decorator's shop in Malo that afternoon carrying looted rolls of wallpaper. His neighbour called out, "But you've forgotten the border for the pattern." The thief thanked him, turned back, and stole the border to match. As an artillery shoot dropped in on Malo, a small crowd gathered to watch the looting of a jeweller's shop. Round the corner came the jeweller, a man they all knew well. The thieves started to apologise, to improvise excuses. "Take it all," said the jeweller. "It's all going to burn anyway."

The real tragedy of this, the last full day of Operation Dynamo, was the failure of the Allies to deter the Luftwaffe. In Britain, the RAF had a first-line force of about fourteen hundred ultra-modern fighters. Over Dunkirk, in the eighteen hours of daylight on June 1st, it flew eight fighter patrols with three or four squadrons each (a squadron had a dozen aircraft; the planes' fuel supply allowed them to wait for up to twenty minutes over the target area). So for most of the day the Luftwaffe had a free run in the air. The surrender at dawn of the French First Army after its long, isolated fight at Lille released the dive-bomber fleet from what had until then been its main task. At 4 p.m., for instance, a little flotilla of four French minesweepers was coming into Dunkirk harbour entrance. The dive-bombers swooped to a couple of hundred feet and sank three of them instantly.

Mr. Churchill declared a motive for withholding the RAF from the fight over Dunkirk. He insisted that if British planes were to be put up against the Germans they must be in superior numbers. He told General Spears on June 1st that this was why more RAF planes could not be sent to cover the evacuation, and it was Spears' job to pass this explanation on to the French government. Churchill put the proposition in encouraging form, saying that "our fighters were bringing down German machines in the proportion of six to one, and that we simply could not accept conditions which would bring the proportion below three or three-and-a-half to one."

Over Dunkirk on June 1st the RAF lost thirty-one planes, mostly Hurricanes and Spitfires, but including a few old planes drummed up from the reserves. Initially the RAF claimed seventy-eight German planes destroyed. Then the pilots' claims were analysed to eliminate double counting, and the figure was reduced to forty-three. In reality the Germans lost twenty-nine planes—ten fighters, nineteen bombers. Probably half of the bombers were brought down by anti-aircraft fire from the ground. The RAF lost three planes for every two German planes they shot down. The Luftwaffe dominated the air over Dunkirk because it had better, more experienced pilots. The fighting experience gained by the RAF over Dunkirk enabled its pilots, flying over home ground and with radar to help them, to face the Germans on roughly equal terms in the Battle of Britain that began in August 1940.

The ground forces in Dunkirk by this time were running seriously short of anti-aircraft ammunition. In the past four days of relatively sporadic bombing the warships too had allowed their anti-aircraft precautions to lapse. They often turned round so fast in Britain to return for more troops that they had no time to take aboard AA shells. HMS *Keith*, for instance, had only thirty rounds for her AA guns when she

was attacked from the air and sunk. But all the same, the
German pilots found the attack on Dunkirk a terrifying ordeal—*"die Hölle über Dünkirchen,"* the hell over Dunkirk,
was how a Luftwaffe propaganda writer described it. In particular the Junkers 87 dive-bombers, the notorious Stukas,
ran deadly risks in their attacks. Soldiers and sailors under
raids saw an unusual number of bombs fail to explode, and
remembered the stories of how, in the Polish campaign of the
previous autumn, the Germans had dropped concrete bombs
for lack of real explosive ones. (But this, of course, may well
have been one of those comforting legends that soldiers often
pass by word of mouth to keep their spirits up.)

All day, despite the bombs and the shells, the boats kept
coming. One of the most remarkable journeys was made by
the sixty-foot yacht *Sundowner*. She belonged to a retired
Naval Reserve commander, C. H. Lightoller, who had won
temporary fame as the senior surviving officer of the doomed
liner *Titanic*. On *Sundowner* he had set out from Chiswick
with a crew consisting of his son and a Sea Scout. At 10 a.m.
they started for Dunkirk, maximum speed ten knots. On the
way over they paused to rescue the crew of the motorboat
Westerly, which had caught fire; then they entered Dunkirk
harbour and packed the men below the decks:

> At fifty I called below, "How are you getting on?"
> getting the cheery reply, "Oh plenty of room yet." At
> seventy-five my son admitted they were getting pretty
> tight—all equipment and arms being left on deck.
> I now started to pack them on deck, having passed
> word below for every man to lie down and keep down;
> the same applied on deck. By the time we had fifty on
> deck, I could feel her getting distinctly tender, so took
> no more. Actually we had exactly 130 on board, includ-
> ing three *Sundowners* and five *Westerlys*.
> Whilst entering [harbour at Ramsgate], the men started
> to get to their feet and she promptly went over to a ter-
> rific angle. I got them down again in time and told those
> below to remain below and lying down until I gave the
> word. The impression ashore was that the fifty-odd lying
> on my deck plus the mass of equipment was my full
> load.

After I had got rid of those on deck I gave the order "Come up from below," and the look on the official face was amusing to behold as troops vomited up through the forward companionway, the after companionway, and the doors either side of the wheelhouse. As a stoker Petty Officer, helping them over the bulwarks, said, "God's truth, mate! Where did you put them?" He might well ask . . .

Other volunteers were less successful in their attempts to take small boats across the Channel. Lieutenant R. H. Meed, RNVR, was put in command of the Walton and Frinton lifeboat, whose crew had not volunteered to go. With two other lifeboats and two civilian-owned motorboats with naval crews he set out at 7:45 a.m. to be towed across to France from Dover. The tow lines broke four times on the way, delaying the convoy for hours. The Eastbourne lifeboat's engine, maintained by a naval rating who did not understand its workings, caught fire and was rendered useless. To spare the tow lines the boats crept dead slow towards the French coast, offering a perfect target for the attack from the air. Duly the Luftwaffe arrived. Meed was killed; his crew, consisting of a retired petty-officer-telegraphist, Mr. Cooley, survived and managed to get a ride home to make his report. The gallantry of the naval crews in the little ships was tragically wasted.

On the evening of June 1st the first cracks began to appear in the brave front put on for so long by the weary crews of the merchant navy. The morning's bombs had been enough to break any normal man's nerve. The master of one Isle of Man steamer refused to sail: "I myself have had 4 hours rest for the week and am at present physically unfit for another trip like what we have had." He added in postscript, "There is two more of the crew going ashore now absolutely nervous wrecks and certified by the naval doctor." Four of the Manx ships refused to sail. So did two other passenger ferries. One Channel ferry simply loosed her moorings and disappeared in the direction of Southampton. The panicking crews were isolated from the main body of the fleet, to prevent the infection from spreading. Royal Navy crews were put aboard, and the ships carried on working.

By now the Royal Navy's manpower—even including the

retired men of the Volunteer Reserve—was running short. Their tempers grew even shorter. The old trawler *Duchess of Fife* was serving as a minesweeper under Lieutenant John Anderson, RNR. His navigating officer was a temporary helper signed up for a month on Form T124, a civilian yachtsman doing his bit. Anderson's report indicates one of the Navy's biggest problems—how to make yourself understood to the French, especially in a broad Scots accent:

> I laid *Fife* alongside. The pier was stiff with French troops. They took my lines and then refused to come aboard. One of my men got one by the leg and hauled him down the brow, but none others would follow. Accordingly I climbed the brow and harangued them in a strange language, which I doubt had little effect. But, as is my custom, I happened to be wearing a beret, and at sight of the familiar headgear some 25 of them followed me down the brow. Again there was a hold up and going on the bridge I hailed to enquire if there was a British Officer within hearing. At the third hail a man forced himself to the rail and replied "Don't be so windy. What do you want?" I replied, "Damn you Sir, I am not windy or I would not be here. Are there any British troops on the quay?" He replied that there were no British troops on the quay, that these "yellow bellies" would not board, and that I might as well let go my ropes and get clear. (5th column?)

Mr. Anderson did not let go his ropes. In time he loaded 550 Frenchmen aboard, sailed them over to Margate, then set his crew to work humping sacks of coal aboard from a lighter, ready for the next trip. For the whole of the next day, in hours of daylight, the rescue was to be halted. But next night—perhaps the last night—it would continue.

15

STOPS AND STARTS: JUNE 2ND

"To VA Dover from SNO Dunkirk BEF evacuated."
—Signal, CAPTAIN TENNANT to Admiral Ramsay,
11:30 p.m., June 2nd, 1940

At 1 a.m. on June 2nd the destroyer *Whitshed* nosed in and tied up at the tip of the East Mole of Dunkirk harbour, from which the greater part of the British forces had embarked over the previous week. There was nobody about, nothing doing save for the sporadic crash of shells and the monotonous whacking of machine-gun fire far inland. It was low tide. The ship would risk being run aground if Commander Conder ventured further in along the Mole. Alone, he climbed up onto the walkway and set off towards the base of the Mole, a mile away. Soon he found a bicycle abandoned against a post. Dismounting at the gaps knocked by shells and bombs, he rode towards the town.

At the base of the Mole the commander met a naval shore party, keeping guard against unauthorised entrants. They assured him that the troops were on their way. So he pedalled on into the town, rounding up small groups of soldiers and speeding them towards his ship. Soon, as the shore party had predicted, a company of British soldiers marched down in good order through the throng of Frenchmen. *Whitshed* packed a thousand men aboard, backed off and sailed for Dover. Other destroyers, arriving before she had left, also found themselves short of a load. The destroyer *Malcolm* resorted to the last, desperate expedient of the British armed forces: her navigating officer played his personal set of bagpipes through the streets to muster the troops.

Orders were strict. To avoid a repetition of the previous day's terrible bombing, all ships were to drop their moorings by 3 a.m., and be clear of the coast by first light. The French were to embark by way of the West Mole and the outer harbour, which, at this state of the tide, were useable only by small vessels; the British were to use their own East Mole. That was the arrangement made at the insistence of Captain Tennant, the senior Royal Navy officer in Dunkirk, with the full agreement of Admiral Abrial. It was not intended to let the British get away while the French waited for a higher tide; but at this phase of the moon, with the tide at its lowest in the darkest hours of night, this was its result.

Just after 3 a.m. the last ship sailed. About a thousand British troops, marching down after disengaging from the front line at Bergues, narrowly missed the final sailing and marched back through the press of Frenchmen to take shelter for the day in the dunes beyond Malo-les-Bains. Nobody quite knew how many soldiers were left in Dunkirk. Admiral Abrial reported that he had 25,000 men in combat positions on the perimeter and another 22,000 in the town. The total of British to be evacuated was reckoned at about 6,000. The Royal Navy, remembering the losses of the previous day, had wanted to close down the Dynamo operation at midnight. The French wanted it to continue, and did not see why it should not do so for as long as they could hold the perimeter—from which all the British defenders were by now disengaged. At dawn, in the sector beside Bergues from which the British had departed the previous day, the French counter-attacked. Ten of their tanks could still move, although several had their turrets jammed so that their guns could not aim. But they rolled off, took by surprise the second-grade German troops facing them, and drove them back across the canal.

Contrary to all expectations, the Germans still failed to

make the final assault into Dunkirk. Their tank force had been withdrawn by Hitler on May 29th to reorganise for the assault on the main body of the French Army. On June 1st they withdrew from the Dunkirk perimeter the last of the 88-mm. high-velocity anti-aircraft guns that could pick out a strongpoint on the ground with the accuracy of a rifle. Almost all their heavy artillery went, too. The massed air assault of June 1st proved to have been their last. The airmen needed a rest before the onslaught on the French airfields around Paris. And with daylight sailings cancelled their observation planes could see clearly that the Allied shipping off Dunkirk offered no target worth a mass attack. During daylight on June 2nd the Luftwaffe harassed, but did not seriously attack, the men in the perimeter of Dunkirk. Presumably—there is no proof of this—analysis of Allied wireless traffic told the Germans that the pace of the evacuation was slacking, now that so few British soldiers remained to be rescued, and they simply did not regard the French forces at Dunkirk as worth their gunpowder.

Along the beaches between Dunkirk town and the Belgian frontier—where the French were now face to face with the Germans—small boats plied all day, hoping to pick up stragglers. The publicity given to the evacuation in the previous day's newspapers and broadcasts, and the partial lifting of censorship on accounts of individual exploits, had attracted several dozen volunteers across the Channel from England. These were the real heroes of the Dunkirk spirit. From this day dates a famous but unsubstantiated anecdote about the absurdity of Frenchmen. The motor yacht *Sea Roamer*, commanded by her ex-naval owner Mr. J. Wheatley, and with a naval crew, spent part of the evening fruitlessly searching for men to rescue from the beach, before fouling her propeller on a rope and getting a tow home. Mr. Wheatley recorded:

> The French, it seems, were not always prepared to wade out and clamber into the dinghies in the surf. A story was told me of a French officer who steadfastly refused to do this. Finally he sent a note to the anxious yacht skipper. It read: "I have just eaten and am therefore unable to enter the water."

One British amateur sailor who went across to the beaches this day was David Divine, author of the classic accounts in English of the naval operations at Dunkirk. He devotes just one page to his own part in the affair. His mission was to help rescue the pocket of British troops who had missed the last boat at the East Mole the previous night, and he starts his tale in Ramsgate with these words:

> Admiral Taylor, who had completed his work ashore, decided to proceed to Dunkirk to supervise the lifting of the pocket from Malo-les-Bains in person. I had at that time stolen a small twin-screw Thames motor cruiser and was ordered to stand by to take the Admiral over. Her name was *White Wing*, she was about 30-foot in length, and she had a speed of approximately 12 knots but, owing to trouble with the starboard engine, did not make this speed all the way across. . . .

Divine and his admiral supervised the lifting off of the British troops in a flotilla of French fishing boats—*Ciel de France*, *Ave Maria Gratia Plena*, *Jeanne Antoine*, *Arc-en-Ciel*—and their ferrying out to a French ship. Then they "went pottering about looking for stragglers," being shelled ("It seemed like pure spite"), visiting the East Mole, where they saw a ship sunk by shellfire, and so finally home. Like Mr. Wheatley in *Sea Roamer*, Mr. Divine did not bring any soldiers home. By the time they had bravely volunteered with their little ships, there were practically no British soldiers left to bring.

During daylight only two large British ships attempted to make the crossing. They were Southern Railway ferryboats converted for use as hospital ships, painted white and with huge red crosses on their upper-works. Captain Tennant had ordered an uncoded wireless signal to be made, confident that the German would intercept it: "Wounded situation acute and hospital ships should enter during the day. Geneva Convention will be honourably observed and it is felt that the enemy will refrain from attacking." They did attack all the same. *Worthing* was damaged and had to turn back. *Paris*, due to leave later, asked Dynamo headquarters whether she should proceed, in view of the fact that the Germans were evidently ignoring the convention of mercy. She was ordered out regardless. "I at once weighed anchor and proceeded to Dunkirk," reported Captain Biles. His ship too was attacked by aircraft. The crew were forced to take to the boats, and the ship returned without reaching the wounded in France.

Many of the Allied wounded were in hospital in the convalescent home by the beach at Zuydcoote. In normal times it was a refuge for tubercular children from the slums of Paris, and it was run by the nuns of the order of the Daughters of the Child Jesus. Jean Beaux tells us of the conduct of these good women: "During a particularly violent bombardment the wounded asked a sister to take shelter against a wall, to save herself from being killed by the shells. She replied by pointing out that the patients were in the middle of the ward. A wounded man called out, 'You, Sister, you are needed. But us . . .' " That day many shells fell into the hospital from the field guns that had moved nearer as the French defenders of the perimeter shortened their line. Two nuns were killed in front of the kitchen range while cooking the patients' dinner.

As dusk drew down, the last remainders of the British Expeditionary Force gathered towards the base of the East Mole for their last chance of escape. A few were stragglers, unearthed from cellars and crannies where they had lain up, drinking if they could scrounge or loot a bottle, trying to forget their danger. Most, of course, were on duty to the end, members of General Alexander's skeleton divisional headquarters, stretcher-bearers, anti-aircraft gunners, signals operators. In Dover they were thought to number 6,000. Alexander thought there were only 2,500. On the western side of the outer port there were at least 25,000 Frenchmen, and many more waiting inland for the hope of rescue.

As evening drew on, the usual motley crowd of ships sailed from the Channel ports of England. *Royal Daffodil*, the Thames estuary excursion steamer, had been on duty since May 20th. In the evening of June 2nd she was first across, filled with troops, and was attacked from the air on her way home. At last, after all her lucky escapes, she was hit, and her engines stopped. There was a big hole on the waterline on her starboard side. Her crew shifted all the ship's gear to port, moved as many troops as possible to that side, and finally lowered the ship's port-side lifeboats and left them hanging full of water at the davits. Thus they raised the hole above the water. Her crew crammed bedding into the hole; the second engineer stood up to his neck in bilge water to keep a jammed valve open, and the chief engineer got the pumps going. With a full load she lurched back to Ramsgate.

Royal Sovereign, Lady of Mann, Autocarrier, St. Helier, Tynwald—from the Thames, the Irish Sea, the Channel, the Channel Isles—they sailed across for their final endeavour. With them went another flotilla, small ships, naval and civilian. The French Channel ferries went over. A cluster of Belgian fishing boats with crews from the French Navy picked up all the men they could; the *Madeleine-Camille* picked up 118 men, her Belgian skipper held at revolver point to persuade him to make the trip. *Onze Lieve Vrouw van Vlaanderen*, out of Antwerp, with French officers and her own Flemish mechanic, set out to carry food and ammunition for the last defence of the town. A shell struck her and blew her to fragments.

Soon after nightfall General Alexander embarked in a small motorboat. In it he toured the beach and the harbour until 11:40 p.m., calling out, "Is anyone there, is anyone there?" He reported that there was no reply, transferred to a destroyer, and went over in the dawn. His destroyer was machine-gunned on the way.

The remarkable fact about Alexander's account of his departure is that, while he made his reported tour of the beach and the outer port, ten thousand Frenchmen were waiting within hailing distance of the water. There were French harbour police boats on the water, and he must have passed within fifty metres of the French anti-aircraft post at the tip of the West Mole. He claimed later that he shouted for troops both in English and in French; his driver, Mr. Wells, confirmed this after the war to Alexander's biographer, Nigel Nicolson.

But anyone who has sailed along Alexander's reported course must find it incredible that he tried, and failed, to locate the waiting French soldiers. It must be the case that, when he said there was no reply, he meant there was no reply from British troops. It was natural enough that his first concern was for his own men; the war diary of his division had even stated: "There was to be no embarkation of the French until the British were finished." But the British government's written order to Alexander was that French troops were to be embarked in equal numbers with his own. The British government showed no displeasure at his apparent disobedience. Mr. Anthony Eden, the Secretary of State for War, recorded in his memoirs Alexander's call on him the following morning: "After he had given me an account of what had passed, I congratulated him and he replied, with engaging modesty, 'We were not pressed, you know.' " It may have been modesty. It was also true.

Muddle, no doubt, was inevitable in this last desperate stage of the evacuation. There was still no proper signals equipment for the shore parties to communicate with the ships at sea. Messages between the Dynamo Room in Dover and the Royal Navy's shore parties in Dunkirk were normally passed over the radios of British destroyers "for the sake of greater secrecy as well as of convenience." But when all British warships were withdrawn at dawn on June 2nd there were, obviously, no destroyers to act as message boxes. Messages had to pass through the French signals centre in Bastion 32. But the French signallers did not have the key to the British naval code, and all important signals were of course coded. The BEF and the French Army relied on the fairly simple Code Franco-Britannique, whose only significant complexity was that you had to know which language the coded message was in before you applied the decoding key. At Bastion 32 they had a copy only of the French-language key. Messages from Dover had first to be put into French, then encoded, transmitted and decoded before being translated back into the original language for delivery. This was easier said than done. One message, sent from Dover at 9 a.m. on June 2nd, was received at the Bastion at 1 p.m. The English text was not available for delivery until 2:30 p.m.

Even more foolish things went wrong. For this final phase French soldiers were to use the East Mole, formerly reserved for the British. British ships were now told to enter the western side of the harbour, which had formerly been reserved for French ships. New navigating instructions were issued. A prominent feature of them was referred to as the Nouveau Avant Port, the Nouveau Avant Pont, even (on some hand-drawn rough charts issued to British sailors), the Noval D'Avant Port. The correct French term was Nouvel Avant Port. Some British ships' masters spent a long time seeking this new place whose name they did not recognise. They all knew it perfectly well under its ordinary English name of the Outer Harbour.

All this may be dismissed as run-of-the-mill military farce. But there was tragedy too. At the start of the evacuation, on May 28th, Captain Tennant had appointed a middle-aged naval officer, Commander J. C. Clouston, piermaster of the East Mole. By trial and error, courage under fire, persistence and sheer unflagging ability he had evolved a reliable system for matching the flow of troops onto the mole to the availability of ships for lifting them. Clouston was indispensable. He understood his French colleagues, and they respected him. After five days of unceasing work he was exhausted.

At dawn on June 2nd the evacuation was suspended until nightfall. Commander Clouston took a motor torpedo boat to Dover, where he had a good meal, a bath, and a few hours' sleep in a clean bed. At 3:30 p.m. he started back to ready the pier and the soldiers for the night's work. He never arrived at Dunkirk. With his shore party, including two officers and two petty officers of the French Navy to ensure liaison, he sailed in two Royal Air Force motorboats, risking—to save time—the short route past the German guns at Gravelines. As the two boats approached the French coast a flight of German dive-bombers appeared and attacked. Clouston's boat was sunk, and all its crew were spilled unhurt into the water. The other boat turned as though to rescue them. Clouston waved them off: the danger of stopping in these waters was too great. Clouston and his companions spotted another boat floating in the water some two miles off. They set out to swim to it. The commander was almost fifty and terribly fatigued. After a few hundred yards he called to his companions that he could not make it, and turned to swim back to the wreckage of his own boat. His drowned corpse was seen floating later on.

Perhaps, if Clouston had survived and his shore party had arrived intact, the disgraceful events of the night could have been averted. The embarkation was to have been controlled by a strong shore party, led by this immensely experienced commander, and manned in such a way as to ensure inter-Allied cooperation. Instead the shore party landed at half strength. The senior Royal Navy officer was a mere sublieutenant, Mr. R. Wake, RN. The French team was led by a somewhat older officer, *Lieutenant de vaisseau* Roux and his imperturbable coxswain, Petty Officer Henri Kroener. None of these men, whatever their qualities, had any experience in the crucial and most difficult task of marshalling men to match the available ships. Nor had any of them the seniority indispensable if orders were to be firmly delivered to the army officers in control of the soldiers waiting on the shore.

The first task for the ships, by agreement, was to take off the final load of men of the British Expeditionary Force. The ferry *St. Helier* had been allocated to evacuation duties on May 20th, and had begun work on May 23rd by picking up British and French civilian refugees from Dunkirk. On June 2nd she had been bombed and shelled, suffering damage to her bows. Only a few of her crew were civilian volunteers; most had been replaced by Royal Navy men. But the vessel carried on, and to her went the honour of lifting the last complete shipload of British soldiers from the East Mole of Dunkirk.

Overloaded and leaking, *St. Helier* winched her hawser inboard at 11:30 p.m. on June 2nd. As she backed off the Mole and inched past the wrecks out of the entrance, Captain Tennant sent his historic signal, "BEF evacuated." This laconic message was, of course, literally untrue. Half the men of the British Expeditionary Force were still in France, scattered leaderless across the countryside to southward of the German line of advance along the Somme to the Channel. Some of them were to surrender, a few to die fighting, most to scramble out to safety in evacuations less dramatic than that from Dunkirk. He and his colleagues of the Royal Navy had done a noble job. In Scotland they still remember that an entire division of their men—the 51st (Highland) Division—was left to fend for itself, and finally surrendered to the Germans.

But Captain Tennant may be forgiven his omission. The final message sent, Tennant embarked in a motor torpedo boat for Dover. The French army, meanwhile, was pressing down to its own side of the port to embark in its turn. But no ships went to meet the French. It was a failure of coordination, caused in large part by the loss of the knowledge

and authority of Commander Clouston. Perhaps the Royal
Navy regarded its work as complete now that the British
army was safe away. Perhaps the fault was simply with the
low tide, which meant that ships could tie up at the East
Mole but not enter the inner harbour where the French were.
Whatever the reason, the British now set to work to block
the port, and to try to ensure that the Frenchmen whose
defence of the perimeter had won safety for the BEF would
have no chance to follow them to freedom.

16

THE BITTER END: JUNE 3RD

"The blockships West Cove *and* Edward Nissen
*entered Dunkirk at 0300 and 0310 respectively. It is
unfortunate that the block was not complete and
navigation in the approach channel is still possible."*
  —Report by COMMANDER E. F. V. DECHAINEUX,
    Royal Australian Navy,
    commanding HM Destroyer Vivacious,
    June 3rd, 1940

At half past midnight a cluster of British ships was gathered
at the tip of the East Mole. The tide was low, a stiff breeze
from the north was blowing into the harbour mouth, adding
to the usual difficulties of navigation among the wrecks in the
narrow channel. Admiral Wake-Walker signalled to Dover at
1:15 a.m.: "Plenty of ships, cannot get troops."

Over on the western half of the harbour the quays and the
Mole were crammed with soldiers. As the crow flies their
central mustering point on the Quai Félix-Faure was about
five hundred metres from the British ships at the East Mole.
On foot, around the head of the harbour, the distance was
almost five kilometres. The soldiers had no signals equipment, and no way of telling the ships that they were waiting
at the wrong place; anyway, only the smaller craft, at that

state of the tide, could have manoeuvred across to pick them up.

As low tide passed and the water rose again, ships tried to move in towards the quays and the Mole on the French side of the port. The paddle steamer *Golden Eagle* of the Thames Local Defence Flotilla was commanded by a man used to working on the tides. At 3 a.m. he moved in to try to pick up French soldiers. Her master recorded: ''At the same time a blockship entered the harbour and told me somewhat emphatically to get out whilst I could.'' He left, empty. So did many other vessels. There were ten thousand unfilled places for soldiers on ships that sailed from Dunkirk without loading that night. Ten thousand French soldiers, at the same time, were left behind on the quayside.

The British army was safe. Much of the French army that had made their escape possible by guarding the perimeter was still on shore. The British decided that the highest priority should be given not to rescuing the French, but to making sure that when the Germans took the port of Dunkirk they should not be able to use it as a base for attack against England. Three old ships had been prepared ready for sinking as obstacles in the approach channel to Dunkirk harbour, and right on schedule at 3 a.m. they moved towards the places where they were to be sunk. But at last the Royal Navy bungled an operation.

The SS *Holland*, the last in line of the three blockships, was rammed and sank about five miles west of Dunkirk. The other two ships moved into the approach channel, holes were knocked in their bottoms, the crews went overside, and they began to sink. But the wind and the tide shifted them out of the channel onto the mud, where they stuck, leaving the harbour entrance clear.* HMS *Vivacious* acted as escort to the blockships, and her commander recorded his disappointment at this failure.

At dawn the harbour was empty. The ten thousand French soldiers before whom the empty ships had sailed off for England marched back into the town to find what shelter and

---

*At the low spring tides of 1980 scrap dealers with acetylene cutters removed from beside Dunkirk lighthouse the last rusty fragments of the blockships *West Cove* and *Edward Nissen*.

what food they could. In an alley off the Place Jean-Bart one baker was still at work, baking flat cakes of dough for want of yeast. A queue formed in front of his shop as he worked. When shells came in the queue stood firm, civilians and soldiers alike, fear dominated by hunger. As the first round of a battery shoot crashed into the street a soldier grabbed a fourteen-year-old boy and pushed him against the wall. Shrapnel killed the man and left the boy unhurt.

In Bastion 32 Admiral Abrial was getting ready for departure, his staff burning code books and records that might be useful to the Germans. His radio-telephone to London was still working. Over it, relayed from Paris, came orders similar to those received by Lord Gort four days previously. He must get out if he could, as his capture would be an unnecessary gift to the Germans. Anyway, added his commander-in-chief, Admiral Darlan, *"On aura encore besoin de vous*—We shall be needing you again."

But Abrial knew that the British had abandoned the evacuation and by the placing of their blockships had tried—but failed—to make it impossible for any more Frenchmen to get away, whatever their orders. The record of the day's messages is naturally incomplete. They were obviously rancorous. The French felt they had been betrayed, that the British had saved their own skins at the expense of the French army. The British felt—or argued, at least—that bad planning by the French ashore had led them to endanger several precious ships in an attempt to rescue French stragglers who refused to be rescued.

In fact, understandably, the rescue fleet was hardly in a condition to carry on. Admiral Ramsay informed the British Admiralty that "the continuance of the demands made by evacuation would subject a number of officers and men to a test which might be beyond the limit of human endurance . . ." He asked for fresh reinforcements if the evacuation was to continue. But, true to form, he also placed all his ships, Royal Navy and civilian, under orders to be ready for work towards dusk. The French Navy too organised all its available craft.

One of Ramsay's problems was that the French had never made clear to him the numbers of men in need of transport. This was the result partly of muddle, partly of a genuine dilemma. At one time Admiral Abrial had provided figures on the assumption that a rearguard of 25,000 fighting soldiers would have to remain behind and face capture, to protect the port while the others got clear. At other times he reported the total number of French troops remaining within the Dunkirk perimeter, including the rearguard, making a total of almost 50,000 men. Finally Ramsay's staff tried to organise cross-Channel transport for 30,000 men, providing they could be got to the embarkation points in the hours of darkness between June 3rd and 4th. This was not nearly enough, but nobody was to blame.

Admiral Ramsay's initial reluctance to mount a further operation was swept away during the day by orders from Mr. Churchill himself. In the morning the news came through to Paris that ten thousand French soldiers had been left on the shore, almost within shouting distance of British ships departing empty. Prime Minister Reynaud was furious. This apparent British betrayal of French interests was just what his critics needed. Reynaud was struggling to keep France in the war, alongside Britain. His defeatist opponents, led by the ancient but unchallengeable Deputy Prime Minister, Marshal Pétain, wanted to break with Britain and make peace at any price.

General Spears, Mr. Churchill's special representative in Paris, saw M. Reynaud in the morning and felt the full weight of his scorn. After lunch Mr. Churchill telephoned Spears, and began to tell him of the disgust felt in Britain about what was being represented as the refusal of the French soldiers to accept the chance of escape to fight again. Spears carefully explained how different things looked from Paris. If no further attempt were made to evacuate more French troops, he said, even the most pro-British of the French leaders would blame the government in London. It would be a great victory for Pétain and the defeatists. Spears won the argument. Churchill gave the orders that, through a reluctant Ramsay and a dispirited fleet, would save the alliance for a week or two more.

The Germans, meanwhile, simply stopped bothering about Dunkirk. They had presumably intercepted the British naval signals ordering the blockships to be sunk in the approach channel. They had all along taken the view—no doubt because they had listened to the BEF's wireless traffic—that the British were concerned only to save their own skins. The last of the 155-mm. medium guns were taken away from the troops surrounding Dunkirk. The Luftwaffe began its offensive on the French air bases surrounding Paris. In the raid on the airfield at Le Bourget, just north of Paris, the German Air Force reckoned that it had shot down over one hundred French planes and destroyed three or four times as many on the ground. (The French, like the British, had clearly held back their planes from the defence of Dunkirk in order to protect their own capital.) With Le Bourget out of action, three hundred German bombers raided the Renault factory making tanks and armoured vehicles in the suburbs of Paris itself.

Dunkirk was more than ever a side issue now. But the French had too few troops, and too little ammunition, to maintain the old perimeter on the main canals surrounding the town. They pulled back. To the west of Bergues, through Spycker, the German infantry found no French soldiers up against them, and advanced along the Canal de Bourbourg towards the centre of the town and the port itself.

As the advancing Germans reached the tall warehouses along the canal by Coudekerque-Branche they were seen from an artillery observation post in the loft. Captain Bièche, the observation officer, watched the German infantry move past at ground level. Carefully he worked out the coordinates for his own position, read them over the telephone, and called his guns to shoot. The gun controller, Captain Durand, checked the coordinates and called back the observation post on the telephone. The conversation deserves to be recorded in the original language: *"Dis-donc, Bièche, il me semble que tu nous fais tirer sur l'observatoire." "Espèce de con, je le sais bien. Tire quand même!"*—("Look, Bièche, I think you are calling fire on your own position." "Silly bastard, of course I am. Shoot anyway!")

The French, evenly matched in weapons now with their depleted German attackers, were at last showing how they could fight. At dusk the Germans broke off their advance, unwilling to get into a house-to-house scrap with defenders who knew every corner of every street. The German infantry was within three or four kilometres of the port, and of Bastion 32 itself. But they did not press forward, and the French were able to retreat quietly in front of them. The shooting died away. Father Lecointe, the young curate at the big Church of Saint-Martin, only fifteen hundred metres from the port, recorded in his diary the strangeness of this night of silence.

As evening drew on, the evacuation fleet sailed out from England. Admiral Ramsay's headquarters counted thirteen destroyers (four of them French), two corvettes, one antique river gunboat, nine passenger ferries (three of them French), thirteen British trawlers, and a flurry of miscellaneous fishing boats, pleasure craft, launches and cutters manned by Royal Navy crews. The Dynamo Room knew of sixty-three French vessels—warships and others—on the way to Dunkirk this evening, to rescue the last of their own people. Most of them were fishing boats and small naval auxiliaries, suitable to go right up to the inner quays even at low tide. The Royal Navy appears not to have known of the additional French convoy of twenty-eight trawlers led by the *Belgica* under Lieutenant Duval. These boats had left in mid-afternoon from off Ramsgate, and had found their way at high tide across the shallows of the Goodwin Sands, by the northerly route which the British had abandoned several days before as too dangerous.

The wind, still brisk, was now in the east, blowing straight across the harbour entrance. The French army had been told to ignore the old demarcation line which reserved the East Mole for the British: they were to use the whole harbour, moles and quays alike. *Lady of Mann* was the first of the personnel ships to arrive, and she headed for the familiar mooring at the East Mole. Her master was astonished, and indignant, to find the Mole lined with French fishing boats, packing in as many soldiers as they could cram aboard. These were the boats of Duval's armada, and it took *Lady of Mann* two hours to clear them off and get alongside for loading.

The larger ships could not approach the Mole without endangering the trawlers tied up there; they struggled to keep their station in the rapid tide of the deep-water channel as the wind pushed them sideways. On past nights of evacuation the Mole had been manned by Royal Navy shore patrols, who regulated the movements both of troops and of vessels. Now it was chaos. The British captains shouted to the trawler skippers that they were more badly needed right inside the harbour, where the big ships could not enter for lack of water under their keels. But the shouts were in English. The trawler men for the most part could not understand, and—after what they had heard of the British "betrayal" of the previous night—they were in any case not minded to obey. Precious time was wasted before the French liaison officers of Admiral Wake-Walker's party could persuade the unscheduled small craft to leave, each with their freight of 100 or 120 men. The destroyers and ferries, after anxious moments in the narrow channel, moved onto station and started to load.

On the West Mole, and at the Quai Félix-Faure inwards from the outer harbour, there was confusion, too. Royal Navy officers and petty officers landed and tried to carry on their duties of mustering the soldiers in appropriate numbers for the vessels available. These Frenchmen too refused to take orders from the British; they insisted on being detailed off by their own officers. One group of French troops filed onto a British trawler, found that there was no room aboard for their commanding officer, and determinedly marched ashore again.

Hitherto, the vast majority of French troops travelling in British ships had been craftsmen, headquarters staff, stragglers and other non-combatants. They had been glad to get away from the confusion of Dunkirk, and happy to accept any offer of transport elsewhere. Now, on the final night, the French were sending down fighting troops straight out of the front line. They were proudly aware that they had held that line for over a week, in face of the enemy. They despised the English who—as they saw it—had sneaked away behind them. Now, defeated but still disciplined, they wanted to arrive on English soil in properly constituted units of the French Army, to which they remained proud to belong.

When they arrived on the quays of Dover or Ramsgate they were disarmed by the British military police, and marched onto trains for the more westerly ports of Southampton and Weymouth, to sail back at once to France. All of them were ordered to surrender by their government on July 16th, without a chance to fight the Germans again.

It is fair to add that, after the fall of France, few of them were keen to continue the fight. In August General de Gaulle, the self-appointed leader of the French in exile, assembled at White City stadium in London two thousand Dunkirk veterans who, because of wounds or other reasons, had not been repatriated with the bulk of the army. He offered them a choice: go home and submit to the Germans or stay and fight with me. Only two hundred of the two thousand volunteered to stay and fight in the forces of *La France Libre*.

17

SURRENDER: JUNE 4TH

*"The whole affair seemed most tame to me,
compared with what I had been led to expect, and
indeed I was disappointed that there was not more
'activity.' "*
> —Report of LIEUTENANT T. JOHNSTON, RN,
> commanding HM Schuyt *Pascholl*,
> Dunkirk, June 4th

*"Where are the English?" "Not here. They are all in
England."*
> —Question by GENERAL VON KRANZ, German Army,
> reply by GENERAL BEAUFRÈRE, French Army,
> Dunkirk, June 4th

"Faut-il recommencer ce soir?"
> —ADMIRAL RAMSAY to Admiral Abrial, Dover,
> June 4th

The ships' orders were categorical: be clear by first light.
Inland, the last weary defenders of the unbroken Dunkirk
perimeter disengaged from their passive enemy. A few
machine-gunners were left in place to maintain a token resis-

tance if the Germans moved. Twenty thousand fighting men set off to march an hour through the night and the shattered town, towards their last chance of safety. It was a race to catch the boats. Their way was blocked by a mindless rabble.

General Barthélémy commanded the *Secteur Fortifié des Flandres*, the ramshackle force of pioneers and infantry who had been the first, and were now the last, fighting defenders of Dunkirk. His men had proved themselves in a week of battle. In the evening of June 3rd he detailed two battalions to guard the canal bridges on the road to Furnes. At ten-thirty the bulk of his force, some eight thousand men, left the front with orders to assemble in predetermined positions near the port for embarkation. As the men neared Malo they were forced to a halt. Jacques Mordal's description of Barthélémy's march is full of bitterness:

> As he approached Malo, he saw a vast crowd of soldiers whose existence suddenly became apparent as news spread of the final departures. From every cellar, from every hole in the ground, unarmed men emerged. . . . Naturally enough, none of the stout fellows who for days had not come out of their shelters were prepared to leave room for those who had done the fighting for them. Marking time, Barthélémy's column waited, while across their front passed these men from the ordnance depots, these truck drivers, these representatives of all the rear echelons.

These stragglers, the non-combatants of the French Army, were the French troops whom the British had grown used to encountering, and by whose deportment the British had come to judge the whole French Army. They had no officers, they had no proper weapons. The stout defence of the Dunkirk perimeter provides the evidence that Frenchmen could fight. The ugly mass of stragglers provides the evidence that many Frenchmen would not fight.

Jacques Mordal wrote:

> All the soldiers in the firing line had been able to disengage without being harassed by the enemy. They were hampered far more by the mass of useless people who

turned up at the moment of the final sailings. Since there was not the physical capacity for everyone to take ship, a ruthless police operation would have been needed to clear the way for the men coming out of the front. Anyone who recalls the appalling confusion of Malo and the approaches to the East Mole must agree that the job could only have been done with machine guns. What commander would willingly have done that?

Admiral Abrial's estimate had been that there were 25,000 men to take to England during the night. Admiral Ramsay organised enough ships to take off 30,000, and there were several hundred more places on French ships independent of Ramsay's command. The total number taken off was almost 27,000. Forty thousand more surrendered to the Germans in the morning.

There were delays in getting the troops to the embarkation points. There were delays in getting ships alongside, too. The unexpected press of volunteer French fishing boats held up the arrival of the large vessels from England; *Lady of Mann*, we have seen, was delayed for two hours. The blockships which the Royal Navy had sunk the previous night, although they did not lie across the approach channel, were an added obstruction. The French Channel ferry *Newhaven* had been earmarked to transport Abrial's headquarters staff from Bastion 32. She struck one of the blockships while entering the channel, and it took her an hour to get clear.

Newhaven and *Autocarrier* between them, at the East Mole, took on board the staffs of Northern Naval Command, of the *Secteur Fortifié des Flandres*, and of Dunkirk port control. They had worked under bombardment all through the great escape, as their town, their ships, their harbour and their army were smashed around them. The *Police de la Navigation* found their own way out. Only three of their pilot boats were still afloat, after the two weeks during which, under bombing and shellfire, they had regulated the coming and going of ships in the western, French sector of the harbour. Two of the boats had their engines out of order, so *Capitaine de frégate* Kernéis ordered the single survivor to take the others in tow, their crews aboard, and they made it to Dover under their own power.

At the base of the West Mole, and on the Quai Jean-Jaurès below the lighthouse, Commander H. R. Troup, RN, and his French liaison officer Captain le Comte Le Chartier de Sédouy, had at last managed to establish their authority over the military. The soldiers waited in ranks, coming forward in disciplined parties to board whatever vessel presented itself—French drifters, the old Thames excursion steamer *Royal Sovereign*, the destroyer *Malcolm*. Lieutenant Johnston, who had taken over command of the commandeered Dutch coaster *Pascholl*, was disappointed that the adventure was so tame. He had evidently been reading too many newspaper stories.

Troup had been told to wait for the arrival of General Lucas, commanding the Thirty-second Division and Captain Le Chartier's superior officer. He was moved to end his report to the Admiralty by quoting the epitaph on the Spartan army after Thermopylae:

> I would like to put on record the wonderful discipline of the French troops when the last ship left about 0300.
> About 1,000 men stood to attention 4 deep about half-way along the pier, the General and his staff about 30 feet away and after having faced the troops, whose faces were indiscernible [*sic*] in the dawn light, the flames behind them showing up their steel helmets, the officers clicking their heels, saluted and then came down to the boat with me and we left at 0320.
> Go, stranger, tell the Spartans that here we lie, having been obedient to their commands.
>
> H. R. Troup, Commander, RN

This last wait for the top brass seemed less glorious for the man in the little motorboat at the foot of the quay. Sub-Lieutenant G. A. Gabbett-Mulhallen, RN, had made one trip to Dunkirk with a string of lifeboats, which all sank before he got there; another with a civilian motorboat whose engine failed, so that he had to get a tow home; another with an army motorboat, during which he made twenty runs in one night, ferrying twenty-five soldiers each time out to bigger ships offshore. He made special mention of this final trip:

I continued this every night until Monday when, having ferried all night and the last transport had sailed with 3,500 troops aboard I waited alongside the pier for Commander Troupe [sic] who was on the pier embarking the men into the ships. Eventually he came aboard with the French General (very relieved at the coming I was to [sic]), for having heard the Jerries had arrived in the town, the wait and the time they took to get down the ladder from the pier seemed interminable. It was about 3:45 a.m. when we finally cast off.

Over at the East Mole, from which most of the BEF had left France, the men of the *Secteur Fortifié des Flandres* had finally made their way through the mob in the town. A first detachment of them hurried aboard the destroyer *Express*. She held on as long as she could, until she had a full load. At 3:18 she backed off. This seemed to be the last chance. The light was growing clear now in the sky towards Belgium. The men on the Mole, exhausted from their days of fighting and their night's march, began to turn back.

Then, from the sea, the old destroyer HMS *Shikari*, rusty, inelegant, spotted the file of soldiers. She was the command ship for the Royal Navy's second attempt to block the port. One of the three blockships had not been degaussed as a protection against magnetic mines; she blew up and sank before entering the channel. Another, the *Moyle*, was swept clear of the deep channel as she sank, and joined the two wrecks from the previous night's attempt, on the sandbank beside the deep water. But *Pacifico*, the third blockship, sank right across the waterway. Only the outer half of the East Mole was now accessible from the open sea.

Shikari, the escort destroyer, had no orders to rescue soldiers. But her commander on his own initiative ran his ship gently alongside the extremity of the Mole. Six hundred men of the *Secteur Fortifié des Flandres* climbed aboard, including General Barthélémy himself. At 3:40 *Shikari* pulled away, low in the water from the human load on deck. So it ended.

Admiral Abrial had begun to wind up his headquarters at seven-thirty the previous evening. It was 3:00 a.m. before he finally left, on *Autocarrier*, together with General Fagalde and his staff from the bastion. He was met on the quay at

Dover with naval honours by his opposite number Admiral Ramsay. "Must we do it again tonight?" asked Ramsay in French. The answer was no. At 2:43 p.m. on June 4th the British Admiralty sent the signal which formally ended Operation Dynamo. On June 5th Abrial was accorded the finest honour the British could think of: he was received at Buckingham Palace to accept the personal thanks of King George VI. Next day he went back to Cherbourg. He surrendered there, along with six other French admirals, on June 18th.

At 8:20 in the morning two German marines, percussion grenades swinging in their hands, moved cautiously up to the sentry on duty outside Dunkirk's pompous Town Hall. Behind them an army colonel in a commandeered black Citroën drove up. He entered the building, and was received in the hall by General Beaufrère, the senior French officer remaining in the town, who had been ordered by Abrial to command the surrender. Beaufrère had put on his gilded képi to mark the occasion. The German spoke excellent French; he was precise, intensely polite. He conducted Beaufrère to his commanding general, von Kranz. The formal discussions on surrender terms continued. Food and water had to be provided for the defeated soldiers, weapons to be stacked in good order.

The German soldiers too needed supplies. James Langley, his arm smashed, was in Casualty Clearing Station No. 12 in the settlement known as Le Chapeau Rouge on the outskirts of Malo-les-Bains. He was the only combatant officer in the casualty station fit to be moved and to speak. Very early in the morning an orderly told him that the Germans were at the gate. He remembered the strict orders given to all platoon commanders of the Coldstream Guards: take no prisoners, unless specifically ordered that they are needed for interrogation. Apprehensively, he instructed the orderlies to carry him out to meet the conquerors. "If we were exhausted, so were the Germans. The small section which wended its way up the drive was reeling with fatigue. Caked with dust, unshaven, two of them sank to the ground as they halted by the stretcher." Soon the captors were offering cigarettes, the captured offering tins of jam. The full courtesies of war were observed.

There was to be one last recorded escape from Dunkirk. The mass of soldiers at the base of the East Mole were worn

out, surly, short on discipline. Their German captors had the
same language problems that the British seamen had encountered. The tangles of the night march were slow to undo.
Lieutenant Le Doze, a medical officer, was just on the Mole
itself. In the water beside him lay a sunken ship, and at her
davits hung a lifeboat which seemed to be floating at that
state of the tide.

With about ten soldiers the doctor climbed onto the wreck
and untied the lifeboat. She turned out to be of the kind
propelled by a screw turned by pedals below the thwarts. Le
Doze and his party pedalled off like so many holiday-makers.
A burst of machine-gun fire followed them, but missed. Soon
they rigged up a sail from a couple of spars and a blanket,
and made better speed. Out at sea they were spotted by an
RAF plane, which summoned a fast patrol boat. And so they
got to England.

One French vessel was less fortunate. The *Émile Des-
champs* was carrying about 500 French escapers, including
several doctors from the field hospitals, and some women,
one with a little baby. The boat was an old hulk, notoriously
unstable. Previously she had carried across the Channel two
loads of German prisoners in French hands. She had not been
degaussed, and her compass was inaccurate. But as dawn
broke she crept across the shoals to within five miles of the
North Foreland on the English coast. There she struck a magnetic mine. Shattered, she went down in ten seconds.

Fewer than one hundred of her passengers survived. One
of them was the naval doctor Hervé Cras, who under the
name of Jacques Mordal later became the chronicler of the
French at Dunkirk. Despite the tangled history of interallied
relations at the time his affection for Britain did not falter.
Whatever some British leaders said or did at the time, he
remembered until his death in 1980 the sailors of HMS *Al-
bury* ''who pulled me from the water under the North Foreland, on June 4th, 1940 at 6:30 in the morning.''

The church of Saint-Martin stands at the inner focus of the
canal system of Dunkirk, about one and a half kilometres
from the port. Father Lecointe, who was then twenty-one
years old and the junior curate of the parish, remembers well
the dawn of June 4th. After two weeks of continuous bombing and shelling, he had slept well that night in the unaccus-

tomed quiet. At first light he began to say Mass in the cellar of the nuns' house where he was lodging, across the square in front of the church. In the middle of the service the dean, the formidable Monsignor Marquis, who had fought at Verdun in the First World War, burst in. ''They're here,'' he cried.

Outside in the square a sergeant was brandishing a revolver and giving orders in a guttural voice. Under his direction men were laying out on the ground a huge swastika flag, about three metres along its sides. They weighted down its corners with bricks, as a sign to aircraft overhead that the Germans had taken over.

The two priests walked unhindered across the cobbles. Father Lecointe remembers:

> We went across to the church. It no longer looked like a place of quiet sanctuary. It was not a ruin, the structure was unharmed. But it was gaping, empty. All the window glass was on the floor, smashed. The doors had been smashed, thrown off their hinges by blast.
>
> We went into the church and were amazed to hear the organ playing. Up in the organ-loft there was a German soldier pumping the bellows, another playing. They stopped as soon as they saw us, stood up, and complimented us on the quality of the instrument . . .

The German occupation of Dunkirk had begun. It lasted very nearly five years. The Canadian soldiers who advanced along the coast into Belgium in the summer of 1944 bypassed the town. Behind its ring of canals it was too strong to be worth a direct attack. The German garrison held on in Dunkirk, as the French had hoped to do in 1940. They gave up the fight in their turn, surrendering finally to a Czechoslovak armoured brigade on May 10th, 1945, two days after the surrender of the main German Army in its homeland.

Part Four
THE DUNKIRK SPIRIT

18

HOW THE NEWS WAS TOLD

*"I'm afraid there is going to be a considerable shock
for the British public. It is your duty to act as shock-
absorbers, so I have prepared, with my counterpart
at the War Office, a statement which can be
published, subject to censorship. . . ."*
— MAJOR-GENERAL MASON-MACFARLANE,
    Director of Military Intelligence, BEF,
    to British correspondents returned from France,
    May 28th

There are some habits that a nation in danger of its life may
be ready to forego. One is the right to be informed, by a free
press, of what its armed forces are doing in its name. The
appalling truth of the defeat leading to the Dunkirk evacuation
was not reported at the time in the British press, partly because there were no journalists at Dunkirk to report it. Not
until the evacuation had been going on for five days, and
almost three-quarters of the surrounded British army had already embarked from France, was the British public told it
was happening. From the deficiency of reported news from
France, the British government and military authorities, with
the willing and patriotic co-operation of the press and the
broadcasters, were able to create a myth whose poetic strength

sustained the morale of the nation at the time, and has survived until today.

The Dunkirk evacuation formally began with the order to commence Operation Dynamo, just before 7 p.m. on May 26th. Over the days that followed, tens of thousands of exhausted soldiers were pouring into the ports of south-east England. Special trains carrying these men were to be seen at almost every station in the south and Midlands of the country. Yet the secret was kept. It was confined to the military, and to a very small group of civilians including the railway organisers—whose work was beyond praise—and certain volunteer workers such as the members of the Women's Voluntary Service who provided, with devotion, comfort to the beaten soldiers. A few journalists were told and sworn to silence, which they preserved. But the secret was not shared even by some members of the government who might have been expected to know.

Harold Nicolson, for example, is best remembered as an occasional author and brilliant diarist. In May 1940 he had just been recruited by Winston Churchill as parliamentary under-secretary—junior minister—in the Ministry of Information, the government department meant to disseminate (and, if necessary, dress up) the news. In his private diary for May 29th, 1940, Nicolson harks characteristically back to the battles of the Peninsular War, and notes: "We are creating a Corunna Line along the beaches round Dunkirk, and hope to evacuate a few of our troops." One-third of the British army in France had already been evacuated.

The evacuation was first plainly announced to the British people just after 6 p.m. on May 31st. Lord Gort, commander of the British Expeditionary Force, had already taken ship from France, and so had some 150,000 of his men. There had been hints before. Public opinion was carefully prepared—without the intervention of the Ministry of Information—for the shock of knowing that its army had been beaten. But the BBC's six-o'clock news was the first to carry the vital announcement in as many words. The newsreader's copy of the bulletin, as read over the air, is signed at the foot: "Approved by MI 17a—S.W. Smithers." MI numbers, then as now, referred to sections of British military intelligence.

The text* is indeed one of which the military could have approved:

> All night and all day men of the undefeated British Expeditionary Force have been coming home . . . From the many reports of their arrival and of interviews with the men, it is clear that if they have not come back in triumph they have come back in glory; that their morale is as high as ever; that they *know* they did not meet their masters; and that they are anxious only to be back again soon—as they put it—"To have a real crack at Jerry."

The newspapers, forced for the first time in a major war to yield primacy as a news source to the broadcast media, had to wait until next morning to tell their readers that the BEF had been beaten out of France. Their tone was equally patriotic, but the name of the liaison officer with the military authorities is not revealed in their printed pages.

It was, of course, both the wish and the duty of the press to support the government and the soldiers in their fight against an enemy whose evil could hardly be doubted. British civil liberties were willingly given up in this struggle. On May 30th, as the real possibility appeared that the Germans might turn away from the final assault on France and attack across the Channel, the Home Secretary was given powers "to suppress any newspaper which systematically publishes matter calculated to foment opposition to the progress of the war." The same day a few British fascists were rounded up and put in prison without trial. (The most influential person arrested that day under the Defence Regulations was the borough surveyor of Guildford, not a key figure in British life.) But the censorship did not need to be imposed. It was voluntarily accepted, even by the news organisations most proud to claim editorial independence of the government.

The British Broadcasting Corporation had somewhat uneasily negotiated an arrangement to preserve its formal independence of the government. It was to be "officially guided" by the Ministry of Information, and its own con-

*See Appendix IV, page 238, for Mr. S. W. Smithers' own account of how the BBC newsroom worked.

troller of programmes was recognised as the organisation's chief censor. The scripts read over the air by the newsreaders give a rather different impression of the corporation's determination to make its own editorial judgements. They bear frequent annotations; "Approved by FO [Foreign Office]," "Referred to Admiralty," "Passed by Home Office," are alternative formulae used in these notes. An account of Norwegian courage in face of the invading Germans, broadcast in the 1 p.m. news bulletin on May 29th, is marked in the margin "MOI Handout" (MOI meaning Ministry of Information). There is some evidence of unease at the use of such handouts. The 1 p.m. bulletin on May 31st carried a story about anti-German riots in, of all places, Buenos Aires. The story runs over two pages of script. Each page is annotated, on three lines: "outlined to Harrison—MOI/FO suggested that we use;/good propaganda." The third line, although still legible today, was prudishly crossed out before the document was microfilmed for the BBC archives.

Some of the journalists propagating this propaganda may not actually have known it to be untrue. Sometimes the soldiers for whom it was the only source of information did. Anthony Rhodes was with his battalion medical officer in France soon after the British Expeditionary Force began the retreat that immediately followed its advance into Belgium.

We listened to the nine o'clock news, to see how our retreat was viewed by the Government, or rather, to see how the Government thought it ought to be viewed. The announcer said we had made "a strategic withdrawal according to plan." It appeared, according to him, that we had always intended to abandon Brussels, it was all part of our devilish scheme. "The bloody liars," said the doctor.

On the other hand the BBC's broadcasts sometimes told the troops more than their officers had. Operation Dynamo began on May 26th. The BBC, then as now, broadcast every Sunday, live, an entire Church of England service. The broadcast service on Sunday, May 26th, was from Westminster Abbey, where the King, the Prime Minister and a host of dignitaries heard the Archbishop of Canterbury pray "for our soldiers in dire peril in France.'' For many soldiers in France this was the first they had officially heard of any dire peril facing the army. It was a nasty Sunday surprise, and did not help the troops in the field to greater faith in their commanders, who had not told them of the danger.

The BBC had set itself an impossible job. It saw its main duty as being to reinforce the morale of the civilian audience at home, its main audience. But falsehoods meant to cheer up civilians could have the opposite effect on the men in the firing line. Admiral Ramsay's final report on Operation Dynamo puts it clearly: ''The formations of our own fighters when operating over the [Dunkirk] area were so outnumbered by the enemy aircraft that it was no surprise to the observer to note that more British machines were shot down than were enemy, and feelings of disgust were engendered on listening in to the BBC report of the same evening, which recounted the opposite story.''

It is fair to say that the British propaganda authorities, including the BBC, learned their lesson from this experience. Later in the war they might postpone or adulterate the news, but they abandoned the Dunkirk experiment of simply telling untruths.

Moreover, what is seen to be untrue now may at the time have been plausible. It is possible, for example, that even some RAF intelligence officers believed the current fantasies about the ''qualitative superiority'' of British planes and their pilots at Dunkirk. The BBC's nine-o'clock news bulletin of May 30th contains a good example of this material. It was carefully constructed to prepare the audience for the planned announcement—it came next day—of the collapse of British resistance in France. It began as follows: ''A battle is now raging on the Flanders coast; a number of troops have now been successfully evacuated with the assistance of the Royal Navy and of the Royal Air Force; they are now back in England. One squadron of Defiant fighters has destroyed thirty-seven enemy aircraft without loss to themselves.''

This story of the Defiants is especially odd. Winston Churchill also used it, both in the House of Commons and in private morale-boosting chats to his intimates. The Boulton-Paul Defiant was a fighter plane looking much like a Hurricane. It had no forward-firing guns, but instead had four machine-guns in a ponderous power-operated turret behind the pilot's seat. The plane proved such a constant danger to its precious crews that it was withdrawn from fighting service as soon as possible after Dunkirk. On the day of its alleged triumph the total of German planes lost on all fronts was eighteen. But the excitement of air combat often provoked air crews to fantastic claims, and it cannot be proven that the Defiant's supporters were deliberately lying.

The role of the BBC as a vehicle for unsupported allegations by government agencies was, however, serious. Then as now, news editors in Fleet Street tended to use it as a quasi-authoritative source of news on official matters. So did the troops in the field, for whom it was not just the best but the only source of information. But then the relationship between the journalists and the soldiers and airmen of the British Expeditionary Force was always unhappy.

When the BEF went off to France, in September 1939, it was accompanied by a high-powered press tail, British and American. The doyen of international war reporters was with them. He was Sir Philip Gibbs of the London *Daily Telegraph*, who had in the Abyssinian War done service as the original of Sir Jocelyn Hitchcock in Evelyn Waugh's documentary novel *Scoop*.* There were plenty of other famous names along with him. Reporters with the BEF had to wear a peculiar uniform, like an officer's but without badges of rank, and with a large "C" for Correspondent instead of a cap badge. (An army wit pointed out that it should have been two initials, for War Correspondent.)

Control of journalists with the army was exercised by the director of military intelligence with the BEF, Major-General Mason-Macfarlane, a fierce and crippled man who had served as a "diplomat" and spy all over Europe as the fascist tide rose. He was in the habit of exploiting his relationship with senior journalists to gather—and, of course, to disseminate—information of a kind useful to his service. But he rarely spoke to ordinary reporters. They were divided up into small

---

*Gibbs swallowed propaganda wholesale. On May 24th, as French morale collapsed, he sent a story from Paris which totally contradicted all other reports from that city. The *New York Times* published this widely syndicated article under the sceptical headline: "Gibbs Finds France Undismayed."

groups under the control of "conducting officers," most of whom appear to have been First World War veterans with an amazing capacity for drink. The chief censor at the War Office was General Ian Hay Beith, author of a famous First War book called *The First Hundred Thousand*. Conducting officers included one Joe Fairley, identified as "the original Bulldog Drummond," and Arnold Ridley, who wrote *The Ghost Train*. Fairly soon the conducting officers found themselves outnumbering the journalists whom they were meant to conduct.

There was no story. Bernard Gray of the *Daily Mirror* put it simply: "The BEF were holding a sector on the Belgian frontier with the nearest German two hundred miles away. We weren't allowed to say so. The censors wouldn't pass it." Most of the senior British journalists, and almost all the Americans except for a few wire service men to file the handouts, left for assignments where they could better earn their expenses. Richard Dimbleby, the BBC's pushing young war expert, set off for the Middle East before the real fighting began.

Bernard Gray recorded before his death in mysterious circumstances in 1941 the frustration of British correspondents at being treated by the Army as though they were potential spies. His constant travelling companion, who vocally shared his indignation, was the man from *The Times*, Kim Philby. Mr. Philby, by his own account (published in 1968) had been an active member of the Soviet Union's intelligence service since 1937; his reports from France in 1939 and 1940 may well have been useful to his masters' allies, the Nazi intelligence services. His memoirs are understandably reticent on the point, although he does record that on his return from France to Britain, having been evacuated twice, from Boulogne and from Brest, he was promptly recruited by the British intelligence service.

The correspondents assigned to report on the work of the Royal Air Force in France had an even worse time than those with the army. The pilots with whom they were in contact were indeed fighting, patrolling, photographing behind enemy lines. But the RAF permitted only the most generalised reporting of their deeds, and strictly prohibited reporters from naming any pilots. Charles Gardner of the BBC was assigned to the Advanced Air Striking Force, the small RAF detachment serving in direct support of the BEF. He recorded an interview with a carefully unnamed "young New Zealand pilot." When this gallant young man, "Cobber" Kain, was awarded the Distinguished Flying Cross by the King, Buckingham Palace gave his name to the press, and he was identified. The RAF's senior officers were furious. Gardner and his colleagues eventually, in March 1940, organised a strike against the stupidity of their censors; the reporters were, after all, loyally trying to present the RAF in the best and most heroic light.

The strike was settled after Gardner had been called in for a frank chat with Air Marshal Barratt, commanding the air striking force. Barratt gave Gardner guarantees of free access to news. Simultaneously his officers proceeded to ban all air crews from talking to any journalist at any time. By April relations between the RAF and the press had got so bad that the newspapers and the BBC withdrew their correspondents from the AASF. Their return was eventually negotiated, but could not be tested in practice. Charles Gardner got back to France on May 8th, and the Germans invaded two days later, before he could join the combat units.

As the German advance began, Lord Gort's first act was to move his headquarters, including his director of intelligence, General Mason-Macfarlane, out of range of the advice of his intelligence staff, and of the journalists they were meant to look after. The journalists were stranded. They had no transport, no information, and nobody to care for them. Soon they were swept away ahead of the retreating army. Bernard Gray recorded a wonderful conversation on Monday, May 20th, in Boulogne. Together with Kim Philby and Evelyn Montague of the *Manchester Guardian* he found himself at a loose end, with nothing to report. The three friends decided to go to Le Touquet for a game of golf. They went along to their public-relations officer to get permission.

"Le Touquet?" said the officer then in charge. "Of course, old boy. Delighted for you to go, normally. But it's a bit difficult at the moment, you know. The Germans are there." We gave up the idea of playing golf.

The correspondents somehow got onto ships, were ferried back to Britain, and on May 28th were summoned to the Berkeley Hotel in London to hear General Mason-Macfarlane tell them, in the words at the head of this chapter, how he wished to employ the press as a shock absorber for bad news. This was a role the journalists willingly played. But Mason-Macfarlane did more then that by way of guidance. In his talk, which was strictly off the record, he told the British press that the BEF was surrounded, and that it was unlikely that it would get away safely. For this he instructed them to blame the French: "It is now no secret that on several fronts, the French failed to withstand the assault. . . . The result of these failures was disastrous from the point of view of the BEF, and led directly to the critical situation with which it is now faced . . . In fairness to the British Army, and its commanders, it cannot be too highly emphasised that it is the Allied High Command that has been outmanoeuvred and the armies of the French that have been outfought—not the BEF."

The general's gloomy ponderings were faithfully reflected in "exclusive" articles in the next day's papers. No source was given for the writers' thoughts. A few correspondents reminded their readers, some days later, that the British army in France had got safely away behind a defensive screen maintained, with great courage, by units of the French Army on the Dunkirk perimeter.

The British press was by now well aware that it had been largely deceived by its source of military information. The public was getting the same idea. The American broadcaster Drew Middleton on May 22nd in a CBS News report spoke of the handling of the news from Norway, where the facts of the Allied defeat had been concealed from the press until, without warning, it was told that the troops were pulling out. This behaviour, said Middleton, "has undermined the confidence of a considerable section of the British public in the integrity and accuracy of its news sources." It is common for journalists who have been deceived by public-relations men to appeal to a wider audience for justice; but Middleton had good sources of information. The Ministry of Information was secretly conducting surveys of British opinion at the time, and their report of May 18th had come to precisely the conclusion reached four days later by the astute American reporter.

As the disaster in France came to look more like the disaster in Norway repeated on a larger scale, the British press became more cautious in its assertions that the British army was ever victorious. *The Times* on May 13th, as the scale of the German offensive became apparent, had a headline on its main news page: "BEF Sweeps On." But the leading editorial opposite had a cautious first sentence: "Now that battle has been joined in the West we must expect the news to be, not indeed meagre, but almost invariably delayed."

On May 22nd, so hopeless were the disparities between the French and British daily official communiqués on the progress of the war, that *The Times* and the other serious newspapers started printing three communiqués side by side: British, French and German too. The German one was more accurate. On May 28th, for example, it reported: "At Dunkirk harbour bridges were set on fire . . . To frustrate the efforts of the British to re-embark parts of their hemmed-in troops for England the Germans attacked ports on the Belgian coast still in enemy hands." Next day the German communiqué claimed that the Dunkirk evacuation had been frustrated by the Luftwaffe. But for the British public there was to be no news of any evacuation at all, even a frustrated one. The almost-truthful German communiqué of May 29th was not printed in any British paper.

For the Germans the truth came easier, since it was telling of their great victory. The role of propaganda in total war was fully acknowledged by the Nazi Party, and German units were accompanied by a staff of reporters in uniform, regarded as full members of the armed forces of the Reich. The reporting units even had their own signals specialists, which is more than most British fighting units had at the time. Neutral war correspondents were attached to these reporting sections, and were given access to skilfully selected scenes of warfare, with just enough ferocity on display to convince foreign readers that the German armies would be—as indeed they were—a formidable enemy to take on. Moreover, the German armed forces were habitually accompanied by film cameramen, often very good ones, and their film was after careful selection and editing made freely available to foreign newsreel chains.

These were powerful weapons for keeping—among other nations—the United States out of the war. Just sometimes they brought advantages to Allied soldiers too. Lieutenant Jimmy Langley, who as we have seen was left behind with the other wounded at Dunkirk, was displayed to neutral reporters by his German captors. "The most helpful visitor was a blonde American press reporter who took a liking to me which was heartily reciprocated when she gave me 100 cigarettes, a pound of chocolate, some sugar and a bag of apples. She told Philip Newman [a doctor prisoner] that she thought he should operate on my arm again and said she would return in two days to see if he had done so." Two days later Dr. Newman cut off Mr. Langley's arm to stop the gangrene from spreading. The reporter did not reappear.

The role of the press, and particularly of the foreign press, was crucial in the weeks that followed Dunkirk. Mr. Churchill, in his immortal speech* to the House of Commons on the day when the successful accomplishment of the evacuation was carried out, revealed that the policy of the British government was to hold on until the day when the United States would put things right in Europe (in Churchillian language, "until, in God's good time, the new world, with all its power and might, steps forth to the rescue and the liberation of the old"). The America to which he was appealing was in the run-up to a presidential campaign: Franklin D. Roosevelt was fighting for election to a third term in office by a nation which—like Britain until 1939—wanted no part of a far-off war.

Most American newspapers cared little about the conflict in Europe. Fortunately for Britain and the world, the relatively cosmopolitan newspapers of the East Coast, and the big radio networks, with their head offices in New York, could afford to send their own correspondents abroad, and had some information about the state of affairs in Europe and the nature

*Churchill's speech of June 4th was a masterpiece of patriotic eloquence (see Appendix III, page 236, for its peroration) that only a fool would describe as propaganda. Interestingly, it contains no reference at all to the armada of "little ships" that later legend describes as having been at Dunkirk.

of the fascist menace. Their proprietors and editors tended to think of themselves either as ethnically "Anglo-Saxon" or as Jewish. In either case, they were no friends of Hitler.

So, while the wire services and the newsreels were well served by the German propaganda machine, the British had on their side the heavyweight commentators of the Eastern press. This was, of course, not sufficient to bring the United States into the war. It took the Japanese at Pearl Harbor to do that. But it did influence opinion in Washington and make it easier for the politicians and the military men to authorise deliveries to Britain of the weapons she so desperately needed after the abandonment of the BEF's armoury at Dunkirk.

The mood of the Eastern press is indicated in *The New York Times* of June 1st, the day when the British authorities first allowed news of the evacuation to be released. A box at the foot of the front page cautioned: "Dispatches from Europe and the Far East are subject to censorship at source." But the paper's editorial had no reservations about the censored news from England: "As long as the English tongue survives, the word Dunkerque will be spoken with reverence," it said. The harsh reality of defeat, the confusion and squalor of the beaches and the harbour, were immediately transmuted for public opinion at home and abroad into an episode of glory. Thus the morale of the British people was sustained, and the supply of new weapons was ensured. If the events of May and early June 1940 had been reported truthfully and blow by blow from the spot—as they undoubtedly would be today—it is unlikely that this great act of faith could have been performed.

19

THE FIGHT GOES ON

With the battle on the Continent well and truly lost, Britain settled down to carry on the war alone. This was how the British preferred it. King George VI royally reflected his subjects' mood when he wrote in a private letter to his mother, Queen Mary, on June 27th after the fall of France: "Personally I feel happier now that we have no more allies to be polite to & to pamper."

Britain's isolation in June 1940 was in practice not so great as it seemed. King George regarded them as subjects, not as allies, but it is worth recalling that as he wrote soldiers were arriving from Australia and from New Zealand to join the Canadians already in Britain. Individuals were coming in from elsewhere in the Empire too. But as a whole Britain's worldwide rôle as an imperial power absorbed more manpower than it provided.

The United States, on whose entering into the war Mr. Churchill relied for Britain's salvation, was prevented from doing so by the will of the people. But as soon as the scale of the Dunkirk disaster became apparent the Americans began to send guns. General George Marshall fixed it, despite the opposition of others high placed in the U.S. Army. On June 3rd the authorisation was given, and by June 11th half a million rifles were on their way across the Atlantic. They had lain in grease since the end of the First World War, and their ammunition was incompatible with anything else used by the

British Army; but at $7.40 each, including 250 rounds of ammunition, they were a bargain. They were a foretaste of all the aircraft, ships, tanks and guns that were to follow. They served as a fall-back arsenal for the Local Defence Volunteers who, armed only with pitchforks, shotguns, and an occasional souvenir revolver, were Britain's principal military force at home. The author's father, as a lieutenant in the L.D.V., was issued with an ancient .45 revolver. It would not hit a bucket at five yards' range, so he carried his shotgun instead.

Churchill was determined to put all Britain, not just its armed forces, into the war. At the head of a coalition government including socialists and conservatives, capitalists and trade-unionists, he succeeded beyond any possible expectation. The example of the volunteers who had joined the rescue at Dunkirk was deliberately exploited as the prototype and symbol of civilian participation in the fight against the Nazis. Rapidly the myth of the Dunkirk spirit overshadowed the confused reality that this narrative has sought to untangle.

During the evil days when the inevitability of defeat in France became apparent, on May 22nd, a Home Morale Emergency Committee was set up to advise the Ministry of Information on how to combat defeatism in Britain. Its chairman was the junior minister for information, Mr. (later Sir) Harold Nicolson, diplomat, author and wit. Another member was Mr. Kenneth (later Lord) Clark, director of the National Gallery and subsequently presenter of the *Civilisation* television programmes. Clark recalls: "We were not ourselves a very warlike body, and I remember one of our members, Harold Nicolson, who was far too civilised a man to be concerned with propaganda, saying several times: 'All we can do is lie on our backs and hope no-one will tread on our tummies.' "

The mood of the nation after Dunkirk made it perfectly unnecessary to have committees on national morale. The appointment of Mr. Churchill as prime minister had been greeted with dismay by much of his own party and—perhaps more seriously—by many in the top ranks of the armed forces and the Civil Service. The head of the Foreign Office was weary of "Winston's rhodomontades." The head of the Admiralty distrusted his former Minister's taste for public relations. Churchill was known to be grandiloquent, impetuous, too fond of large brandies and larger but emptier gestures. But he passed in a speech on his eightieth birthday the definitive verdict on his own rôle at the time, in words that can still irritate as they inspire: "It was the nation and the race dwelling all around the globe that had the lion's heart. I had the luck to be called upon to give the roar."

This was the mood that followed Dunkirk. It matters not how many lies were told to sustain it. The finest chronicler of those times is of course not an historian but a novelist, Evelyn Waugh. At the end of *Put Out More Flags*, in the hot summer of 1940, Lady Seal is lunching with her dull old friend Sir Joseph Mainwaring, the eminent civil servant. Sir Joseph fears that, once again, Lady Seal will ask him to save her disgraceful son Basil from a scrape. Instead she tells him:

> "He has joined a special corps d'élite that is being organised . . . I am not sure what they are going to do, but I know it is very dashing and may well have a decisive effect on the war."
> The grey moment was passed; Sir Joseph, who had not ceased smiling, now smiled with sincere happiness.
> "There's a new spirit abroad," he said. "I see it on every side."
> And, poor booby, he was bang right.

APPENDIX I

EVACUATION:
Numbers of Soldiers Arriving in British Ports

DATE	DAILY TOTAL	RUNNING TOTAL	FROM PORT	FROM BEACH	BRITISH	FRENCH/ ALLIED
May 27th	7,669		7,669		3,373	
May 28th	17,804	25,473	11,874	5,930	13,948	
May 29th	47,310	72,783	33,558	13,752	38,188	655
May 30th	53,823	126,606	24,311	29,512	39,858	8,616
May 31st	68,014	194,620	45,072	22,942	43,438	14,874
June 1st	64,429	259,049	47,081	17,348	25,190	35,013
June 2nd	26,256	285,305	19,561	6,695	15,378	16,049
June 3rd	26,746	312,051	24,876	1,870	7,208	19,803
June 4th	26,175	338,226	25,553	622	6	29,989
			239,555	98,671	186,587	124,999

None of the available sets of figures on the evacuation gives the same total. Soldiers and sailors had more important work than the compiling of accurate statistics. The totals given here, and the figures for the port and the beaches, are from Mr. Churchill's history and are probably the best available. The figures for British and other arrivals are from Admiral Ramsay's report of 1940. Taken together they at least give a measure of the flow of troops, and an idea of the priority given to the British forces.

APPENDIX II

EVACUEES–by Type of Vessel

ROYAL AND FRENCH NAVY VESSELS		197,139
Fighting warships	113,490	
Minesweepers	48,472	
Dutch *Schuyts* (RNVR)	22,698	
Other RN	12,479	
CIVILIAN VESSELS		135,094
Passenger ferries	87,810	
Trawlers (including trawlers under French naval command)	28,709	
Other civilian craft	18,575	

The table understates the role of small craft in the evacuation from Dunkirk. Most of the 98,671 soldiers rescued from the beaches were ferried by small craft to larger ships that carried them to England. Equally, the table overstates the role of civilians in the evacuation, since many civilian vessels, including passenger ferries, were taken over by Royal Navy crews when their own crews were worn out.

APPENDIX III

The prime minister, Mr. Winston Churchill, announced in the House of Commons on June 4th, 1940, the safe return from France of the British Expeditionary Force. "We must be very careful not to assign to this deliverance," he said, "the attributes of a victory. Wars are not won by evacuations." And he closed his speech with the following words:

I have, myself, full confidence that if all do their duty, if nothing is neglected, and if the best arrangements are made, as they are being made, we shall prove ourselves once again able to defend our island home, to ride out the storm of war, and to outlive the menace of tyranny, if necessary for years, if necessary alone. At any rate, that is what we are going to try to do. That is the resolve of His Majesty's Government—every man of them. That is the will of Parliament and of the nation. The British Empire and the French Republic, linked together in their cause and in their need, will defend to the death their native soil, aiding each other like good comrades to the utmost of their strength.

Even though large tracts of Europe and many old and famous States have fallen or may fall into the grip of the Gestapo and all the odious apparatus of Nazi rule, we shall not flag or fail. We shall go on to the end. We shall fight in France, we shall fight on the seas and oceans, we shall fight with growing confidence and growing strength in the air, we shall defend our island, whatever the cost may be. We shall fight on the beaches, we shall fight on the landing grounds, we shall fight in the fields and in the streets, we shall fight in the hills; we shall never surrender, and even if, which I do not for a moment believe, this island or a large part of it were subjugated and starving, then our Empire beyond the seas, armed and guarded by the British Fleet, would carry on the struggle, until, in God's good time, the new world, with all its power and might, steps forth to the rescue and the liberation of the old.

APPENDIX IV

The way in which the British government influenced the flow of news through the British Broadcasting Corporation in the Second World War has never been fully explained. Indeed the official chroniclers have persistently stated that no such influence was directly exercised. When this book first appeared, in April 1980, excerpts from it were published by the *Sunday Telegraph* of London. In response to the passage (see page 221) describing the BBC newsreaders' scripts and the annotations in their margins referring to official sources, Mr. S. W. Smithers wrote to the Editor. I have the kind permission of the Editor of the *Sunday Telegraph* and of Mr. Smithers himself to publish this letter:

Dear Sir,
Nicholas Harman named me as the BBC journalist who, in May 1940, wrote the bulletin story which gave the public the first news of the Dunkirk evacuation (6 p.m. news, May 31st). He also reproduced my footnote (not, of course, meant for broadcast): "Approved by MI 17a— S. W. Smithers" (correctly, I think, that should have been MI 7a). This was the branch of Military Intelligence to which we in the newsroom had easy access when we felt we needed it.

We had equally easy contact with A16 at the Air Ministry, the Chief of Naval Information at the Admiralty and with staff at the Ministry of Home Security. I do not recall a single occasion when any of these services made calls to us, save to answer an inquiry we had made. There was certainly no attempt at any time to influence anything we had written.

But although there was no requirement for us to consult the Intelligence Services or anybody else we sometimes did so, and for two main reasons: one was to ensure, before a broadcast, that in collating pre-censored information from a number of sources (sometimes a great heap of it) we had not, by any mischance made any factual error; the second was because we always kept in the front of our minds the fact that at the very moment our stories were on the air to the vast public in Britain, they were also being heard by the enemy in Europe. It was, after all, the first major war in which broadcasting had played an important part.

The only directive we had during the whole war was given to a small crowd of us in the newsroom by the news editor, R. T. Clark, on the day it began. He shuffled into the room in his slippers, his shirt-cuffs flapping at his wrists. He climbed on to an old wooden chair, clapped his hands, a little diffidently, for silence, and said: "Well, brothers (and he really did regard his staff as brothers), it is now war, and your job will be to tell the truth. If you're not sure it is the truth don't use it." That was all.

From then on, the BBC newsroom not only had total editorial independence, but I thought it had also amply demonstrated it. It had certainly never occurred to us that the BBC, as Mr. Harman says, "saw its main duty as being to reinforce the morale of the civilian audience at home." If the BBC did, I never heard about it, and we in the newsroom had never to take anything of the kind into account. Had we been asked, or told, or advised to do so, I can well imagine what the final and definite answer from all of us would have been: "Our job is news and nothing else." We never were asked.

—S. W. Smithers, Sussex.

NOTES ON SOURCES

The heart of this book is the personal memories of the veterans of Dunkirk. I spoke and corresponded with many of them in 1978 and 1979. After the original publication, in 1980, I presented a BBC television documentary based on this book, and extracts from it were published in the *Sunday Telegraph* of London; more than 200 other veterans wrote in response. My gratitude to these generous informants is immense. I mourn the death of many of those to whom I am indebted.

In particular I was helped by several dozen members of the 1940 Dunkirk Veterans Associations, both in Britain and when I travelled as a respectful observer with their annual pilgrimage to the town and beaches in 1979. Their general secretary, the late Mr. Harold Robinson, was at all times helpful. I am sure that he and many other members of the DVA will dislike this book. I hope they will nevertheless believe in my respect for and my gratitude to them.

In and around Dunkirk I spoke with many who remember the events of the spring of 1940. I was much helped by Serge Blanckaert of *La Voix du Nord*, and by the archivists at the Musée de la Ville de Dunkerque. The museum's conservator, M. Kuhnmunch, very kindly provided the photo of the sinking of the *Bourrasque*.

The evacuation and the events surrounding it were the subject of several instant books, have been explained and counter-explained many times, and are mentioned in dozens of memoirs and biographies. It would be merely tedious to list all the books I have consulted. Instead I describe in this section the main sources I have found especially interesting. I have relied on some publications and archives throughout the book, and these I describe first.

The British official history of *The War in France and Flanders* (published 1953), by Major L. F. Ellis, is a splendid and, by its nature, selective account of the battle. Ellis' main sources are in the Public Record Office (PRO) at Kew near London, in several dozen volumes of headquarters papers, war diaries and other military documents of the British Expeditionary Force classified W0167 and W0197. Since 1971 they have been available to students who promise to reveal nothing of a personal nature contained in them. It is intriguing to spot what the official historians left out.

The other official British war histories, of the Royal Navy and the Royal Air Force, are also valuable. Captain Roskill's official naval history, incidentally, is wonderfully well written. The Admiralty papers on Dunkirk are in the Public Record Office under ADM 199, in some confusion.

A scholarly German work is Adolf Jacobsen's *Dünkirchen* (1958). Jacques Mordal's *La Bataille de Dunkerque* (1948) is as pro-British an account as a Frenchman could possibly write; Mordal was in Dunkirk in May 1940. Under his real name of Hervé Cras this author published a fuller version of the story in *Dunkerque* (1960). Dr. Cras, an eminent and prolific naval historian based at the *Musée de la Marine* in Paris, most generously helped me with his personal memoirs and knowledge.

An indispensable source is David Divine's *The Nine Days of Dunkirk* (1959). Divine behaved bravely in a small boat at Dunkirk and was throughout his life connected with the British armed forces (for many years as defence correspondent of the London *Sunday Times*, where this writer was briefly among his colleagues, and learned to like him a lot). He was always accurate and always intensely patriotic; however, comparison with his source material in the Public Record Office shows that, although he contributed much to our understanding, he also left things out.

On the political events and their interaction with military decisions, Baron Jacques Benoist-Méchin's encyclopaedic *60 Jours qui ébranlèrent l'Occident* (three volumes, 1956) is amazingly useful and only occasionally slips on a fact. (The English-language edition is unfortunately an abridgement.)

Of the myriad reminiscences of the period, the most imposing are those of Sir Winston Churchill, the best written those of General de Gaulle. Paul Reynaud and General Maxime Weygand both wrote their own accounts of events. That of Reynaud (published 1960) is largely an attempt to make peace between Britain and France and to wipe out the Vichy Government's lies (with which some truths go, too). Weygand's (1950) is a monument of ossified French prose, presumably ghost-written, but tells some good stories and reprints some valuable documents in its appendix.

General Sir Edward (Louis) Spears, in *Assignment to Catastrophe* (1954), wrote a brilliant book which deserves to be read, if not always believed, by everyone interested in how the British and the French viewed each other. *Gort: Man of Valour* (1972), by Sir John Colville, is far better than its title promises.

There are several fascinating memoirs by British officers who retreated to Dunkirk. The classic of the genre is Gun Buster's *Return via Dunkirk* (1940), a hugely patriotic work. Gordon Beckles' *Dunkirk and After* (1940) is somewhat similar but had less success. Anthony Rhodes' *Sword of Bone* (1940) has far greater literary merit and seems undeservedly forgotten. (It ends with the famous description of an officer's reaction to the Dunkirk beaches: "My dear, the noise! And the people!") Peter Hadley's *Third Class to Dunkirk* (1944) is revealing. Lieutenant-Colonel Ewen Butler and Major J. Selby Bradford called their loyal reminiscences *Keep the Memory Green (1950)*. Patrick Turnbull, by contrast, called his *Dunkirk: Anatomy of a Disaster* (1978). *Before the Dawn* (1957) by Brigadier Sir John Smyth, VC, is good on atmosphere.

Colonel James Langley's *To Fight Another Day* (1974) contains in its early chapters an outstanding account of how the fighting seemed to a very brave young officer; the rest of the book is enthralling on the subject of how to escape from prison. Colonel Langley lent me some valuable documents, for which I am most grateful.

My friend and colleague Gordon Lee at *The Economist* read the manuscript, disagreed strongly with its tone, and suggested amendments, of which I have adopted a few. Richard Natkiel, also of *The Economist*, is a rigorous cartographer who helps to make things clear. Harry Hastings of the BBC, who produced the film we based on this book, was the best of producers.

I have used throughout the French version of Belgian place names (Nieuport, not Nieuwpoort, for example), because the British did so at the time. But the river Meuse becomes the Maas when it flows into Dutch-speaking country.

Chapter 1

Alan Bullock's *Hitler: A Study in Tyranny* (1952) and Captain Liddell Hart's *A History of the Second World War* (1971) are required reading. *Mein Kempf* (1924) is indispensable. General Warlimont's *Inside Hitler's Headquarters* (1964) describes what it was like working loyally for a criminal psychopath who kept on winning victories. *The Rommel Papers* (edited by Liddell Hart, 1953) are thrilling and need to be read alongside various biographies of Rommel. The same goes for Heinz Guderian's *Panzer Leader* (1951), although as a corps commander he had less exciting adventures than Rommel. Captain Liddell Hart collected stories from various surviving Nazi generals in *The Other Side of the Hill* (1951); the interviewees clearly sought to flatter their captors in general and their interrogator in particular. German Army headquarters published a fascinating propaganda tract, *Sieg über Frankreich* (1940); *Der Panzerkrieg* (1965), by Eddy Bauer, is more truthful. I have already credited Jacobsen's excellent *Dünkirchen*, which uses the diaries and other documents meticulously kept by all German formations. The Imperial War Museum in London has a scrappy but interesting collection of German war diaries and other papers.

Chapter 2

I have relied heavily on the works already listed by Benoist-Méchin, de Gaulle, Liddell Hart and Churchill. The Admiralty records of operations off the Low Countries are in the Public Record Office. Sir John Wheeler-Bennet's *King George VI* (1958) tells the story from a royal perspective, with use of the Kings' diaries; there are several Belgian accounts of their King's adventures. The standard Belgian work on military events in 1940 is *La campagne de l'armée belge en 1940*, by de Fabribeckers. I was kindly helped at the *Musée de l'armée* and the *Centre de documentation de la Deuxième Guerre Mondiale*, in Brussels.

Chapter 3

There is an enormous amount of material on the collapse of France in 1940. Much of it is based upon, or is in reaction against, the Riom "trials" held by the Vichy regime to try to pin the blame on the democratic politicians. Both the Riom evidence and its rebuttal are dubious. Between them, Benoist-Mèchin, Reynaud and Weygand provide most of the direct evidence I have used, although all three often contradict the others. *The Battle of France* (1958), by Colonel A. Goutard, and General d'Astier de la Vigerie's *Les Cieux n'étaient pas vides* (1950) helped me to understand how the defeat felt for French military men. Colonel Jean Beaux's *Dunkerque* (1967) does much to explain how the French Army saw its British Allies. General Spears is always interesting.

Chapter 4

The official British histories, taken with a pinch of salt, provide much of the evidence for this chapter, although much material about signals and radar was still secret when they were published. Colville's life of Gort is useful; *The Private Papers of Hore-Belisha* (1960) by R. J. Minney is intriguing. Both were written without access to the BEF papers in the Public Record Office. A brilliant light is shed on the operations in France by *British Army Signals in World War II* (1953), by Major-General R. F. H. Nalder. Captain Liddell Hart's regimental history *The Tanks* (1959) corroborates the general's information about signals deficiencies. I have read several standard biographies of British generals involved in the campaign; the most misleading is that of Lord Alanbrooke by Sir Arthur Bryant (*The Turn of the Tide*, 1957), the most fascinating *Montgomery of Alamein* (1976) by Alun Chalfont. Many histories of British regiments are interesting, often because of their omission of what the war diaries said at the time. The memoirs of journalists with the BEF were useful, but the newspapers themselves were more so. I read mainly in *The Times*, the *News Chronicle*, the *Illustrated*

London News and *Picture Post*. Hitler's admiration for Britain is documented both in *Mein Kampf* and in his *Table Talk* (1953).

Chapter 5

This is where I start to make use of personal reminiscences kindly given to me by veterans of the BEF. I also rely heavily on the war diaries and other papers in the Public Record Office. I have consulted, and sometimes disagreed with, Gregory Blaxland's monumental *Destination Dunkirk* (1973). The Reverend Leslie Aitken in 1977 published *Massacre on the Road to Dunkirk*, about the SS murders of British soldiers; he has some valuable original material. The Imperial War Museum has a folder of German papers on the same incidents, classified AL 1520, from which I have quoted in translation.

Chapter 6

The Arras adventure has been described often, and many writers have followed Rommel's exciting account of what it was like on the receiving end, at which he got the impression that larger British forces were involved than the four battalions actually engaged. I was generously helped at the Durham Light Infantry Museum and the Light Infantry Office in Durham city. The war diaries of the units concerned are fascinating. Those who consult them in the PRO must promise not to reveal information about individuals named. I have treated some personal interviews about the fighting on the same basis; notably, those concerning the murder by British soldiers of their German prisoners.

Chapter 7

Dover Castle and its underpinnings are now mostly open to the public. The British official histories and David Divine's *Nine Days of Dunkirk* both have much information on the preliminaries to Operation Dynamo. Cabinet papers in the Public Record Office tell the story of Neville Chamberlain's committee; I was guided to them first by Benoist-Méchin, then by P. M. H. Bell's *A Certain Eventuality* (1974). *The*

Ironside Diaries, 1937–1940 reveal the thinking of the most pro-French of British generals; I also used them for my account of the preparations for war in France. The War Office and Admiralty papers in the Public Record Office contain a mass of material that I have not seen used before. The Reynaud-Churchill meeting of May 26th is variously described by the participants, both of whom agree that the Dunkirk evacuation was never mentioned at the meeting; Martin Gilbert's vast edition of Churchill's papers confirms this by omission. The significance of Commandant Fauvelle's trip to Paris was impressed upon me by M. Jacques Mordal: the memoirs of Weygand, Reynaud and Spears all describe the event in contrasting lights. The minutes of the Council of War of May 31st are printed in facsimile in General Weygand's *Rappelé au Service*, and there are other descriptions (including that of General Spears) of what happened; there are no disagreements of substance. The abortive role of the First Canadian Division is described in Colonel C. P. Stacey's excellent official history (1957) of the Canadian Army in World War II.

Chapters 8 to 17

The day-by-day account of the evacuation is assembled from many sources, including verbal accounts by eyewitnesses. David Divine's *The Nine Days of Dunkirk* is indispensable. He was there and, more important, he interviewed many participants who are now dead. I have used his information only when there was strong supporting evidence, which came mainly from the documents he used. They are in the boxes under ADM 199 in the Public Record Office, very roughly sorted. It is no criticism of Divine to say that he tended to accentuate what was positive about British actions at Dunkirk. Jacques Mordal's *La Bataille de Dunkerque* is only slightly less pro-British; Jean Beaux's *Dunkerque* is heartily pro-French. Albert Chatelle's *Dunkerque: Ville ardente* (1956) is illuminating on the plight of the civilian population. The papers he used are in the Dunkirk city museum. Jacques Blankaert's *La Guerre à Dunkerque* (1971) is vivid; M. Blankaert kindly helped me to find some valuable information in the town. Father Lecointe, almoner of the Hôpital Maritime Vancauwenberghe at Zuydcoote, was immensely kind and generous with his time. The Royal Air Force's claims and performance are recorded in various official publications, post-war.

Chapter 18

The main sources here are the British newspapers of the period, and the microfilmed BBC radio news scripts in the corporation's archives at Caversham, next to the place where they still monitor other people's broadcasts for intelligence purposes. Professor Asa (Lord) Briggs' history of the BBC (Volume II, *The War of Words*) does not help to explain how the scripts came to bear annotations attributing stories to propaganda sources. Several journalists with the BEF wrote memoirs, of which the most revealing are Bernard Gray's, published posthumously in 1942. He took a shorthand note of General Mason-Macfarlane's unattributable briefing at the Berkeley Hotel. Mason-Macfarlane's biography, written in 1972 by Ewan Butler, does not mention the incident. Charles Gardner of the BBC in *AASF* (1940) is good on Air Force censorship. Philip Knightley's *The Last Casualty* (1975) is an interesting study of the perpetual trials of war reporters. Jonathan Dimbleby's filial *Richard Dimbleby* (1975) is also revealing, as are Harold Nicolson's diaries. The official story of the Defiant fighters is told by Churchill and Spears, among others; the unofficial truth was later revealed in various technical publications. I consulted in particular the *RAF Flying Review* for 1956 in the Imperial War Museum. On the United States connection, various memoirs of the period were helpful, and Joseph P. Lash's *Roosevelt and Churchill* (1977) was indispensable for this and the following chapter.

Chapter 19

The memoirs of the time, and the personal memories, all bear witness to the extraordinary change of mood in Britain at the beginning of June 1940. It is to give the flavour, rather than because they are unusual, that I have used the diaries of Sir Alexander Cadogan and Sir Harold Nicolson, and the au-

tobiography of Lord Clark. The House of Commons debates
of the time, and articles and pamphlets galore, tell the same
story. Perhaps the most naive, and therefore revealing, propaganda pamphlet of the time was called *Guilty Men*: its
leading co-author was a well-known journalist, Michael
Foot.

INDEX

THE BEST IN WAR BOOKS

__**DEVIL BOATS: THE PT WAR AGAINST JAPAN**
William Breuer 0-515-09367-X/$3.95
A dramatic true-life account of the daring PT sailors who crewed the Devil Boats—outwitting the Japanese.

__**PORK CHOP HILL** S.L.A. Marshall
0-515-08732-7/$3.95
A hard-hitting look at the Korean War and the handful of U.S. riflemen who fought back the Red Chinese Troops.
"A distinguished contribution to the literature of war."—New York Times

__**THREE WAR MARINE** Colonel Francis Fox Parry
0-515-09872-8/$3.95
A rare and dramatic look at three decades of war—World War II, the Korean War, and Vietnam. Francis Fox Parry shares the heroism, fears and harrowing challenges of his thirty action-packed years in an astounding military career.